Contents

National Identity

Edited by
Keith Cameron

intellect™

EXETER, ENGLAND

intellect – EUROPEAN STUDIES SERIES

General Editor – Keith Cameron

First published in Great Britain by **Intellect Books**
School of Art and Design, Earl Richards Road North, Exeter EX2 6AS

Series Editor:	Keith Cameron
Copy Editor:	Lucy Kind
Cover Design:	Yahia Badawi*
Production:	Annegret Rösler, Julie Strudwick

A catalogue record for this book is available from the British Library

ISBN 1-871516-05-6

* Yahia Badawi Graphic Design (ybad@btinternet.com)

Printed and bound in Great Britain by Cromwell Press, Wiltshire

Introduction

Keith Cameron

As the European Union becomes more unified through its legislation and interstatal trade and movement, there is a centrifugal movement in a number of Member States as individuals begin to feel threatened and to think that they are losing their national identity. What is, however, national identity? It is one of those terms which is used frequently but which often beggars definition.

In an earlier collection of essays,[1] we showed how difficult it is to define a nation, how the concept of the nation varies according to the historical moment, geographical situation, linguistic affiliation, political climate, etc. Is national identity something of which we ourselves are aware or is it an identity which others bestow upon us? In the world press, England (which often includes the British Isles) is, or has been, referred to as John Bull, a nation of shopkeepers, devourers of beef and fish and chips, perfidious Albion, etc. Is national identity synonymous with stereotypes? The French eat frogs and snails, wear a beret, carry a baguette in their shopping bag, flaunt their government by organising stoppages on the motorway; the Germans consume vast quantities of beer, lounge on all the best seats around pools in expensive hotels in exotic resorts; the Don Juans of Spain; the dour Scots and Scandinavians; the yoik British football supporters. Or is it 'the awareness of self within a defined national context'?[2] The relationship we establish between ourselves and the ambient society, the way in which we identify with objects, institutions, behavioural patterns, common traditions and history. This process of identification is often one of which we are not consciously aware until it is challenged. Recently, I enquired of two people in their twenties why they felt they were British. Their response was not immediate but studied. They eventually offered that they had a British passport and spoke English. And yet a British passport does not bestow 'Britishness' on its holder and to speak English is a pleasure to be shared with many millions of varying nationalities who feel that they have their own distinct national identity. My two informants also said that they 'lived in Britain', and it is certain that 'geography and identity are inextricably tied up with each other'.[3]

Is the acquisition of national identity a spontaneous process or can it be manipulated? To what extent can historians or politicians mould a national identity? In a recent study, Stefan Berger has highlighted the role of historians in the creation of German awareness of their national identity:

> The commitment of historians to nation-building can look back on a long tradition in German historiography, its major function being to uphold national honour and glory and create national identity.[4]

The history of European States is narrated differently from state to state. Depending upon the degree of government control, school textbooks, which have such a powerful influence on our attitudes in later life, can be designed to fit in with the political objectives of the ruling party or with a particular ideology. Teams of scholars from the West are currently assisting teachers and scholars in the republics of the former Soviet Union to rewrite the history of their respective countries. Not only historians but the Churches,[5] the political parties, and the various media can all play an important part in forming national identity and can in turn be associated in our minds with *our* national identity. We know that political parties in the run-up period to an election seek the advice of psychologists and publicists to make their policies more accessible or perhaps more acceptable, so that they appear to reflect the mood of the nation and thus encourage electors to identify with their party.

The present collection of ten studies looks at national identity from five different perspectives — language, the political entity, the arts, money and the public figure. It is designed to provoke awareness of how great a role national identity plays, and has played, in our daily attitudes and our *Weltanschauung*. It is not a frivolous role (although perceived traits of national identity are often the stuff of caricature), but one which is associated with political decisions that govern our lives. The essays, which reveal the advantages of the multi-disciplinary approach, cover a wide geographical area and draw attention to some of the important factors which underlie our concept of being able to identify with a nation. Nation and state are not synonymous, and generally, as a result of growing national awareness, nations seek autodetermination, in fact, statehood. Yet there is a common tendency to believe that nation and state do coincide and many governments adopt a policy which seeks to forge one state out of different nations.

One of the big factors in the configuration of our own identity is the language we speak. In many states there is one official language which is not the native language of all its inhabitants. Lynn Williams examines the language policy in Spain and takes as a parallel the position of Welsh in Britain. People see in their language the testimony of their cultural heritage, it assumes the role of a cultural 'label'. The more a minority feels threatened by the political majority or by a more powerful economic power, the more it will tend to assert its own culture and language. Similarly, it will try and protect its culture from outside influences by trying to ban the language of the other in favour of its own. States, too, can try and ensure 'national' unity by insisting that only one language be taught in the schools. In both cases, whether it be the super power or the minority group, compulsory use of only one language can have counterproductive consequences. People are reluctant both as individuals and as groups, as Williams tells us, 'to abandon one linguistic identity in favour of a new one', if they are to do so they must do so of their own accord.

Even though people may use the language of another majority group, they can still use it in a distinctive way and create their own version, as it were, of the imported tongue. Over the years, the English spoken in North America, Australia,

India and elsewhere has evolved in such a way that each country has its own 'national' English, in pronunciation, in lexis and in syntax. Diane Davies takes a close look at the relationship between a literary form, poetry, and the Anglo-Welsh identity. Ironically, the Welsh poets writing in English have, over the last years, used English as a means of gaining support for 'Welshness' and for the Welsh language. They have helped create an awareness amongst the Welsh of their identity and have succeeded in increasing a sense of pride in being Welsh. They are now moving away in their interests from the small world of Wales to problems and subjects outside, thereby establishing internationally their reputation and that of their nation.

Europe has witnessed over the last decade the phenomenon of the break up of the previous USSR into a series of smaller states, thus reversing the integrationist policy of Lenin, Stalin and their followers. Yugoslavia has been the scene of a bloody war which has seen fervent nationalism lead to political disintegration. West Germany has been reunited with East Germany, fulfilling the visionary policies of its post-war Chancellors. To what extent can such momentous historical events be linked with national identity? Mark Blacksell, who maintains that 'nationalism and a sense of national identity are recent creations', traces the history of the reunification of Germany and stresses that for half a century the aim to bring together the two halves of the nation was a stimulus to persevere and provide the *raison d'être* of the mission. Once they were reunited, however, the former two sides discovered that over the 50 years they had developed different identities and different attitudes, based on different ideologies and different lifestyles.

Conflicts in the former state of Yugoslavia have highlighted the problems of ethnic identity. John Vincent, a sociologist, has studied the symbols of nationalism in Bosnia and Hercegovina where people have been having to rethink their identities on an almost daily basis. As we have seen, language and religion can be seen as ethnic symbols. In modern Europe, people may speak the same language but belong to a different religion, or to a different religious sect, from their neighbour. When they decide to separate for religious, or for a combination of religious and linguistic reasons, great and bitter hardship can ensue. Not only does this constitute a problem in Bosnia and Hercegovina but the separation of Cyprus or troubles in Northern Ireland also remind us of the misery and enmity that can come into existence when such factors are given political status.

National identity has a wide variety of facets and it is interesting to observe how some countries become associated with certain activities – bull fighting or flamenco dancing in Spain, beer drinking in Britain, cycle races in France. In Austria, as Gar Yates amply illustrates, it is the theatre with which the Austrians identify. The Austrians speak a distinctive German but it is nonetheless a language which it shares with its bigger and economically greater neighbour, Germany. The Austrians are fearful of being dominated by the Germans and consider that they constitute a threat to their own national identity and it is often to the theatre that they look to preserve it. It is not a new phenomenon and the importance of the theatre goes back to at least the last century. In England, at the end of the 19th and

at the beginning of the 20th centuries, there was a feeling that music in England
lacked 'Englishness' and that the musical scene was too much under the influence
of German composers. Following the example of Grieg and Dvorák, English
composers such as Vaughan Williams and Peter Warlock attempted to create a
music inspired by their English ancestors and, in so doing, resorted to archaic
phraseology in their wish to reinstate a national music, as Fiona Clampin
underlines. Yet even in the muscial domain we get the impression that national
identity is a fairly nebulous term as it is possible for the musicologist to detect in
much of the 'English' music of the beginning of the century a definite French
influence.

What allows people to assert that something belongs uniquely to them and
could be termed a national characteristic, may be merely based on familiarity and
what they believe because of thought or cultural associations to be the product of
their nation, irrespective of those 'foreign' influences which have helped mould its
shape and existence. Their views can also be formed because of propaganda at
either the local or the national level. To what extent, for example, is the British view
of themselves and of other ethnic groups formed by the cinema and the television
film? To see a film of 50 years ago can often cause a comic reaction to the way in
which the British have been portrayed. Such films did much to promote the image,
amongst others, of the 'stiff upper lip', the intrepid nature of the British, their sense
of humour in the face of adversity, their excellence in dignity and decision-making.
Susan Hayward looks at film from a fascinating angle. She takes the French cinema
and examines to what extent it reflects 'the texture of society at a national level'. As
she shows, the cinema exploits national myths and creates them, it is a dual process
and one which is in a constant state of change. New social and political conditions
create new situations which the cinema portrays and which can in turn form part of
a new myth.

Myth is inextricably linked with the concept of national identity. Many of the
symbols which people seize upon to denote their national allegiance are shared
with the people of other nations who do not attribute to them the same significance.
Their value is in the mind more than in reality. The mind and our deep
psychological reactions can govern our attitudes and often enable us to seek
justification for them in logical arguments based upon an uncertain premise. Carole
Burgoyne and David Routh are both psychologists and they have studied the
relationship, from the point of view of their discipline, between national identity,
European identity and the new European currency, the Euro.

One of the big issues in creating the European Union is to get people to feel a
sense of loyalty to this grouping of diverse states and nations. As individuals we
support our local and regional sporting teams when they play against those of
neighbouring localities and regions within our own state and yet when a team,
which in the national context we may have opposed, finds itself in the position of
representing the state we tend, to transfer our allegiance to it. In a competition
between a European team and ones from other parts of the globe, would we be
inclined, irrespective of our ethnic origins, to identify with the Europeans? If this is

the case, it suggests that national identity is often not a fixed concept but one of which the definition can vary according to the circumstances. The symbols of our identity change according to our concept of what constitutes the 'nation'. And money, is it an ethnic symbol, is it associated with national identity? Apparently, the countries that make up the European Union can be seen as falling into two distinct camps, those that see the Euro as a potential threat to their national identity and those that do not. This poses a considerable problem for those governments who support the Euro as they will have to embark upon a campaign to make sure that the introduction of the new currency will not alienate more than it will encourage national and European cohesion.

It would appear that people need familiar symbols to feel reassured and even to give shape to their existence. Such symbols are not necessarily inanimate but can be people or institutions. Into this category can be placed the British monarchy, and closely associated with that institution, the late Princess of Wales. Bruce Coleman and Joy Thompson, in turn, cast light upon the role the British monarchy has played in public life over the last few centuries and the way in which Diana became an object of national grief which was virtually without precedent. The attitude of the British public has not been constant over the centuries and feelings towards the Royal Family have waxed and waned, ranging from hostility to profound respect. At times, 'the Royals' have been looked upon as remote figureheads representing the nation and, at others, as creatures of flesh and blood who because of their worldly attitudes were not worthy of the nation's respect. The death of such a well-known personage as Diana was not only considered by many who had come to know her through the popular image projected by the media as a tragedy in general terms, particularly for her family, but it quickly became a matter for individual public concern. Throughout the country the manifestation of grief and the ensuing anger at the way in which the Royal Family showed its own sense of bereavement assumed alarming proportions. Could it be that the people were seeking an opportunity to exercise a sense of despair which hitherto had been without focus? Did this loss resurrect an atavistic need for a collective display of feeling more befitting the cult of the Madonna? What is certain is that many within this nation, and outside, saw in Diana a symbol with which they could identify and which they felt belonged to them.

The chapters of this collection open up the avenues towards reflection on the paradoxes, the contradictions, the vagueness which often surrounds the concept of national identity. It is obvious that it is easier to define the concept than the reality. From an individual point of view national identity seems to be a conscious and often unconscious identification with a symbol, be it language, political system, gastronomic activity, religion, etc., which is within that person's perception common to the small or large community to which she or he belongs. The unique quality of such symbols can be illusory and, on investigation, be of more widespread significance than just within the local or national context. It has been suggested that the symbol is perceived as one of unity yet, at the same time, its diffusion can be the object of political designs so as to achieve unity but which may exacerbate matters and lead to disunity. The factors constituting national identity do not have fixed parameters but evolve in the same way as any society evolves but not always at the same speed. When they are identified the factors can often be assimilated to a myth of man's creation for his own satisfaction and one which once created can impede his reasoning and deform his perception of reality. National identity, the elements which compose it and the forces which can control it, need much more investigation. This book paves the way.

Notes

1   Keith Cameron (ed.) (1994)*The Nation: Myth or Reality?* Exeter: Intellect.
2   Salma Sobhan (1994) 'National identity, fundamentalism and the women's movement in Bangladesh', in Valentine M. Moghadam (ed.), *Gender and National Identity. Women and Politics in Muslim Societies*. London & New Jersey: Zed Books; Karachi: Oxford University Press, p. 63.
3   David Hooson (ed.) (1994) *Geography and National Identity*. Oxford: Blackwell, p. 11.
4   Stefan Berger (1997) *The Search for Nationality. National Identity and Historical Consciousness in Germany since 1800*. Oxford, Providence: Berghahn Books, p. 3.
5   See Stuart Mews (ed.) (1982) *Religion and National Identity*. Oxford: Blackwell.

National Identity and the Nation State:

Construction, Reconstruction and Contradiction

Lynn Williams

Introduction

The ultimate objective of nationalist movements is to make the nation and the state co-extensive.[1] In other words, as they become conscious of their national identity, nations almost invariably claim the right to govern themselves. That they are entitled to do so is something which has long been widely accepted. In 1861, for example, John Stuart Mill declared: 'Where the sentiment of nationality exists in any force, there is a *prima facie* case for uniting all the members of the nationality under the same government, and a government to themselves apart.'[2] The position represented here by Mill seems, on the surface, to be perfectly reasonable. However, there lurks beneath a very real difficulty, namely, the inescapable fact that there is no generally accepted view of what constitutes nationality or national identity. Whereas some would point to objective indicators like language, race, religion or territory as essential criteria for marking off membership of a particular national group, others, like Mill, give greater prominence to subjective factors such as the perception which group members themselves have of the national category to which they belong and also the strength of feeling which they evince in support of their unique identity.[3] One of the problems with Mill's position, as I see it, is that even when there exists within a given collectivity a strong sense of identity (as is the case today among most Welsh), it may well be that a larger group (e.g. Britons generally) denies it national status on the grounds that the parameters of the nation are, in fact, much broader than claimed and extend to include peoples and territories outside the limits of the original self-defining group.[4] Such discrepant perceptions of the national category have helped to spawn, and perpetuate, a good deal of terminological muddle in the sense that some people understand nation and state to be one and the same thing, whilst others see them as being very different creatures indeed. For reasons which, I hope, will become apparent, the dominant trend today is to confuse the two terms and to use national as an adjective and/or post-adjectival noun relating not only to nation but also to state (consider, for example, the sentence 'X is a British national',where national clearly means attachment to the British State, not British nation). In fact, one may even go so far as to say that the confusion has become institutionalised. For instance, it is perfectly possible to argue that had it not been for the existence of The United States of America (more commonly known simply as The United States), The United Nations might easily, and perhaps more accurately, have been designated The United States. The indifferent use of the terms nation and state which English allows has given rise, on this occasion, to a very curious situation in which, on the one hand, a collection of sovereign states or political entities whose respective citizens may or may not share a close sense of identity is known as the United *Nations* and, on the other, a political entity known as the United *States* of America claims, under the flag to which all its citizens swear allegiance, to constitute a nation.

The doctrine that nation and state must coincide has led multicultural states to engage in the construction of a single nation by devising new symbols of collective identity like the flag, which in the United States has assumed huge importance, and also by attempting to assimilate the minority cultures within their borders, integrating them into the culture of the politically dominant group. Conversely, it has led minority cultures to defend their separate identity (often described as their national identity) by seeking political control over their own affairs. In other words, some groups wield the political power they have in order to construct a national identity, whereas others seek political power in order to protect and even reconstruct a national identity which they believe already exists. The same theoretical objective of achieving isomorphism between the nation and the state thus often has completely different motivations and these motivations, as we shall see later, not infrequently result in antagonism and conflict.

As is well known, nationalism is a comparatively modern phenomenon. According to Benedict Anderson, it was the arrival of print languages that permitted national consciousness to develop.[5] Through their print language, people were invited to imagine a national community, to assume a collective identity whose limits they could not possibly define on the basis of their particular personal experience. The bonding and, where necessary, assimilatory functions of language are thus crucial to nationalist ideology. In fact, they are crucial not only to those collectivities engaged in the construction of a national identity but also to those which set out to protect or reconstruct a national identity which already exists. The purpose of this paper is to discuss the role of language in these two different types of nationalism and also to look at the relevance of some of the elements often associated with national identity. The frame of the discussion will be a comparison of nationalism in Spain and the United Kingdom.

Constructing national identity

Some time after political union, the non-English regions of the United Kingdom and the non-Castilian regions of Spain were subjected to a process of assimilation by the official culture.[6] The clear objective in each case was to use language to

construct a single cultural identity to match the new single political identity.
However, policies of assimilation proved to be less than wholly effective so that
regional cultures in these kingdoms were never entirely extinguished but
continued, in some measure, to attract the loyalty of the local populations. In
particular, their stubborn persistence in the Spanish periphery eventually
persuaded Madrid to grant them official recognition. Accordingly, the Constitution
of 1978 divided Spain up into 17 autonomous communities and by so doing
allowed regions like Catalonia, the Basque Country and Galicia to re-establish their
local cultures as official cultures alongside the dominant Castilian culture.

The Spanish decision in 1978 to move from the highly centralised state that had
existed under General Franco to one whose basic structure was the autonomous
community was, in fact, a logical one. The dictatorship had long been synonymous
with highly centralised government and the active suppression of regional identity.
Democracy, therefore, almost inevitably implied, in post-Francoist Spain,
decentralised government and the recognition of regional cultures. This does not
mean, however, that all autonomous communities were invested with the same
powers. Whereas the Basque Country and Catalonia were granted unusually high
levels of control over their own affairs, other regions, including those like Galicia
with their own very distinctive personalities, were given a lower level of autonomy.
In fact, it is probably fair to say that traditionally Galicia has not been taken terribly
seriously by Madrid and was only really granted autonomy because it was decided
to extend the Catalan and Basque solution, albeit watered down, to the rest of the
country.

The strikingly different attitude displayed by Madrid towards Galicia, on the
one hand, and the Spanish Basque Country or Catalonia, on the other, is especially
relevant to the question of what precisely constitutes national identity and,
therefore, invites explanation. If we compare Galicia with the Spanish Basque
Country, we discover that approximately 90 per cent of those who lived in Galicia
in 1986 claimed to be able to speak Galician, whereas the proportion of Basque
speakers in the Spanish Basque Country at that time was around 21 per cent.[7] These
figures demonstrate convincingly that the Spanish Basque Country is much more
culturally integrated into the Spanish State than is Galicia and yet, as has been
noted, it is the Basque Country, with its largely diluted Basque cultural identity,
which has received, and continues to receive, from Madrid the greater attention and
recognition. As it happens, the reasons for such differential treatment are, I think,
not too difficult to discern and have to do, in part, with a concept of nationhood
which attaches only limited significance to cultural identity. In addition to its
economic importance, the Basque Country has two obvious advantages over Galicia
in connection with the national question. First, a hard core of its people has been
extremely vociferous, and even violent, in pursuance of the right to govern
themselves. One has only to think of the activities of the Basque terrorist
organisation ETA since the early 1960s to get some idea of just how aggressively
they have articulated their demands. Second, the Basque Country has a political
history that, by and large, remained separate from that of the rest of Spain for many

centuries. Despite sharing with Castile, since medieval times, the same sovereign lord, each Spanish Basque province was governed according to a unique foral regime or set of laws and institutions, which was abolished only following the first and second Carlist Wars. Significantly, Galicia has scarcely been vociferous in its demands for home-rule and has never really had a separate political history. In fact, the absence of a separate political history is something that was exploited as long ago as 1888 in order to reject Galician claims to nationhood. On the occasion of his entry into the Academy of History, the academician Sánchez Moguel had the following to say:

> ¿Qué nacionalidad es esa que tratan de establecer los regionalistas gallegos, si su hermoso y leal país, fuera del fugaz reinado de D. García, no fué nunca reino independiente?[8]
> [What nationality are Galician regionalists trying to establish if their beautiful and loyal country was never, apart from the fleeting reign of D. García, an independent kingdom?]

It would seem from this assessment that subjective and objective indicators of national identity, in whatever combinations, count for little or nothing unless accompanied by a history of political separateness. Without this, the argument runs, a collectivity cannot legitimately lay claim to nationhood. Now, the belief that a separate political history is an essential ingredient of nationality is not unique to Sánchez Moguel. It is also the view which appears to prevail in Madrid and, therefore, helps to explain why Galicia has never been recognised in quite the same way as Catalonia or the Spanish Basque Country. Of course, if one accepts that Galicia has traditionally been denied national status by Madrid largely because it has never enjoyed a separate political history, one must also accept that there is a certain irony in the fact that Spain has failed dismally to construct, from the centre outwards, a single cultural identity to match its new political identity.

The situation sketched out here for Spain offers a number of parallels with the United Kingdom, where we also witness the failure of a powerful political entity to complete the construction of a suitable, corresponding cultural identity. The survival of a Welsh culture and a Scottish culture provides unequivocal evidence of a residual desire, alive today in some parts of the British Isles, to resist the spread of an English cultural identity. Perhaps influenced by the Spanish experience, a United Kingdom government showed at last, in 1997, a willingness to accept the distinctiveness of Wales and Scotland and to mark this acceptance politically by offering the former a national assembly and the latter its own parliament. Replicating, to a large degree, the different treatment accorded by Madrid to the Spanish Basque Country, on the one hand, and Galicia, on the other, Westminster has resolved to invest a Scottish parliament with powers which far exceed those granted to a Welsh assembly. Hardly surprisingly, this decision, on the part of Westminster, is disconcerting to many Welsh people. Although there are many colourful symbols of Scottish identity like the kilt, the bagpipe and whisky, whose association with Scotland is recognised all over the globe,[9] it has to be said that these are ultimately rather superficial manifestations of cultural separateness and hardly compare with, say, language, which few would deny, constitutes the bedrock of collective cultural identity.[10] In terms of the latter, Wales has much the stronger claim to nationhood. Its autochthonous language enjoys considerably more vitality than does Gaelic in Scotland and is experiencing something of a renaissance even in the south and east of the country, where traditionally it had retreated in the face of an ever-advancing English language.[11] Indeed, it would seem safe to conclude, on the basis of linguistic comparisons, that the decision taken in Westminster to offer Scotland a parliament and Wales merely an assembly was scarcely prompted by notions of cultural distinctiveness. Had this been the case, Wales would surely have been offered no worse a deal than Scotland. But if this assumption is correct, how does one explain the way in which these two regions are perceived in Westminster and, no doubt, elsewhere? The answer probably lies in the fact that Wales suffers from two clear disadvantages with regard to Scotland in connection with the national question. First, Wales, like Galicia, has never been especially vociferous in demanding control over its own affairs, whereas Scotland, like the Spanish Basque Country, has spoken out rather more loudly on this issue, particularly since the discovery of North Sea oil which both raised economic expectations and, no doubt, aroused a measure of concern over the impact the discovery would have on Scottish life.[12] Second, Wales, like Galicia, does not have a strong history of political separateness, whereas Scotland, like the Spanish Basque Country, does. Confirmation of the relevance of this latter point may be found in an article penned by Simon Jenkins and appearing in *The Times* the day before the referendum on the Welsh national assembly was conducted. The section of particular relevance reads as follows:

> The case for a Welsh assembly was never strong. 'Wales was never conquered', says the slogan, but the reason is that there was never a nation to conquer. Since the birth of the modern state under Henry Tudor, Wales has been ruled from England. There is unquestionably a Welsh people, a religion, a language and a culture. But these do not in themselves constitute a nation, though they do validate a degree of regional autonomy. Wales's handicap is that it has never enjoyed a political entity to match its cultural identity.[13]

Whilst accepting that Wales has its own very distinctive cultural identity, Jenkins (no doubt ultimately of Welsh stock himself) nevertheless argues that the Welsh are not entitled, in the words of Mill, to 'a government to themselves apart' precisely because they have no history of political independence.[14] Scotland, on the other hand, joined the Union only in 1707 and retained subsequently a measure of control over its own affairs. It is this fact which, apparently, qualifies it today for a parliament with the power to raise taxes. Like Sánchez Moguel, then, Jenkins too argues that a separate political history is an essential ingredient of nationhood and, if we are to believe him, the same view would appear to be dominant in Westminster. This means, of course, that in Britain, as in Spain, there is a view that neither objective indicators like language, race and religion nor subjective indicators like national sentiment, taken either separately or together, are enough to constitute nationhood. Political experience across a span of history is the crucial factor.

The kind of reasoning adopted by Sánchez and Jenkins seems to me to be not merely unenlightened but also seriously flawed. It simply makes no sense to acknowledge individuality and yet withold freedom. Slavery, for example, would never have been abolished had freedom to govern oneself depended, in the last analysis, on having enjoyed freedom at some time in the past. Nor, by the same criterion, would children ever be allowed by parents to take charge of their own lives. And what is self-evident for individuals seems to me also to be self-evident for collectivities. To the objection that silence suggests contentment with one's lot and that the Welsh or the Galicians must always have been largely happy to endure English or Castilian rule since they have never demanded loudly the right to control their own affairs, it may be contended that this is not the real issue. The real issue is that a large collectivity which inhabits its own discrete territory and possesses its own highly distinctive personality should be given the freedom to choose its own level of self-government. In other words, Wales ought to have been given the choice between a parliament, a national assembly and the status quo. Political experience, after all, has to start somewhere.

All of the above is evidently extremely important, especially for minorities like the Welsh and the Galicians. Just as important, however, are its implications for a new Europe. If it is true that powerful political entities do not always prove able to construct a cultural identity to match their political identity and that fracture lines, when they appear in the body politic, frequently follow cultural/racial contours, the European Union should beware of introducing over-centralising policies and be clear about the need to respect not only current state/political identities but also regional/cultural identities. Recent events in former Yugoslavia bear eloquent testimony of the strength of regional centrifugal forces, especially where race and/ or religion are involved. Nation-building or the construction of national identity is thus fraught with danger and this is something which needs to be borne very much in mind by Europe if it is intended one day to undertake the construction of a European identity.

Reconstructing national identity

Without exception, the smaller nations of Spain and the United Kingdom have watched their native culture either retreat or suffer dilution as the official culture of the State has infiltrated their territory and penetrated their class system. Obviously, displacement of local cultures has been greatest in urban and industrial areas and this has left an exceedingly uneven cultural spread over the territory as a whole. For example, the 1991 census for Wales reveals deep divisions between Cymric North Wales and Anglophone South Wales, with 61 per cent of the population of Gwynedd and a mere 2.4 per cent of the population of Gwent claiming to speak Welsh.[15] Needless to say, this kind of pattern is not peculiar to Wales and may be found, in more or less extreme form, in all the bilingual regions of Spain, as well as in Scotland. The real significance of such patterns is that they generate confusion within the nation over national identity and can lead to a certain amount of discrimination of natives who do not speak the local language but whose national pedigree otherwise stretches back over as many generations as can be counted. In this context, it is surely safe to say that the label Anglo-Welsh is hardly intended to be flattering and that the place, within the nation, of those who do not speak the local language is certainly considered to be problematic by at least some of those who continue to speak it as their mother tongue.[16] However, when asked whether non-Basque-speaking Basques could really be considered Basques, the radical Basque nationalist, Alvarez Emparantza, underlined the need to draw a distinction between objective and subjective attachment to an ethnic group, arguing that the Swedish-speaking inhabitants of 19th century Helsinki claimed a Finnish identity, just as the intellectual elite of Prague identified with Czechoslovakia despite being speakers of German.[17] Competence in the local language, he maintained, is merely one measure of identity and may not be evident in all members of the group, especially when dealing with nations which are in crisis and thus find themselves in a period of transition or transformation.[18]

The uneven spread of the indigenous culture within small nations of the type being discussed is also important for another reason. As soon as they achieve some level of control over their political destiny, such groups often seek to regenerate their ailing culture by extending knowledge and use of the local language, which is taught not only to young children at school but also, in evening classes, to adult natives who do not speak it, and to immigrants. In other words, these smaller nations do what multicultural states so frequently do. They attempt to assimilate linguistically and culturally all those who live within their borders. The Catalans of Spain have been singularly energetic, in recent years, in working towards this objective. In particular, they have introduced, in the public school system of Catalonia, a programme of linguistic immersion in Catalan, which is compulsory for all children between three and eight years of age. This means that unless they are able to attend a private institution, children in Catalonia can no longer receive, in their early years, an education in Spanish. The importance of such a policy for the Catalan Government is that the children are exposed principally to Catalan at a critical time in their linguistic development, with the likely result that they will come to favour the Catalan language over the Spanish language and a Catalan identity over a Spanish identity.[19] In imitation of the Catalan experiment, Galicia introduced a modified version of the linguistic immersion programme into its public education system in September 1996, presumably with similar hopes of making the local language the preferred language of the next generation. Now, although such measures are, in practice, no different from those employed by multicultural states seeking to assimilate minority cultures into the official culture of the State, the justification for them is completely different. Whereas multicultural states set out to generate or construct a single cultural identity to match their political identity, smaller nations like the Catalans clearly see themselves as being involved in the regeneration or reconstruction of a cultural identity which history has usually left seriously damaged. Their gaze, then, rests not on the future but, primarily, on the past as they strive to restore the congruence between culture, territory and self-government that they imagine existed in a by-gone age.

One naturally feels some sympathy for smaller nations struggling to secure their national identity. Even so, it has to be recognised that programmes of cultural assimilation, whatever their inspiration, almost inevitably meet with resistance. Unless the advantages of cultural migration are so obviously huge that they completely neutralise all feelings of allegiance to the original group, most members of the group will resist the imposition of a new tongue and all that goes with it. The more vigorous the policy of assimilation, the stronger will normally be the resistance it meets. Such, at least, is true in contemporary Spain, where resistance is strongest in Catalonia and comes both from Spaniards whose roots ultimately go back to Spanish-speaking Spain and from those whose names unmistakably betray their local origin. An example of the former is Antonio Robles, president of the *Asociación por la Tolerancia y contra la Discriminación*, whose strenuous efforts to defend the rights of Spanish speakers in Catalonia regularly make headline news in some of the more right-wing Spanish dailies;[20] examples of the latter include Trías de Bes and Aleix Vidal-Quadras. Trías de Bes is actually a former leader of the Catalan nationalist party *Convergència Democràtica de Catalunya* and has represented the Catalan coalition party *Convergència i Unió* in the Spanish parliament. He deserted to the Spanish centre-right *Partido Popular* in 1995 because he could no longer support the kind of linguistic policy which the Catalan government has been promoting in recent years.[21] Similarly, Aleix Vidal-Quadras, former president of *Partido Popular* in Catalonia, spoke out unequivocally against the Catalan programme of linguistic assimilation during a conference held in Santander in the summer of 1996. By the end of September, he had been dismissed from office as a direct result of pressure on Madrid from the Catalan government, which is currently lending its support to the Spanish Prime Minister, whose party (PP) lacks an overall majority in the Spanish parliament.[22] However, removal from office has not silenced Vidal-Quadras on the matter of linguistic rights. In fact, when the Catalan parliament approved, in December 1997, a revised Law of Linguistic Normalisation, Vidal-Quadras actually appealed to the Catalan people to engage in civil disobedience, an appeal which, it has to be said, has so far gone largely unheeded.

Although resistance to this kind of cultural assimilation is more common in Catalonia than in any of the other regions discussed in this paper, there is, nevertheless, evidence of it elsewhere. The *Asociación Gallega por la Libertad de Idioma*, for example, was established, among other things, precisely to limit the use of Galician in the public school system of the region and to defend the right of Spanish speakers to opt for an education in the language of the State.[23] On a more localised scale, there has been resistance in Wales, specifically in Merthyr Tydfil, to local council plans to make the Welsh language compulsory in nursery classes. Apparently, a petition of more than 700 signatures has been collected in the borough of Quaker's Yard, where English is the dominant language, and is to be forwarded to the Welsh Office as part of a campaign to thwart plans to make nursery education in the borough monolingual in Welsh. Significantly, local residents claim not to be anti-Welsh but insist that they are unwilling to see their children learn Welsh as a first language. In response to this protest, bilingual nursery provision in the area is currently under consideration.[24]

When multicultural states engage in the assimilation of the minority cultures located within their borders, they often discriminate against whole nations by denying them the right to use their mother tongue for official purposes; when small nations embrace similar policies, they tend to discriminate against individuals and, perhaps, specific sections of the population such as immigrants or those living within certain well-defined areas. There can, of course, be no doubt that there is something of a contradiction in what small nations do when they pursue policies of cultural assimilation in order to reconstruct their national identity. At its simplest, the contradiction entails indulging in precisely the kinds of behaviour they condemn in multicultural states which seek to construct a single cultural identity to match their political identity. This should come as no surprise. The struggle to achieve cultural homogeneity necessarily means that the rights of the individual are swallowed up in those of the collectivity. The reason for this is that nationalism, whatever its point of origin, is basically about territory. It is about transforming the culture of a given territory and steering it either back towards the past or towards a new future.[25] Either way, it exhibits scant regard for the habits and customs, linguistic or otherwise, of those individuals who currently inhabit the land. Reconstructing national identity may, therefore, turn out to be just as risky a business as constructing it.

Conclusion

Nationalist ideology dictates that there should be congruence between nation and state, between cultural identity and political identity. Accordingly, many powerful political entities have engaged in the construction of appropriate, corresponding cultural identities and many minority cultures have sought political power in order to protect or reconstruct identities under threat. As we have seen, the role of language in shaping national identity is of crucial importance. Perhaps the most eloquent exponent of the view that nationalist movements of all persuasions 'invite' individuals and collectivities to imagine a particular kind of community through a particular print language is the North American scholar, Benedict Anderson. Referring specifically to the power of language to provide entry into the target community, he writes:

> Language is not an instrument of exclusion: in principle, anyone can learn a language. On the contrary, it is fundamentally inclusive, limited only by the fatality of Babel: no one lives long enough to learn *all* languages.

And:

> From the start the nation was conceived in language, not in blood, and [...] one could be 'invited into' the imagined community.[26]

Language is, without doubt, a fundamental component of our identity and most individuals are perfectly happy to imagine a particular national community through a particular print language, so long as the print language concerned is basically the same language as their native tongue. However, Anderson seems to refer here to the assimilatory function of language, to the way in which it may incorporate, or permit to be incorporated, linguistically into the community of those individuals or groups who belong to some other community. It is, of course, true, as Anderson maintains, that, in principle, anyone can learn a language. But it would be wrong to pretend that anyone can learn any language perfectly at any time in his life. Children obviously can learn any language perfectly and, presumably, this is why the Catalan government has introduced a programme of linguistic immersion in Catalan schools for pupils between three and eight years of age. Adults, however, rarely, if ever, come to speak a language acquired after childhood quite like native speakers. We can think, for example, of Giulio Mazzarini, who became a naturalised Frenchman in 1639 but who never felt at ease in French and never succeeded in persuading the French that he was anything but Italian. Noteworthy too is the fact that some individuals or groups are reluctant to embrace a language that is not their mother tongue and may even refuse to allow their children to acquire it as their first language. This is something which is currently being enunciated in the most unambiguous terms by the mothers of Merthyr Tydfil. What this means, of course, is that the role of language in providing access to the community is not altogether so straightforward as Anderson appears to suggest. As well as functioning as a gate through which the individual or group may pass, language also constitutes a very real barrier for those who desire to enter the community but never manage to become linguistically naturalised and for those who, out of loyalty to their roots, choose not to trade their native tongue for a new one. The reluctance of individuals and groups to abandon one linguistic identity in favour of a new one, regardless of the type of nationalism with which the transfer is associated, is something which this study has sought to underline. Even so, the language barrier, in most instances, need apply only to the first generation. The next generation will always prove linguistically able to enter the new community. Whether or not it chooses to do so will, of course, depend on a variety of factors, especially on the kind of image of the target culture which is transmitted to the new generation by the collective memory of the group to which it belongs. For this reason, it is essential that entry into the new community is by invitation, never by compulsion.

References

ABC, 16. VIII. 95; 17. VIII. 95; 20. VIII. 95; 21. VIII. 96.

Anderson, Benedict, *Imagined Communities. Reflections on the Origin and Spread of Nationalism.* London & New York: Verso, 1991.

Argelaguet i Argemí, Jordi, 'L'impacte dels partits polítics en la política lingüística de la Generalitat de Catalunya en l'ensenyament obligatori.' Unpublished doctoral thesis. Universitat Autònoma de Barcelona, 1996.

Gaskell, John, 'Welsh fight to keep English language.' *The Sunday Telegraph*, 4. I. 98.

Gorostidi, Iñaki, 'El bilingüisme és la mort de la llengua.' *El Temps*, 5. VIII. 96.

Hobsbawm, E.J., *Nations and Nationalism since 1780.Programme, Myth and Reality.* 2nd ed. Cambridge: Cambridge University Press, 1992.

Jenkins, Simon, 'A Dragon, not St David.' *The Times*, 17. IX. 97.

Mill, John Stuart, 'Considerations on Representative Government.' In *Essays on Politics and Society. Collected*

Works of John Stuart Mill, vol. XIX. Ed. J.M. Robson. Toronto: University of Toronto Press / Routledge & Kegan Paul, 1977.

Neath Guardian, The. 15. IV. 97.

País Digital, El. 30. XII .97.

Robles, Antonio, '¿Lengua propia de Cataluña?' *ABC Cataluña,* 17. IV. 97.

Sánchez Moguel, Antonio, *El movimiento histórico regionalista de Cataluña y Galicia. Discurso leído ante la Real Academia de la Historia en la recepción pública de D. Antonio Sánchez Moguel.* Madrid: Imprenta de la Viuda Hernando, 1888.

Siguan, Miquel, *La España Plurilingüe.* Madrid: Alianza Editorial, 1992.

Williams, Lynn, 'The Elastic Nation, or, When is a Category not a Category?' In *The Nation: Myth or Reality?* Ed. Keith Cameron. Exeter: Intellect, 1994, pp. 39-49.

Williams, Lynn, 'Percepciones de identidad: el problema de la denominación lingüística en España.' *Tesserae,* vol. 1, no 2, 1995, pp. 263-75.

Notes

1   E. J. Hobsbawm, *Nations and Nationalism since 1780. Programme, Myth and Reality.* 2nd ed. Cambridge: Cambridge University Press, 1992, p. 9.

2   John Stuart Mill, 'Considerations on Representative Government.' In *Essays on Politics and Society. Collected Works of John Stuart Mill,* vol. XIX. Ed. J.M. Robson. Toronto: University of Toronto Press / Routledge & Kegan Paul: Toronto, 1977, p. 545.

3   For more on the question of national self-perception, see Lynn Williams, 'The Elastic Nation, or, When is a Category not a Category?' in Keith Cameron, ed., *The Nation: Myth or Reality?* Exeter: Intellect, 1994, pp. 39-49; and Lynn Williams, 'Percepciones de identidad: el problema de la denominación lingüística en España.' *Tesserae,* vol. 1, no 2, 1995, pp. 263-75.

4   Mill himself falls into this category, arguing, rather disparagingly, in favour of the absorption of small nations by larger ones when it is beneficial. He gives as examples the Welsh and the Scots who, as originally inferior and backward collectivities, now share, as members of the *British nation,* 'the ideas and feelings of a highly civilized and cultivated people'. See Mill, *op. cit.,* p. 549. This is very much the same view as we find in post-revolutionary France, where Bretons and Occitans were, for their own benefit, 'invited into' the new French nation through the French language.

5   Benedict Anderson, *Imagined Communities. Reflections on the Origin and Spread of Nationalism.* London & New York: Verso, 1991, p. 134.

6   The prestige of English culture led to a certain amount of spontaneous cultural assimilation in non-English parts of Britain prior to political union and the same may be said of Castilian culture in Spain which had started to penetrate the Basque Country in the Middle Ages. But there is, of course, a world of difference between willingly embracing an alien culture and having it forced upon one.

7   Miquel Siguan, *La España plurilingüe.* Madrid: Alianza Editorial, 1992, pp. 218, 233.

8   Antonio Sánchez Moguel, *El movimiento histórico regionalista de Cataluña y Galicia. Discurso leído ante la Real Academia de la Historia en la recepción pública de D. Antonio Sánchez Moguel.* Imprenta de la Viuda Hernando: Madrid, 1888. Rather surprisingly, this is a view which appears to be shared by a number of prominent Catalans. At least, it is implied in statements they have made to the effect that the Spanish State includes only three nations: the Catalans, the Basques and the rest. See, for example, *El País Digital,* 30. XII. 97. Jordi Pujol, president of the Catalan government, has also made statements of this kind to the Spanish press.

9   Obviously, the bag-pipe is a feature of Galician and other cultures and, therefore, cannot be said to be exclusively Scottish.

10   See Anderson, *op. cit.,* pp. 133-34.

11   According to the 1991 census for Wales, the age-group from 3-15 years old shows the highest proportion of Welsh speakers, with a figure of 24.3%. This represents an increase of 6.7% since the census of 1981. For more information, see 'Fewer People Living in West Glamorgan.' *The Neath Guardian,* 15.IV.97, p. 12.

12   The different levels of self-government envisaged for each territory probably have no direct relation to the relative strength of national feeling in Scotland and Wales. Although Wales has never been strongly

in favour of home-rule, it has to be said that the choice between an assembly and a parliament was not, on this occasion, given to the Welsh. They were simply required to say whether or not they wanted an assembly. The small margin in favour of an assembly may have something to do with the fact that many felt that an assembly of the kind proposed was nothing short of an insult or, more probably, that among the Welsh of South Wales class identity has precedence over national identity.

13 Simon Jenkins, 'A Dragon, not St David.' *The Times*, 17. IX. 97, p. 18.

14 Mill himself sees 'identity of political antecedents' as one of the strongest causes likely to generate a feeling of nationality within a group. See Mill, *op. cit.*, p.546. However, this is not the same as saying that a separate political history is a pre-requisite for nationhood.

15 See *The Neath Guardian*, 15.IV.97, p.12.

16 The presence of immigrants of non-white ethnicity does not, on the whole, complicate the question of national identity in Wales. According to the 1991 census, white ethnic groups formed 98.5% of the country's population. See *The Neath Guardian*, 15.IV.97, p. 12. Clearly, however, there may be individuals who are not white but who, in a very real sense, feel themselves to be Welsh.

17 Iñaki Gorostidi, 'El bilingüisme és la mort de la llengua.' *El Temps*, 5. VIII. 96, p. 44.

18 Members of the nation who do not speak the national language clearly do not have a national identity which is as undiluted as those who do speak it. Similarly, those who are bilingual in the national language and in the language of the State have a national identity which is more diluted than that of monolingual speakers of the national language. Among the Welsh, Scots, Basques, Catalans and Galicians it is difficult today to find individuals who speak only the national tongue. This means, of course, that the national identity of just about every member of the nation is, to some degree, diluted.

19 This is just one of the conclusions to emerge from a recent study of Catalan society. See Jordi Argelaguet i Argemí, 'L'impacte dels partits polítics en la política lingüística de la Generalitat de Catalunya en l'ensenyament obligatori.' Unpublished doctoral thesis. Universitat Barcelona: Autònoma de Barcelona, 1996.

20 See, for example, Antonio Robles, '¿Lengua propia de Cataluña? *ABC Cataluña, 17.IV.97, p. 6.*

21 See *ABC,* 16, VIII, 95, p. 20; *ABC,* 17.VIII. 95, p. 15.

22 See *ABC,* 21. VIII. 96, p. 42; *El País Digital,* 30. 12. 97.

23 See *ABC,* 16, VIII. 95, pp. 50-51; *ABC,* 17. VIII, 95, p. 63; *ABC,* 20. VIII. 95, p. 47.

24 John Gaskell, 'Welsh fight to keep English language.' *The Sunday Telegraph,* 4. I. 98, p. 15.

25 Clearly, it may also involve transforming the political system of the territory. However, this is not my principal concern here.

26 Anderson, *op. cit.,* pp.134 and 145.

Towards Devolution:

Poetry and Anglo-Welsh Identity

Diane Davies

In the Spring of 1996 *The Western Mail*, subtitled 'The National Newspaper of Wales', ran a series of articles on what people from diverse walks of life understood by a sense of Welsh identity. One contributor, the BBC journalist and newsreader John Humphrys, attempted to diagnose a condition he referred to as the 'lack of interest in all matters Welsh syndrome', in so doing making some forthright comparisons between Welsh and Scottish identity:

> The Scots are taken seriously. We, by and large, are not. We are defined in the English mind by our national caricature. The daftest cliché in the film director's manual – coal-dust covered men singing in perfect harmony as they trudge back to the cottages from the pit – may fade away now the pits have closed. But don't bank on it. To a large extent we connive in the creation of our cultural caricature. Why, if a play or short story comes from Wales, must the plot invariably be set in a Welsh village peopled entirely by women called Bloddie and men called Dai Coffin-Maker or Jones-the-Something-or-Other? And why must they all have IQs of 10 but be very, very cunning? And why must half the characters sound as though they're Peter Sellers imitating a doctor from Madras?[1]

We do not have to look far, especially in the case of TV programmes, for some illustration of stereotypical Welshness. The BBC series, 'Mortimer's Law', about a coroner called Rachel Mortimer who gives up a high-flying professional life in London to work in rural Wales, clearly seemed to associate the Welsh mind with a degree of cunning and eccentricity, and this was not just in the portrayal of the criminals. Much of the series was taken up with a sub-plot concerning the disposal of the ashes of Rachel's mentor, the former coroner, who declared they should be scattered at a place of ancient oak trees apparently with druidic associations. The problem was that the precise location chosen turned out to have been concreted over and turned into a shopping precinct. Finally, the cunning widow resolves the issue by deviously burying the ashes under pot plants in the garden centre within the precinct. Light relief from the formality of the coroner's inquests this may be, but it also amounts to an all too typically off-beat representation of Welshness.

My concern here, however, is not with Welshness on TV. What I wish to do in this chapter is focus on how Welsh identity has been interrogated in Anglo-Welsh poetry after 1945. If stereotypes of Welshness can still sometimes be found in the popular media, poets in Wales have continually questioned and challenged them, and never more determinedly than in the last 20 years. Anglo-Welsh identity is of the problematic, hyphenated sort, a split personality that has often seemed doomed to self-destruct, yet which has gradually emerged with a new confidence and sense of purpose. The heavily politicised period between the Devolution Referendum of 1979 and that of 1997 can, I think, be seen as an important interval in which writers and critics in Wales explored the relationship of literature and national identity with a new honesty.

Those familiar with Anglo-Welsh writing (now often referred to more sensitively as 'Welsh writing in English') will recall where the stereotypes trotted out by Humphrys in my opening quotation originated. Farcical and grotesque portraits of Welsh peasantry can be traced back to Caradoc Evans (1878-1945) whose bestseller *My People* (1915) entertained a metropolitan market and angered Welsh readers in equal measure. Evans has gone down in history as the father of Anglo-Welsh literature, yet other writers (e.g. Rhys Davies, Glyn Jones and Dylan Thomas) were happy to take up a similar vein of fantasy and eccentricity in their representation of the Welsh character. These were writers of the so-called 'first flowering' of Anglo-Welsh literature, and for those connected specifically with the South Wales Valleys (e.g. Gwyn Thomas), absurdism and farce to some extent provided a necessary diversion from a harsh world of poverty and the dole. Writers like Gwyn Thomas were also disinclined to be more sensitive in their representation of Welshness when, in any case, they regarded the nonconformist culture of rural Wales as puritanically repressive and the Welsh language – which was in rapid decline in the industrial valleys – as largely anachronistic in the context of the international cause of the worker.

It was really not until after the Second World War and the beginning of the 'second flowering' of Anglo-Welsh literature that the question of Welsh and Anglo-Welsh identity and the survival of Welsh culture and nationhood became a central concern of the majority of writers with Welsh affiliation working through the medium of English. Certainly the most influential figure of this generation was, and still is, R.S.Thomas, a poet who is regarded by some as one of the most important poets writing in English anywhere today, and by others as a provocative nationalist and Anglophobe. These lines from 'Reservoirs' typify the uncompromising stance taken by Thomas on both the actions of the English and the partial complicity of the Welsh in their own cultural demise:

Where can I go, then, from the smell
Of decay, from the putrefying of a dead
Nation ? I have walked the shore
For an hour and seen the English
Scavenging among the remains
Of our culture, covering the sand
Like the tide and, with the roughness
Of the tide, elbowing our language
Into the grave that we have dug for it.[2]

Thomas was not brought up Welsh-speaking but learnt the language as an adult. He uses Welsh in preference to English whenever possible and has written a number of prose works in the language, including the autobiographical *Neb* (*No One*).[3] He believes there can be no diluting of Welsh identity, that 'the only justification for the Anglo-Welsh movement was that it should be a stepping-stone back to the vernacular'. For R.S., as he is often called, 'Hyphenisation is betrayal. Whatever the situation may be in other countries, in Wales we have by now only the language to distinguish us'.[4]

Many of the poets of the second flowering, with Thomas to lead the way, shared the sense that it was the Welsh language that they should rediscover, if possible, if they were to be fit custodians of Welsh culture. Sam Adams's poem, 'Hill Fort, Caerleon', typifies the theme of alienation from language and heritage that was frequently foregrounded:

From this tree-finned hill
Breasting the breeze –
Leaf shadows like water shifting,
Sounds of water always moving
In the preening of so many leaves –
I can look down over old Caerllion.

In the aqueous rush of bracken fronds
Breaking round, and in a sound
Clearer now, once heard,
An unbroken hum
Like some instrument endlessly strummed
On one low note, or the tone

Of wires looped from pole
To pole vibrating through wood
Where we pressed our ears,
There is a sense of something living,
Breathing, watching here
As I push towards the rampart mound.

The path is blocked. A swarthy
Sentry bars my way, his spear-
Tip sparks with sunlight.
He challenges in accents I know well;
The words I recognise, but the sense eludes.
I am ashamed and silent. He runs me through.[5]

In the first stanza Adams establishes an expectant but non-specific atmosphere: the continual movement of leaves and water suggests the poet feels the natural world as a 'presence' as he looks down at the town, referring to it by its wholly

Welsh name 'Caerllion' rather than the partly anglicised 'Caerleon'. The strange 'preening' of the leaves seems to be echoed in the second stanza by the image of the 'unbroken hum / Like some instrument endlessly strummed', suggesting now a more insistent sense of unbroken sound. The run-on line bridging the second and third stanzas seems to mimic orthographically the image of electrical current carried between telegraph poles. Now the poet begins to connect these images to the ghostly presence of a 'sentry' from Caerleon's Romano-Celtic past, one who evidently uses a Celtic language remotely familiar to the poet but which, to his shame, he no longer understands. Unable to communicate with the 'silent' intruder, the sentry judges him to be a threatening outsider and kills him. Despite this melodramatic ending, the poem is interesting in its representation of the shadowy origins of Welsh national identity. There is an irony, intended or otherwise, in the fact that the voice challenging the poet to answer must itself be something of a hybrid, the speaker being both Celt and Roman citizen. What, then, is the sentry expecting of the poet, if not that he should declare allegiance to a Romano-British identity? Yet the poet is 'ashamed and silent', because although he is familiar with the sentry's 'words', their 'sense eludes': he cannot fully comprehend or accept the subjection of his tribe to the pragmatic invader. The unpalatable message of the final sentence 'He runs me through' is, therefore, that the modern Welsh nationalist should be ready for martyrdom rather than cede to the demands of a colonial power. However, the poem's attempt to draw a parallel between the Celts under Roman occupation and the subordination of the modern Welsh to their English neighbours is, from today's perspective, both simplistic and troubling. After all, the poem presupposes the existence of a clearly definable Welsh nation prior to the Romans' arrival on the scene, whereas in fact there had been at that time, not one identifiable Celtic nation, but a number of separate, warring tribes. It was only after the departure of the Romans that, as the historian Gwyn A. Williams points out, it became strategically necessary to forge a sense of a Welsh nation:

> For a further four hundred years they [Celtic-speaking tribes] lived under Rome; for half that time, their freemen as Roman citizens of Britannia, in at least three city-state Romano-British commonwealths. With the breaking of Britannia, they emerged in a welter of little British kingdoms.... By the eighth century they found that Britain had been removed. They were stuck in their peninsulas behind a great dyke and rampart raised by an alien people who called them foreigners – in that alien language 'weallas' – Welsh. By that time they themselves were beginning to call what was left of the Britons 'Cymry' or fellow-countrymen. Pretty soon there was nobody left to call 'Cymry' except themselves. Their stronger kings started to hammer the whole bunch together and to make a country called Cymru: Wales.[6]

The second flowering, rooted in Welsh nationalism, tended to be inward-looking, hostile to England and the metropolis and, consequently, was ignored by the English critical establishment. The fact that during the 1950s and 1960s new poetry magazines were founded in Wales specifically to foster Anglo-Welsh writing

(*The Anglo-Welsh Review* in 1957 and *Poetry Wales* in 1965) only further marginalised some of these writers, from the British point of view, since there was no need for them to look for publishing outlets beyond Welsh borders. The editors of the anthology *Twelve Modern Anglo-Welsh Poets* (1975) seemed to be aware of the deficiencies of this kind of entrenchment when they suggested that there was a danger in 'the tendency to narrowness, the failure to look beyond the Welsh pale to the wider perspectives of world literature'.[7]

Commitment to a distinctively Welsh inheritance, and particularly to the role of the Welsh language in its representation, was to become more tenuous with the next generation of writers. Indeed, in his introduction to *Green Horse: An Anthology by Young Poets of Wales*, published just one year before the 1979 Devolution Referendum, the critic and historian Roland Mathias notes that many of the poets featured in the collection have been brought up without any contact with the Welsh language and 'against backgrounds...in which life is not merely anglicised but remarkably little different (...) from that experienced in any region of England outside the Home Counties...' He goes on to claim that 'commitment to the Welsh heritage, where it appears, is the result of involvement...with other enthusiasts or representatives of the Welsh heartland. In other words, it is acquired, no longer indigenous'.[8]

Although *Green Horse* does show that, for some poets born and resident in Wales, there was still a sense of nostalgia for a forgotten Welshness associated with childhood or the accounts of older relatives who had experienced a richer and supposedly more wholesome community life, many voices are openly hostile towards the modes of writing of the R.S.Thomas generation. In 'How to Write Anglo-Welsh Poetry' John Davies taunts the would-be apprentice with merciless sarcasm:

First, apologise for not being able
To speak Welsh. Go on: apologise.
Being Anglo-*any*thing is really tough;
Any gaps you can fill with sighs.

And get some roots, juggle names like
Taliesin and ap Gwilym, weave
A Cymric web. It doesn't matter what
They wrote; look, let's not be naïve.

Now you can go on about the past
Being more real than the present-
You've read your early R.S.Thomas,
You know where Welsh Wales went...[9]

The mere existence of such jibes, or rather their publication in anthologies, tells us that by the end of the 1970s the validity of Anglo-Welshness as a genre was being seriously doubted. For poets like John Davies, Steve Griffiths and Robert

Minhinnick there was no inclination to be circumscribed by Wales. Indeed their way of knowing 'home' was often by looking at it from a cultural distance (e.g. through writing about travel and residence abroad) or by turning their attention to specific communities and to what they encountered through their professional work. Stylistically, too, the younger poets were open to influences far beyond those of the Welsh tradition, with Peter Finch in particular absorbing the energy of the avant-garde with a spirit of innovation that has remained undaunted, and Tony Curtis acknowledging his admiration for Browning's dramatic monologues as well as contemporary American poetry. Sheenagh Pugh, one of the best women writers living in Wales, adopts the subtlety and reserve of the English Movement poets, but is also influenced by other literature, for example, through her own translation work from German. Here is 'The Use of the Field' by Pugh (from her most recent volume) which shows how even an apparently traditional Anglo-Welsh subject may have more of Larkin in it than R.S. Thomas:

> On the turn of the railway line after Taffs Well
> lies a triangular field, a handkerchief.
> It seems smoother, its green deeper, than most;
> a Persian glow to it under the morning sun.
> It is sheltered by cliffs, enclosed in a river's arm,
> and it grows no crop. I have never seen it grazed
> by sheep or cattle; no horses are pastured there.
> Yet the grass is a lawn almost; close and gleaming,
> -tended? For what? I look at the field, thinking,
> always, *What is its use?* If not arable
> nor pastureland; if nobody ever camps there,
> if nobody rides trail bikes or flies kites?
> What farmer, for a whim, grooms a field
> and leaves it watching its face in the water,
> its only witness, unless you count the windows
> that mirror it a moment in passing?[10]

In the referendum on St David's Day in 1979 only about 12 per cent of those who voted were in favour of a Welsh Assembly, four out of five people voting against devolution. Looking back both at this vote and the subsequent massive swing to the Conservatives in Wales in the General Election of that year, Gwyn A. Williams concluded that 'a majority of the inhabitants of Wales are choosing a British identity which seems to require the elimination of a Welsh one'.[11]

Through the 1980s and much of the 1990s there has been continued discussion in literary and cultural journals about the increasing Anglicization of Welsh writing in English. But perspectives have widened, and it is the blandness of an all-embracing Anglo-American culture that some commentators now fear most, rather than a specifically English influence. Yet, fortunately, there is also less deference to the notion of an Anglo-Welsh canon and the younger writers, be they poets, novelists or dramatists, are clearly mapping out their own cultural landscapes. For

Robert Minhinnick the Wales of R.S.Thomas is 'largely unlocatable': of the famous hill-farmers of Thomas's best-known poems, he writes that 'Prytherch, the Puws, Cynddylan, etc. are mere cyphers created to make a point'.[12] Similarly, in a recent critical study of several post-war poets, Edward Picot notes Thomas's tendency to avoid detailed observation and that his 'often-declared allegiance to Wales and to the traditional lifestyle of the Welsh hill-farmers is undermined by the fact that his poetry works to disembody both the landscape and the people who live there'.[13]

What many of today's writers and critics realise, I think rightly, is that there is no future in imagining an artificial Wales, but only in engagement with the real nation in all its diversity. And there is plenty of evidence that this is the way that Welsh writers, whether writing in English or Welsh, can continue to have a distinctive voice. Indeed, there is more collaboration between the English-language and Welsh-language writers of Wales now than ever before. A leading poet in Welsh, Menna Elfyn, has had her poetry published with parallel translation in English (interestingly, translated by Anglo-Welsh poets like R.S.Thomas and Gillian Clarke),[14] and has given many readings at home and abroad alongside poets writing in English. Also, Wales now has several poets (e.g. Gwyneth Lewis and Huw Jones) writing in both languages. In his introduction to a new anthology of writing from Wales,[15] Minhinnick goes so far as to suggest that the next generation of English-language writers in Wales might be, not from the 'old spawning grounds' (Glamorgan and Gwent), but 'bilingual, from Gwynedd, Clwyd or Dyfed'. It seems, then, that new bridges are being built and crossed between what used to be two polarised, and at times mutually distrustful, language communities. Even the unthinkable appears to have happened: the Welsh language has actually become more popular, with the demand for bilingual schools increasing and learners of the language growing in number. It is the general assumption in Wales today, and not just in the Welsh-speaking heartland, that the ability to speak Welsh as well as English is likely to enhance the prospects of most of those in local government, education, the arts and media-related professions. As Robin Reeves points out in his editorial to the *New Welsh Review* published in the Spring of 1997, this upturn in the fortunes of the Welsh language has, with an ironic reversal of history, been brought about by the now global currency of the English language:

> The explosion in telecommunications and the creation of the world-wide village is resulting in languages the world over having to learn to live alongside English as a dominant imperial language – something Wales has experienced for many centuries. And English's international footlooseness is paradoxically making Welsh more popular as a key badge of Wales's identity.[16]

If the trend towards bilingualism continues, Welsh writing in English will be able to build on its refreshing new links with the Welsh language, but it may also acquire a new distinctiveness in the way it uses the English language. When Anglo-Welsh writers felt obliged to entertain an English metropolitan readership, they would use dialect forms to ridicule, for example, the speech of an ill-educated peasantry. As they have become more confident in their own cultural roots, they have begun to use Welsh English dialect without wishing to stereotype and demean those who use it. Before looking at an example of this, however, it may be worth drawing a few comparisons between Wales and Scotland in this context. Scotland has three broad traditions of writing through which Scottish identities may be represented: a Gaelic tradition; a Standard Scottish English tradition, and a tradition of writing in Lowland Scots vernacular which goes back to the medieval period, was revived by Robert Burns and championed by Hugh MacDiarmid in the first half of this century. Today poets like the Glasgow-based Tom Leonard are the inheritors of a Scots voice which is distinct from both Gaelic (a different language) and Standard Scottish English. Scots has its own formal and spelling conventions (e.g. 'frae' for 'from'; 'cannae' for 'cannot', etc.), as well as an extensive range of vocabulary to distinguish it from Standard English. Now in Wales, by contrast, writers have only two traditions to choose from: the Welsh language tradition and the so-called 'Anglo-Welsh', which critics have traced back to metaphysical and devotional poets like Henry Vaughan and George Herbert, but which does not have anything like the formal linguistic distinctiveness of Scots. Anglo-Welsh poets are generally recognised as such because of their allusions to Welsh places, communities or individuals, or occasional use of traditional poetic forms borrowed from the Welsh language tradition (e.g. the awdl, or englyn). Thus the Anglo-Welsh tradition is defended on the basis of largely non-linguistic criteria. Anglo-Welsh poetry cannot easily convey its cultural origins unless its subject-matter is connected to Wales in some way, whereas Scots writing reveals where it comes from no matter what it is about. And what it reveals is not, of course, just a matter of linguistic code, but also a specific cultural and political standpoint. As Robert Crawford makes clear in his compelling study *Devolving English Literature,* the use of a provincial vernacular automatically gives a voice to the 'barbarian'. Crawford writes of poets like Tom Leonard being 'able to use non-standard forms as part of a gesture of solidarity with lower-class speakers…, as well as using these forms as a means of interrogating the established structures of linguistic and cultural power'.[17] Some Anglo-Welsh poets have attempted to create their own vernacular, giving it dialectal spellings, but, as we can see from these opening lines to a poem in Swansea dialect by Stephen Knight, the lack of established conventions for Welsh-English dialect can produce obscurity:

Ow footbawlTeem wares blackenwhite:
a angz a reds, a looks kuntrite
fuhlOozin, Homer N'weigh,
buhstill aisle go unwatchum-play
in Winter wenner Windsor blowin
9gaylz offaSee unthrowin
rubbish rowndee airmTee stanz,
blowin ice throo my airmTee ands.[18]

Such lack of recognisable forms for the dialect is, of course, Knight's point in this poem, but how much more difficult it is for him to illustrate this than it is for Tom Leonard when he uses a more familiar provincial demotic:

this is thi
six a clock
news thi
man said n
thi reason
a talk wia
BBC accent
iz coz yi
widny wahnt
mi ti talk
aboot thi
trooth wia
voice lik
wanna yoo
scruff.[19]

Of course, poets like Stephen Knight could establish new directions for English-language poetry in Wales, but it is debatable whether this would open up, or in fact restrict, the scope of Anglo-Welsh writing. Knight has himself admitted that poetry representing local dialect in this way would be incomprehensible to a reader outside Britain and that the most successful context for it is the live poetry reading, where copies of the published poem can be handed out before it is heard.[20]

Today there is no controlling group of writers speaking for the Welsh nation as there was in the 1960s and 1970s, and artists of very different backgrounds and styles, working in a range of genres (and with new strengths in the novel and film production), are all pursuing their own interests with varying degrees of connection to Welsh life. The satires of the typical Anglo-Welsh voice (by John Davies, Harri Webb and others) are no longer topical and so not half as entertaining as they used to be. Increasingly, poets are orientating themselves to the Wales they know, which is often the post-industrial Wales of lost community values and opportunities made or destroyed by the faceless multinationals. It can also still be a rural Wales, though there is now less of a sense of remoteness from urban influence. Connections are made between Wales and elsewhere and poets write as citizens, not only of a small nation, but also of the world, aware of how the whole planet needs to be respected. Even one of Wales's most rooted poets, Gillian Clarke, has written impressive poems on the importance of seeing the nation, ultimately, from an internationalist and global perspective. Her 'Neighbours' is here quoted in full:

That spring was late. We watched the sky
and studied charts for shouldering isobars.
Birds were late to pair. Crows drank from the lamb's eye.

Over Finland small birds fell: song-thrushes
steering north, smudged signatures on light,
migrating warblers, nightingales.

Wing-beats failed over fjords, each lung a sip of gall.
Children were warned of their dangerous beauty.
Milk was spilt in Poland. Each quarrel

the blowback from some old story,
a mouthful of bitter air from the Ukraine
brought by the wind out of its box of sorrows.

This spring a lamb sips caesium on a Welsh hill.
A child, lifting her face to drink the rain,
takes into her blood the poisoned arrow.

Now we are all neighbourly, each little town
in Europe twinned to Chernobyl, each heart
with the burnt fireman, the child on the Moscow train.

In the democracy of the virus and the toxin
we wait. We watch for bird migrations,
one bird returning with green in its voice,

glasnost,
golau glas,
a first break of blue.

(*golau glas* - blue light)[21]

In the early hours of 19 September 1997 the final result of the second Referendum came through: by the smallest of margins the Welsh had voted in favour of an elected Assembly for Wales. The 'Yes' campaign, as well as their opponents, were left bruised and humbled by the closeness of the fight. Writing only a few hours later, Robert Minhinnick weighed up both the change and the challenge thus:

> ...very carefully, and with considerable reluctance, Wales is remaking itself. What changes this morning, imperceptibly but permanently, is a sense of a people's esteem for itself. With that must come tolerance – indeed, celebration – of the difference of others. [22]

Minhinnick's basic principle of 'tolerance' was shared by Robin Reeves, editing the post-referendum *New Welsh Review*. He writes that 'multiculturalism is a fact of life in Wales', hoping that 'all sides...help forge new, more balanced and mutually beneficial relationships between the multi-cultural nations which make up the United Kingdom as it enters the 21st century'.[23] Other, more recent, commentators have felt sufficiently confident about the outcome that they have declared that the future now looks very promising for Wales and Welshness. They argue that the success of actors like Anthony Hopkins and rock bands like Manic Street Preachers and Super Furry Animals, and the opera singer Bryn Terfel, is only the most obvious sign of an increasingly buoyant Welsh culture. Jan Morris predicts that in 'another couple of generations, with luck, released from London's apron-strings, this can be a truly modern small country, bilingual (multilingual, perhaps), progressive in its outlook, ancient in its loyalties, proud of itself and content with its place in the wider community of Europe'.[24] Stirring stuff indeed.

As Wales shakes off its cultural cringe (to use a term normally applied to Australia), poetry may have begun to lose its traditional function as a voice of the Welsh nation. But poetry can, in any case, be ill-served by too predictable a role. Good poetry demands that we look askance and question our assumptions; it discourages us from relying too heavily on familiar points of reference, preferring to cast us adrift to take new bearings. For the poet, ultimately, identity is better deferred than shouted from the hill tops; poets are more witnesses than leaders. What Marina Warner writes of the Caribbean and international poet, Derek Walcott, could surely be a goal for the Anglo-Welsh poetry of the future. Walcott, she writes, 'reproduces the dense mesh of modern identity, with its multiple compass points, its layered experiences; he stands witness to a rich – and painful - story made in common by both invader and invaded, coloniser and colonised, migrants and residents'. For Warner, Walcott can show us a new way of 'talking about home', because his 'acts of remembering, his quest for identity are grounded in generosity.'[25]

Further Reading

Conran, Anthony (1982) *The Cost of Strangeness: Essays on the English Poets of Wales*. Llandysul: Gomer.

Jones, Glyn (1968) *The Dragon Has Two Tongues*. Dent: London.

Johnston, Dafydd (1994) *The Literature of Wales*. Cardiff: University of Wales Press.

Lloyd, David T. (ed)(1994) *The Urgency of Identity: Contemporary English-Language Poetry from Wales*. Illinois: Northwestern University Press.

Mathias, Roland (1987) *Anglo-Welsh Literature: An Illustrated History*. Bridgend: Poetry Wales Press.

Stephens, Meic (ed) (1986) *The Oxford Companion to the Literature of Wales*. Oxford: Oxford University Press.

Stevenson, Anne (1995) 'Identity, Language and Welsh Poetry', *Poetry Wales* 31(2): 38-43.

Thomas, M. Wynn (1992) *Internal Difference: Twentieth-Century Writing in Wales*. Cardiff: University of Wales Press.

Thwaite, Anthony (1996) *Poetry Today: A Critical Guide to British Poetry 1960-1995*. Harlow: Longman. (See chapter 11, 'Scotland and Wales')

Notes

1   Humphrys, John (1996) 'Time to blow all the coal-dust clichés away'. 13. Western Mail, 20 March.
2   Garlick, Raymond and Roland Mathias (1982) *Anglo-Welsh Poetry1480-1990*. 183. Bridgend: Seren.
3   Translated by Jason Walford Davies in Thomas, R.S. (1997) *Autobiographies*. 27-109. London: Phoenix.
4   Thomas, R. S. (1992) *Cymru or Wales*. 30. Llandysul: Gomer.
5   *Anglo-Welsh Poetry*: 280-281.
6   Williams, Gwyn A. (1985) *When Was Wales? A History of the Welsh*. 3. Harmondsworth: Penguin.
7   Dale-Jones,D.and R.Jenkins (1975) *Twelve Modern Anglo-Welsh Poets*. 16. London: University of London.
8   Introduction to Stephens, Meic and Peter Finch (1978) 18-19. *Green Horse: An Anthology by Young Poets of Wales*. Swansea: Christopher Davies.
9   *Green Horse*: 52-53.
10 Pugh, Sheenagh (1997) *Id's Hospit*. 34. Bridgend: Seren.

11 *When Was Wales?*: 303.
12 Minhinnick, R. (1993) 'Living with R.S. Thomas', *Poetry Wales* 29 (1): 12.
13 Picot, E. (1997) *Outcasts from Eden: Ideas of Landscape in British Poetry since 1945*. 122. Liverpool: Liverpool University Press.
14 Elfyn, M.(1995) *Eucalyptus: Selected Poems 1978-1994* . Llandysul: Gomer.
15 Minhinnick, R.(ed) *Drawing Down the Moon:Poems and Stories 1996. 8*. Bridgend: Seren.
16 Reeves, R. (1997) 'Welsh versus English', *New Welsh Review*. 36 (IX/IV):1
17 Crawford, R. *Devolving English Literature*. 284-285. Oxford: Clarendon Press.
18 Knight, Stephen (1996) 'At the Foot of Division Four', in *The Sandfields Baudelaire*. Smith/Doorstop Books.
19 Leonard, Tom. (1984) *Intimate Voices: Selected Work 1965-1983*. 88. Newcastle: Galloping Dog Press ('Unrelated Incidents (3)').
20 See the interview with Stephen Knight in *Poetry Wales*. 32(1): 30-34.
21 *Twentieth Century Anglo-Welsh Poetry:* 175.
22 *Poetry Wales* (1997) 33(2): 2.
23 *New Welsh Review* (1997) 38 (X/II): 1.
24 Morris, Jan (1998) 'The Dragon Still Breathes Fire'. 3. *The Times Weekend*, 28 February.
25 Warner, Marina (1994) *Managing Monsters: Six Myths of Our Time*. 93-94. London: Vintage.

Acknowledgements

The author, editor and publisher wish to thank the following for permission to quote copyright material:

Sam Adams – for 'Hill Fort, Caerleon' from *The Boy Inside* (Triskele Press).
Carcanet Press – for Gillian Clarke's 'Neighbours', from *Letting in the Rumour.*
Dent – for extract from R.S.Thomas's 'Reservoirs' in *Collected Poems.*
Gomer Press – for extract from John Davies's 'How to Write Anglo-Welsh Poetry', from *At the Edge of Town.*
Stephen Knight – for extract from 'At the Foot of Division Four', from *The Sandfields Baudelaire* (Smith/Doorstop Books).
Tom Leonard – for extract from 'Unrelated Incidents', from *Intimate Voices: Selected Work 1965-1983* (Galloping Dog Press).
Seren – for Sheenagh Pugh's 'The Use of the Field', from *Id's Hospit.*

State and Nation:

Germany Since Reunification

Mark Blacksell

National Identity, nationalism, and the state

Nationalism and a sense of national identity are recent creations; products in Europe of the period since the end of the 18th century. Ernst Gellner (1993), one of the most prolific analysts of political and socio-economic change in modern Europe, argues forcefully that the close identification of culture with the state, in other words nationalism, is not a feature of pre-industrial, agrarian societies and has only developed as industrialisation and advanced technology have increasingly come to dominate the way in which people live and work. The new forces bring with them an unavoidable commitment to economic growth and occupational mobility, which have combined steadily to erode feudal hierarchies and, consequently, forced peoples' cultural identities to be much more closely bound up with the state and an over-arching national identity.

Gellner identifies five stages in the transition. The first, the Congress of Vienna stage, refers to the territorial carve-up of Europe between Britain, Russia, Prussia, Austria and the defeated France after the end of the Napoleonic Wars in 1814-15, which attempted to reverse the disruption to the 18th century political order, by compensating the four ultimately victorious empires at the expense of France (Davies, 1997, 762). The second, national irredentism, lasted into the 20th century at the end of the First World War, but had little direct impact on the political geography of Europe. Nationalist aspirations were not in general translated into wholesale territorial reapportionment, the only significant exception being the Balkans, where a number of new highly nationalistic states were created, but as much as a consequence of the implosion of the Ottoman Empire as the coherence and vibrancy of Serbian and other nationalisms in the region.

The third stage embraces the period between the two World Wars when in the bulk of Europe the peace settlement brokered at the Treaty of Versailles finally replaced the shattered remnants of the pre-industrial dynastic empires in central Europe with a patchwork of small states, the boundaries of which were largely drawn specifically to reflect culturally homogenous regions. It was intended, in this way, to engender a stronger sense of national identity and to make cultural allegiance synonymous with the state. By and large, the experiment was a dismal failure: the small, politically and militarily weak states were unable to stand up for themselves, thus enfeebling Europe as a whole, yet at the same time they fostered rabid nationalist yearnings. Subsequently, in the fourth stage, these aspirations were translated into calls for cultural, ethnic and religious homogeneity, leading to mass movements of population across the new national borders and, more sinisterly, the emergence of genocide as an instrument of national policy.

On Europe's eastern border, of course, there was the very different model of the Soviet Union which, under the umbrella of Communist ideology, set out specifically to suppress national identities and subsume them into a homogenised socialist state. At the end of the 20th century this too was to fail, leading to many of the former Soviet Republics on the eastern fringes of Europe emerging, or re-emerging, as culturally distinctive independent states, eager to rejoin the Western European political mainstream.

Since the end of the Second World War, the fifth stage has been characterised by a broad-based movement, originating in western Europe, aimed at creating what might be termed 'collaborative nationalism'. The calls for a spurious reawakening of long-suppressed national identities, which had emerged so forcefully in the inter-war years and with such politically disastrous consequences, were generally rejected in favour of a multi-nationalism, based on a family of nationally distinct states bound together by common values and economic interests (Milward, 1992). The cornerstone of European collaborative nationalism is the European Union, an experiment in economic union that has developed in the last four decades of the 20th century into a vehicle for far-reaching political, social, and economic integration. It already has 15 members, with the prospect of at least a further 11 states joining in the early years of the next millennium.

The European Union, together with other multi-national organisations, such as NATO and the Council of Europe, is a powerful force for change in the political landscape, but it has also raised important issues of policy which have yet to be resolved. The most fundamental of these is the future of national identities and the extent to which a pooled sense of European self-esteem is compatible with a host of smaller national self-esteems? Certainly the lessons of nationalism and policies based on the primacy of national identities in Europe as a whole over the past two centuries suggest that such exclusivity is a recipe for conflict and political instability.

Creating Germany

During 1990, when frantic preparations were being made for a united Germany, there was some debate as to whether the process should be referred to as 'reunification', or 'unification', the distinction being that the former embodied an explicit historical continuity, including a single national identity, while the latter signalled a new beginning. In this chapter 'reunification' has been used quite intentionally, because the new Germany is clearly an extension of the FRG as originally constituted, and the FRG itself claims to have evolved directly from the Deutsche Reich of 1871. Such an outcome was not always a foregone conclusion, but the complete collapse of the Communist party and its hegemony in the USSR and in its satellite states (including the GDR) in Eastern Europe, ensured that reunification occurred on the FRG's terms.

To understand the force of the drive for reunification in Germany, it is necessary to explain, briefly, how the modern state of Germany emerged and how the FRG relates to the other German states that have existed in the course of this century. An element of continuity has been an essential component of each successive manifestation of the German state and the most recent change has served to strengthen, rather than weaken, historic links.

After the defeat of Napoleon at the Battle of Waterloo in 1815 and with it the effective collapse of his European Empire, a long process of political amalgamation began, which was to lead eventually to the founding of the Deutsche Reich in 1871. From the beginning, it was recognised that what was being created was a German state with a pivotal position in central Europe, which could act as a focus for a more integrated European system of states (Jäckel, 1990), but the nature of that state was fiercely disputed and the road to its creation beset with difficulty. The Deutsche Bund, established in 1815 at the Congress of Vienna, united 39 German princedoms and independent cities, but it rapidly disintegrated after 1849, when an ambitious attempt to create a unified administration came to nothing, following the Emperor of Prussia's refusal to become head of the unified state.

At issue was a conflict at the heart of the search for a generally acceptable definition of German identity and one which has haunted Germany right through the 19th and 20th centuries in a number of different guises, Großdeutschland versus Kleindeutschland. Großdeutschland is a concept that envisages a single state, embracing all the major German-speaking political areas in central Europe, including Austria. Kleindeutschland, on the other hand, envisages Germany and Austria as two separate states (Winkler, 1990).

Throughout the 19th century, and even before, there had been much academic speculation about the physical extent of a German-dominated Mitteleuropa, but once the Deutsche Reich became a reality the debates became much more focused on the issue of the ultimate boundaries of a German nation state (Schulz, 1989). At the same time, a separate debate was also in train about what should be the nature and extent of Germany's imperial ambitions overseas. The distinction between the two is often very blurred, with the same people contributing to both. But the world and national views they generated were important, because they provided a basis, and often a justification, for specific territorial ambitions.

The Prussia-dominated Norddeutsche Bund, founded in 1867, was clearly in the mould of Kleindeutschland, even though Austria as such did not exist at that stage, and this was still the case when the Deutsche Reich came into existence four years later. Bismark's achievement was to incorporate Bayern and a number of other entities, mainly in the Catholic south, into a single, Prussian-dominated, state. It was symptomatic of the extent of that domination that the large Prussian landowners in the Protestant east of the country enjoyed a virtual veto in government, a privilege that only finally disappeared after the Second World War.

Defeat in the First World War and the subsequent collapse of the Deutsche Reich saw the effective end of most of the imperial dreams, but the severity of the settlement agreed at the Treaty of Versailles in 1919 served to sharpen Germany's territorial ambitions within Europe. It also focused the main thrust of foreign policy on the extent to which Germany could, and should, be a state for all Germans and the embodiment of the German national identity.

The terms of the treaty meant that much of what had been Preußen was included in Poland, Lithuania, and the USSR; the Sudentenland became part of Czechoslovakia; while in the west the Rheinland was internationalised, and the Saar ceded to France. Taken together, these losses provoked a strong sense of grievance, which certainly contributed to the subsequent collapse of the Weimar Republic. They also rekindled enthusiasm for an all-embracing Großdeutschland and, ultimately, fuelled the rabid nationalism and the expansionist goals of the Third Reich.

The extent of the land-grab undertaken during the Third Reich is astounding (Figure 1). The Saar was re-incorporated as the result of a plebiscite in 1935, the Rheinland re-militarised in 1936, Austria annexed through the medium of the Anschluß in 1938, the Sudentenland annexed in 1938, the area around Memel on the Baltic coast annexed in 1939, and a protectorate established in what is now the rest of the Czech Republic in 1939. The war that followed saw German troops occupying the Netherlands, Belgium, Luxembourg, much of France, Denmark, Norway, Estonia, Latvia, Lithuania, Poland, the USSR to a line running roughly from St Petersburg (what was then Leningrad) to Rostov, Yugoslavia and Greece; all by the end of 1942. Whether it was ever envisaged, if the Second World War had been won, that all these territories would form a single German super-state is unclear. It is certain, however, that whatever Germany emerged would to all intents and purposes have more than fulfilled the demands of the all-embracing Großdeutschland concept described above.

German inter-state relations after the Second World War

The creation, in 1949, of the two German states, the FRG and the GDR, out of the bulk of the Allied-occupied territory of the Third Reich marked a decisive break with the past. For the first time since the early years of the 19th century, Prussian dominance of the political process was neutralised, and two-Germany political solution, excluding Austria, was a reality. Nevertheless, the FRG and the GDR incorporated radically different conceptions of themselves, each other, relationships with third party states and, crucially, what it meant to be German.

The FRG was a federation, with a Constitution laying down a strict division of political power between the national government and the Länder. From the outset, it clearly aimed to represent all Germany, with specific provision in the Constitution (Article 231) for further Länder to join the original nine, as and when the opportunity arose. After lengthy deliberation, the Constitutional Court also clarified the relationship between the FRG and Germany as previously constituted. In a judgement on 31 July 1973, it ruled unequivocally that the state was, in legal terms, a continuation of what had gone before, including all Germany (von Münch,

Figure 1

1992). The FRG never recognised the GDR as a state, arguing that it was not legitimised by free and democratic elections and, until the early 1970s, not recognised by the vast majority of other states across the world. It followed that the FRG also always considered its dealings with the GDR to be an internal matter, not constrained by foreign policy considerations. In practice, the FRG's stance amounted to a long-term goal of unification on its own terms.

The GDR was a centralised, Communist totalitarian state, which based its legitimacy on a complete break with the past. The fact that there had once been a single German state was of no relevance to the political situation after 1945; the existence of two separate, and radically different, states was quite in order, indeed it coincided better with the conclusions of the Potsdam Agreement of 1944, when the Allies agreed the outline of a post-Second World War settlement in Europe. As a result, the GDR always recognised the formal legitimacy of the FRG, even though it found its government and society deeply flawed, and was only ever prepared to consider reunification on the basis of there being two Germanies. It also viewed the provisions in the FRG Constitution providing for the eventual reunification as unacceptable interventions in the affairs of a sovereign state.

Despite the explicit policy of reunification, the issue was always extremely fraught in the FRG, with different factions attaching varying degrees of importance to its realisation. The strongest political pressure came from the 2.3 million displaced Germans living in the FRG, who had been forced to leave their homes in the east and many of whom still had family and friends living there. In this regard it should be stressed that initially reunification by no means only referred to the GDR; it encompassed all the territories of the former Third Reich lying outside the FRG and the ultimate hope was that, at some unspecified point in the future, they would all be brought together in a single state – the FRG. Unquestionably such a hope was fostered by the Constitution of the FRG (Article 116), which gave an unrestricted right of citizenship to anyone living within the boundaries of Germany as of 31 December 1937, or the child of anyone living within Germany at that date. Article 116 also allowed anyone forced to leave Germany during the Third Reich (30 January 1933 - 8 May 1945) for political, racial or religious reasons the same right of citizenship.

In practice, the policy of reunification was pursued by the Government with a combination of superficial public enthusiasm and considerable practical caution. The first Chancellor of the FRG, Konrad Adenauer, was primarily concerned to secure the position of the new state firmly within a politically united Western Europe and he eschewed any policy likely to jeopardise its membership of the fledgling European Union, though this did not prevent him campaigning vigorously in elections with the promise of eventual reunification (Korka, 1990).

The exception to this cautious approach by the Government was in relations with the GDR. In the course of the mid-1950s, the then Foreign Minister, Walther Halstein, developed the so-called Halstein Doctrine, which reaffirmed that relations with the GDR were a matter of FRG domestic policy and went on to proclaim that any state officially recognising the GDR would not be recognised by the FRG. Between 1957 and 1971, only 16 of the states recognised by the FRG, all of them in the developing world, established diplomatic relations with the GDR (Blacksell, 1982). The reaction of the FRG was to break off, or suspend, relations and to end, or freeze, all aid programmes. More important was the total success with which the FRG persuaded its NATO and OECD partners not to recognise the GDR in the first place. The only major breach in the Halstein Doctrine was when the FRG established diplomatic relations with the USSR in 1958. The inconsistency was acknowledged at the time, but was justified in the interests of German service personnel held prisoner in the USSR since the end of the Second World War.

After 1969, however, when the socialist SPD replaced the conservative CDU as the senior partner in the ruling coalition, FRG policy towards the GDR underwent a decisive change. The new Chancellor, Willi Brandt, gradually introduced what became known as the Ostpolitik, a policy of détente with the GDR and the other Communist states in Eastern Europe. The policy never involved formal recognition of the GDR by the FRG, but it did seek to deepen and extend bilateral relations between the two, and diplomatic relations were established with other states in Eastern Europe, notably Poland and Czechoslovakia, even though there were still serious outstanding territorial border disputes with both countries.

The Ostpolitik broke the mould of FRG policy towards the GDR and Eastern Europe generally, heralding a gradual acceptance of the political status quo. Twenty years later it was being claimed that '...the modern discussion about a unified Germany is to be seen against the background of Ostpolitik'. (Ossenbrügge, 1989: 391) and, although this was undoubtedly true insofar as it ushered in an era of new realism in the FRG, the practical results are harder to quantify. The GDR remained a very separate and closed society, insisting on its own sovereignty and still allowing citizens of the FRG on only a very restricted basis (Blacksell and Brown, 1983). Indeed, by the late 1970s and early 1980s, when the Cold War enjoyed a brief renaissance, it would not be an exaggeration to claim that the Ostpolitik became somewhat discredited, because of its lack of concrete results.

Reunification

Throughout the 1980s the momentum for change in the USSR and Eastern Europe mounted steadily, with the super-power summit meetings between the USA and the USSR acting as a backdrop to what can now be seen as the crumbling of Communist totalitarian control in one state after another. Whereas in 1961, the completion of the Berlin Wall was an undeniable symbol of state power, dictating where people could, and could not, move and representing a dividing line between two very different conceptions of Germany, by 1989 it was increasingly an irrelevance. Germans in their thousands streamed into the FRG from the GDR and from elsewhere in the GDR and the USSR, no longer physically prevented by border controls from voting with their feet. In 1989 and 1990 more than half a million GDR citizens fled to the FRG, their number swelled further by 300,000 from other parts of the fast-disintegrating Communist bloc.

Nevertheless, the collapse of the GDR and with it a very particular conception of the German state took nearly everyone by surprise. Although *die Wende* – the internal process of change in the GDR which gathered momentum throughout 1989 – had mobilised widespread popular support for greater democracy and openness in government, it was not aimed at overthrowing the state as such (Blacksell, 1997). *Wir sind das Volk* (We are the people), the slogan of the demonstrations, is indicative of the mood for internal reform and a loosening of the stifling and oppressive rigidity of the Communist Party machine over people's lives. However, the removal from power of Erich Honecker, the nation's leader, on 18 October and the symbolic breaching of the Berlin Wall on 9 November, not only had a terminal impact on the government of the GDR, they also brought about a decisive shift in public opinion. For the first time reunification became an explicit popular objective, the mass slogan changing from *wir sind das Volk* to *wir sind ein Volk* (we are one people) and, with brilliant political opportunism, Chancellor Helmut Kohl seized on the new mood to realise the long-term FRG national goal of reunification and a single German state.

On 3 October 1990, less than a year after the collapse of the Berlin Wall, reunification of the two Germanies was a fact. The tide of events during the first ten months of 1990 had been breath-taking. Free elections were held throughout the GDR on 18 March and resulted in a decisive majority for non-Communist parties in favour of unification with the FRG, preparations for which began immediately. However, further progress was complicated by the residual involvement of the four Second World War Allied Powers in the government of Germany and the continuing absence of a comprehensive peace treaty.

Anticipating the problems for any substantial political change, the Foreign Ministers of the United Kingdom, France, the USA, and the USSR, together with their FRG and GDR counterparts, met in the Canadian capital, Ottowa, on 13 February to agree a framework for reunification. The first issue to be settled was the boundaries of the new state. The Third Reich had occupied 114,549 km^2 to the east of the GDR which was now in Poland and there had never been any settlement of the outstanding territorial issues. On 21 June the Bundestag in the FRG and the Volkskammer in the GDR both simultaneously agreed to renounce any claim to lands east of the rivers Oder and Neiße. This paved the way for a comprehensive treaty with Poland. On 17 July the two Germanies and Poland reached an agreement in principle, to be guaranteed by the four Second World War Allies. The new country was to comprise the FRG and the GDR, together with Berlin; any reference which could be construed as implying that the Polish-German border was provisional was to be removed from the laws of the new state; and the united Germany was to sign a formal treaty confirming the Oder-Neiße line and abandoning all territorial claims. The treaty itself was signed on 14 November, once the reunified country was a reality.

The second issue was membership of military alliances. At the time the FRG belonged to NATO and the GDR to the Warsaw Pact and it seemed that this would be a major problem in reaching international agreement. In the event, the USSR withdrew its objection to the new state being in NATO on 16 June. This was in return for a phased withdrawal of its troops, a reduction in the size of the new German military force, a promise that no German troops would be stationed in what had been the GDR until 1995, and a substantial financial contribution from Germany to the USSR in the form of trade credits and monies to help defray the costs of Soviet troops so long as they remained in Germany. Subsequently, the question of membership of military alliances became almost academic when, in 1992, the Warsaw Pact was dissolved as a consequence of the break-up of the USSR.

The third issue was the need to conclude a treaty formally bringing to an end the state of war between the Second World War Allies and Germany. This was achieved by the Treaty on Final Settlement with Respect to Germany, now universally referred to as the Two plus Four Treaty, in which the Allies relinquished all their rights as occupying powers and allowed Germany to be established as a fully independent state.

Finally, the reunified FRG concluded three partnership treaties with the USSR (9

November 1990), Poland (17 June 1991), and Bulgaria (9 October 1991), pledging mutual friendship and co-operation.

Internally, the preparations for reunification were equally complex, but three key pieces of legislation formed the basis of the new state. First, an agreement on economic union was concluded on 18 May 1990 and crucially provided for the currency reform, whereby the Ostmark was exchangeable on a one to one basis with the Deutsch Mark for individual GDR citizens, and generally on the basis of two for one. Second, the legal basis for all the Germany elections which took place on 2 December was provided by an agreement on elections concluded on 3 August. Thirdly, reunification itself was covered by an agreement concluded on 31 August. This created five new Länder, broadly along the lines of those abolished by the GDR in 1952, and re-established Berlin as the capital of the united Germany (Figure 2). The agreement also confirmed the status of the Treuhandanstalt, the organisation set up by the GDR government to manage the sale of the state-owned economic infrastructure to the private sector, and another key feature of the transformation engendered by reunification.

The meaning of German reunification

Against the background outlined above, the reunification of Germany on 3 October 1990 undoubtedly signalled one of the most significant changes in the political geography of Europe in the second half of the 20th century. It transformed West Germany – the Federal Republic of Germany (FRG) – from a state in the front line of the Cold War confrontation, to one at the heart of a new Europe, where the political certainties of the post Second World War division into East and West, have been replaced by a multitude of differing national interests striving to accommodate themselves to the new international order. The German nation, for nearly half a century divided between two separate states, has been brought together as one, and the outstanding territorial disputes with Poland and other East European states have been officially resolved.

The speed with which reunification actually occurred took everyone by surprise. In little more than a year, East Germany – the German Democratic Republic (GDR) – disintegrated and its territory was absorbed into the FRG with no serious opposition and amid widespread public rejoicing, both at home and abroad. That this was possible, owed much to the fact that such a reunification has always been a central political goal of the FRG itself, not least because the Preamble and Article 23 of the Basic Treaty, the state's Constitution, specifically provided for the five pre-war Länder which comprised the GDR – Brandenburg, Mecklenburg, Sachsen, Sachsen-Anhalt, and Thüringen – to join the FRG federation[1]. However, until 1989, though widely desired and much discussed in the course of the preceding four decades, reunification had apparently become a distant and ever dimmer prospect, despite a continuing ritual adherence to it on the part of all the major political parties in the FRG.

Now that the initial euphoria has died down and the practical realities of forging a new Germany at the centre of a much-altered map of Europe are clearer, it is

Figure 2.

possible to place the expanded FRG more firmly within the emerging wider political context. First of all, it is crucial to stress the obvious point that this is a new Germany, and the latest in a line of 'new Germanies' that have come and gone in the course of the 20th century (Figure 3). Since the Deutsche Reich, the Second Empire and supposed successor to Charlemagnes's mediaeval Holy Roman Empire, was realised by chancellor Bismark in 1871, there have been at least six different states called Germany, each with its own raison d'être, population, society, economy, government, and international boundaries. They range from the triumph of Prussian will that extended the Norddeutsche Bund to include Bayern and the other south German states in the Deutsche Reich (1871-1918); through the post First World War political and economic uncertainty of the Weimar Republic (1919-1933); the National socialism of the Third Reich (1933-1945); the years of division, with the FRG representing the western rump of what had been Germany (1949-1990) and the GDR purporting to be a new beginning in the Communist mould (1949-1990); right up to the reunified FRG (1990-) which now represents all Germany, if not all Germans. Even this list is incomplete, in that it fails to take account of the important territorial additions during the Third Reich, and the administrations of the four Allied Occupying Powers – France, the former USSR, the United Kingdom and the USA – after the Second World War.

Each of these earlier Germanies fostered German identity. In every case, with the notable exception of East Germany, they purported to represent all Germany and embrace a single national identity, although in every case with a different emphasis. The new, enlarged FRG, which is the actual outcome of reunification, is yet another such attempt and one which will define the nature of Germany and Germans in the multi-national, pan-European political institutions that are the defining feature of Europe as a whole at the end of the 20th century.

The state of Germany

In retrospect, the timing of reunification can be seen to have been crucial. Success depended entirely on international agreement being reached in that period of little more than a year between the opening of the Berlin Wall and the demise of the USSR. The whole reunification process hung upon the willingness of the Second World War Allies to end formally the state of war with a peace treaty and, thereby, allow a fully independent German state to emerge. Once the USSR had collapsed, such a treaty would have been difficult, if not impossible, to achieve. Trying to forge agreement on such a sensitive international issue amongst the multiplicity of rival states that have replaced the USSR would, almost certainly, have been beyond the powers of the other Allied statesmen and the whole reunification project would have foundered, or have been concluded without the full participation of all the parties concerned.

The FRG that emerged from reunification is markedly different from the state that preceded it. Although it only covers roughly two thirds of the area of the Deutsche Reich, it is unequivocally the one and only German state, and clearly the locus of the German nation within the framework of the Kleindeutschland concept.

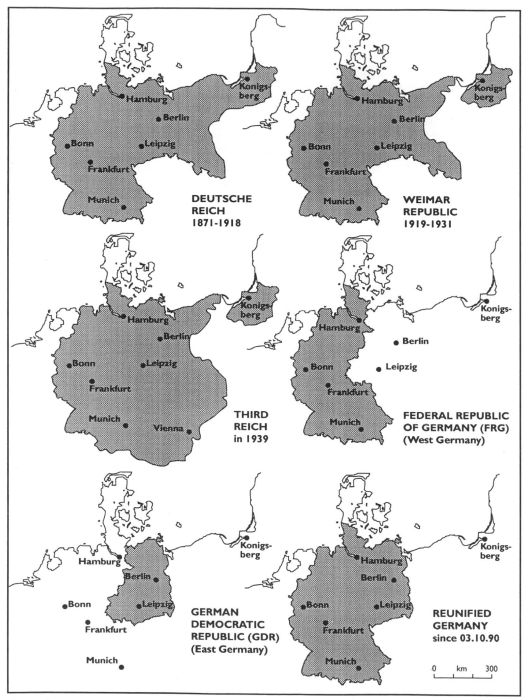

Figure 3.

It is unencumbered by the restrictions imposed by the fall-out from the Second World War, something that it has sometimes found hard to accommodate. There was, for instance, a fierce debate about FRG involvement in UN military activities outside the NATO area. The new state has also explicitly relinquished further territorial ambitions, both with respect to lands which were part of earlier German states in the 20th century, as well as elsewhere. The Constitution has been modified to reflect this and, as a result, the FRG is now a very different political entity to its original incarnation.

Nevertheless, the links with the past are still there and remain important. Germany once more occupies a key position in central Europe and this brings with it new responsibilities, as well as raising the spectre of old neuroses (Schmidt, 1993) The FRG shares land borders with nine other independent European states – Austria, Belgium, the Czech Republic, Denmark, France, Luxembourg, the Netherlands, Poland, and Switzerland – more than any other European state. Geographically it occupies a cross road in Europe between west and east and between north and south. The importance of its central position is further emphasised by the fact that all but one of its neighbours are, or soon will be, members of the European Union. It is also the most populous state in Europe (80.3 million) and the most powerful economically. All these factors taken together give the FRG unparalleled scope for influencing the course of events in continent, especially because alone amongst European states the FRG today combines the experiences of both sides of the Cold War division into a single, unified, state.

Throughout the 1990s, however, the most problematic question has been whether the FRG would be able to reform its internal political structures sufficiently quickly to measure up to its new international status. At the point of reunification in 1990 the expectations of reform were high, probably unreasonably so, but progress on restructuring in a number of key areas has been frustratingly slow and conservative. The bold move to change the Constitution to make Berlin the capital has been followed by indecision and self-doubt, although the transfer of both houses of parliament and the government should be complete in time for the new millennium (Laux, 1991; Smith, 1992). Even so the status of Berlin itself remains uncertain, with the voters rejecting a move to incorporate it into the Land of Brandenburg in 1997, a change that would have embedded the city more firmly into the FRG's federal political structure. Indeed, the whole way in which the five new Länder were constituted, harking somewhat slavishly back to the pre-Second World War pattern and ignoring the weight of academic evidence in favour of a more rational economic and political structure was disappointingly reactionary (Rutz, 1991).

The underestimation of the economic problems to be faced, both within the former GDR and the former FRG, as a result of the speed with which reunification was completed brought with it serious charges of political irresponsibility at an early juncture (Schmidt, 1993) and the strictures appear, at least in part, to be justified. The costs of reunification, in particular the DM 500 billion that has been received by the five new Länder as a result of transitional aid and financial equalisation (Hingorani, 1997), have not only caused internal resentment, but also threatened Germany's economic leadership in the European Union. This will be vital in the next few years as further expansion extends membership to 28 countries from the present total of 15, not least because most of the new members are facing similar economic problems to those in the former GDR.

Finally, the issue of German nationality and citizenship still haunts the enlarged FRG. Over the four decades that the two separate states existed, their respective populations grew apart and forged their own national identities and after reunification Germans from both sides have found that they have less in common than was initially supposed. The *Wessies* from the former West Germany, especially those who have taken jobs or reclaimed property in the new Länder, are deeply resented by the *Ossies* in the former GDR. On the one hand, the *Ossies* are despised by many West Germans who see them as cut-price competitors in an increasingly competitive job market throughout the reunified FRG.

The resentment on both sides is often very deeply felt and is somewhat surprising in the light of the readiness of the FRG, both before and after reunification, to accept and care for anyone claiming German ancestry and refugees of all persuasions, in a way that most other European states have conspicuously failed to emulate. Nevertheless, Germany's open door policy has begun to pose increasingly serious problems, which at times seem to threaten the stability of the state. Renouncing all outstanding territorial claims as Germany agreed to do as part of the reunification settlement is one thing, but regulating and managing the flow of those wishing to settle in the FRG as a result has proved to be quite another. The large numbers of non-German economic migrants, who have so far been refused dual German and their native nationality, have created a very visible and disenfranchised minority, which is in danger of acting as a focus for economic and political discontent amongst the wider population in the FRG. The problems have been especially acute in the former GDR, where many people lost their jobs after reunification and unemployment has remained stubbornly high ever since.

The most obvious evidence of a growing xenophobia, which has been particularly concentrated in the new Länder, is the rise in right wing extremism and in racist attacks (Skrypietz, 1994). Since reunification the federal government has banned four neo-Nazi political organisations – Nationalistische Front, Nationale Offensive, Deutsche Alternative, Kamaradenbund – for inciting racial violence, but at least four others, including the National-Demokratische Partei Deutschlands and the Deutsche Volksunion are suspected of lending their support to extreme right-wing protests (Weissbrod, 1994).

Despite having to face these serious challenges, the reunified FRG shows no sign of succumbing to an early demise. The enlarged federal state is being peacefully governed and the eastern boundaries of the new country, a critical part of the political map of central Europe, have been decisively redrawn without recourse to armed conflict, a success that is by no means universal in other parts of the continent struggling to emerge from their Communist pasts.

A new German identity?

The sixth significant manifestation of Germany in the course of the 20th century appears to offer a better prospect for long-term political stability in Europe than any of its predecessors. The geographical boundaries of the modern state are agreed as never before, and the idea that all the German-speaking areas in central Europe should be united in a single state has been firmly rejected from the national agenda. The emotive and destabilising debate about the relative merits of Großdeutschland and Kleindeutschland has been resolved by creating a Germany which, internally, has a strong democratic constitution and, externally, is bound closely to the European Union and accepts, by treaty, the legitimacy of the states that surround it. German national identity is bound up with the reunified FRG in a way that has never been true of any of its more overtly nationalistic predecessors.

References

Blacksell, M. (1982) Reunification and the political geography of the Federal Republic of Germany. *Geography* 67, 310-319.

Blacksell, M (1995) Germany as a European power. In Lewis, D. and Mckenzie, J.R.P. *The new Germany. Social, political and cultural challenges of unification.* Exeter: University of Exeter Press.

Blacksell, M. (1997) Partition, *die Wende*, and German unification. *Applied Geography* 17, 257-265.

Blacksell, M. and Brown, M. (1983) Ten years of Ostpolitik. *Geography* 68, 260-262.

Davies, N. (1997) *Europe. A History* revised edition, London: Pimlico

Fulbrook, M. (1991) *Germany 1918-1990. The divided nation*. London: Fontana Press.

Gellner, E. (1993) Nationalism and the Development of European Societies. In Iivonen, J. (ed.) *The future of the national state in Europe* Aldershot: Edward Elgar, chapter 3, pages 19-28.

Hingorani, S. (1997) Territorial justice in unified Germany: financial equalisation, the Länder and the Federal Constitutional Court. *Applied Geography*, 17, 335-343.

Jäckel, E. (1990) Furcht vor eigenen Stärke? *Die Zeit* 45 - 2, 10.

Kaiser, K. (1990/1) Germany's unification. *Foreign Affairs* 179-205.

Korka, J. (1990) Nur keinen neuen Sonderweg. *Die Zeit* 43 - 19, 11.

Laux, H.D. (1991) Berlin oder Bonn? Geographischer Aspekte einer Parliamententscheidung. *Geographischer Rundschau* 43, 740-743.

Milward, A.S. (1992) *The European rescue of the nation state* London: Routledge.

Ossenbrügge, J. (1989) Territorial ideologies in West Germany 1945-1985. Between geopolitics and regionalist attitudes. *Political Geography Quarterly* 8, 387-399.

Rutz, W. (1991) Die Wiedererrichtung der östlichen Bundesländer. Kritische Bemerkungen zu ihrem Zuschnitt. *Raumforschung und Raumordnung* 49, 279-286.

Schmidt, H. (1993) *Handeln für Deutschland* Berlin: Rohwolt.

Schulz, H.D. (1989) Fantasies of Mitte. Mittellage and Mitteleuropa in German geographical discussion in the 19th and 20th centuries. *Political Geography Quarterly* 8, 315-339.

Skrypietz, I. (1994) Militant right-wing extremism in Germany. *German Politics* 3, 133-140.

Smith, F. M. (1992) Changing significance of space. Politics, population and German reunification. Discussion Paper 92/4, Applied Population Research Unit, University of Glasgow.

Von Münch, I. (1992) *Die Verträge zur Einheit Deutschlands* München: C.H. Beck.

Weissbrod, L. (1994) Nationalism in Reunified Germany. *German Politics* 3, 222-32.

Winkler, H.A. (1990) Mit Skepsis zur Einigung. *Die Zeit* 40 - 28, 8-9.

Note

1 The Basic Law (Grundgesetz) was altered, with effect from 21st December 1992 and a new Article 23 was inserted on the European Union. This was first because reunification had removed the necessity for the Basic Law to make provision for further Länder to join the federation; and, second, to take account of the the provisions on European unity in the Treaty on European Union (the Maastricht Treaty).

Symbols of Nationalism in Bosnia and Hercegovina

John A. Vincent

Introduction

This chapter is not an account of the current conflicts in the former Yugoslavia directly, it is an attempt to understand the construction of ethnic identity in the Republic of Bosnia and Hercegovina. In particular, it is about the development of the symbols through which solidarity and opposition are expressed in the continuing crisis situation as it existed up until the summer of 1992.[1] I am not going to deal with the horrendous genocide (Gutman, 1993), ethnic cleansing and the systematic use of rape and terror for political ends used to destroy the multi-ethnic country I lived in. However, the chapter does provide a context for understanding how political change and personal identity become intertwined.

The central problems addressed in this chapter are the ways in which the particular symbols of ethnic identity used in Bosnia and Hercegovina have become salient and powerful. I will attempt to trace links between the changes and conflicts on the level of national political institutions and those on the interpersonal level of identification of self and others. Bosnia is the key republic in the middle of former Yugoslavia in which the three largest national groups are Moslems, Serbs, and Croatians, in that order of size. How do people 'tell' who is a Serb, Croat, Moslem, or Bosnian? People in Bosnia and Hercegovina are having to renegotiate their identities and sense of self daily, indeed it becomes a matter of personal safety how, and to whom, the labels are attached. In Bosnia in 1991 it was possible to see people waving the red, white and blue flag of Yugoslavia with its official version of a red star in the middle but also with the red checkerboard Croatian symbol and ones with the four Cyrillic 's' cross of the Serbs and of the crescent moon of the Moslems in the middle of the tricolour. The Serbian red, blue and white tricolour made an increasing appearance and the white, with blue fleur-de-lis shield, flag of Bosnia was launched with independence in 1992. These colours and flags now adorn uniforms and tanks to identify combatants, territory, and inspire identity and loyalty. The newness of the nationalist phenomenon is perhaps exhibited by the range of various flags and banners which have been waved, the lack of standardisation indicating an incomplete 'invention of tradition'. As the conflicts have accelerated, the symbols have crystallised more sharply. Increased ethnic awareness and nationalism in contemporary Bosnia is manifest not only in politics

Orthodox Cathedral: Sarajevo

but also in individual identifications of the self in terms of the styles of dress and address people use, and the way in which interpersonal relationships have responded to the nationalist social movements.

Some approaches to ethnicity

There is considerable literature on approaches to nationalism and ethnicity, which can be drawn on to provide a theoretical framework to formulate potential explanations for the resurgence of militant nationalism. This section is not in any way an exhaustive review of that literature but rather a selection within which to locate a discussion of the specific situation in Bosnia and Hercegovina. Three key areas need to be addressed. Firstly, what is the nature of the boundaries between ethnic groups? Secondly, what factors influence the growth of national and ethnic sentiments? And, thirdly, the relationship between the state and ethnic identity. Wallman (1978) specifies a number of 'boundary processes' by which ethnic differentiation is socially created. Ethnic boundaries are social relationships which change over time and can become rigidified, or can be shown to be flexible, permeable, or context specific. Ethnic boundaries relate to the perceptions of those involved in differentiating 'us' from 'them', but as Wallman points out there is no necessary common perception between the parties as to the nature of the ethnic boundary and where it lies. It is rare that the groups on each side of an ethnic boundary have equal ability to have their definition of the situation accepted as 'real' or legitimate. John W. Coles (1985) suggests that historically there were gradual shadings of cultural difference (which he calls 'clines') across much of Europe such that there were no sharp cultural breaks, merely subtle shifts of tone as one moved across the social landscape. However, in practice, boundaries have become identified, as a consequence some of these shades of cultural difference become more salient than others. Nationalist and state formation political processes have endeavoured to make geographical and social boundaries coincide. In this process of differentiation into 'we' and 'they' certain patterns of behaviour are selected as identity markers to distinguish each group from its neighbours. 'While sharing a wide range of cultural characteristics, articulating groups will inevitably celebrate their uniqueness in terms of contrasting cultural elements and promote these contrasts so as to make these differences a reality' (Coles, 1985 p.5).

The usefulness of this approach is that it does not over concretise ethnic groups, it complements the 'invention of tradition' idea in the sense that a group's claim to a history and to historical symbols is part of the process of demarcating social boundaries. The protagonists in Bosnia and the former Yugoslavia are busy throwing various histories at each other. What matters is not so much the particular historical story but the use made of selected parts of a history to mark and legitimise a boundary. There is nothing *a priori* about the tenacity of ethnic tradition, 'there is nothing more real about an ethnic movement of venerable antiquity than one recent derivation' (Coles, 1985).

Some writers, for example, Anthony D. Smith (1981), while acknowledging the changing nature of ethnicity, want to stress the historical reality of self-perpetuating social groups. One of their concerns is to examine the relationship between ethnicity and modernising processes. The significant point we can take from Smith's analysis is that although these two processes of modernisation and ethnic group formation are, in many ways, incompatible, they nevertheless have a cyclical relationship. He argues that the social processes of modernisation including geographical and social mobility, the systematisation of administrative procedures and the concept of citizenship (and other universalistic values associated with the European nation state) undermine the particularism of ethnicity. However, he also sees the converse of this process, in that the anomic tendencies within modernising societies lead to a search for community which is found in ethnic revival. 'The political myths of the post-revolutionary modern period have proved to be insufficient to the task of welding poly-ethnic states together, even in more mono-ethnic states, there have been periodic rediscoveries of an historic culture as an indispensable basis for communal regeneration. The advance into the future has frequently taken the route of a return to an ethnic past' (Smith, 1981, p.193). In other words the economic and development failures of Yugoslavia in the 1980s and 1990s increased levels of anomie, leading to a renewed search for community in ethnic nationalism.

For others, ethnicity is a modern phenomenon which is linked to the development of the nation state (Ringer & Lawless, 1989; Grillo, 1980; Rex & Mason, 1986). The processes by which nation states have emerged across Europe and then the world includes the social dynamic which consolidates cultural expression of national solidarity. The consequence is seen to be increasing concern about those who do not conform to these patterns of cultural identity and who are thus differentiated ethnically. There are two useful points to take from this approach. Firstly, to note the ways in which national and ethnic symbols come to achieve their potency:

> Certain symbols, values, and beliefs in taking on a sacred character may come to represent the very essence of the concept of folk [or nation] and give a sense of mission and destiny. (Ringer and Lawless, 1989, p. 7)

Secondly, to observe that the relationship between state formation and ethnic identity retains its importance when states disintegrate and are replaced.

Historical background to Bosnia

In order to understand the situation of Bosnia in the 1990s it is necessary not only to look at contemporary events, but also at the history of the region, to look at its long term patterns of change and the range of historical symbols which are available. The history is a symbolic resource for defining contemporary identities. Any history is going to be seen by one party or another in former Yugoslavia as ethnically biased. So the origin of the population of the area through the migration

This city scape shows the strong Turkish influence in Sarajevo. The people are indistinguishable, in terms of national/ethnic affiliation, by their appearance.

of south Slavs is itself a matter of debate. Did the Serbs and Croatians arrive separately or as one Slav people? What is clear is that at the end of the Roman empire and, in particular after the fall of the Eastern empire and Constantinople, the Ottoman state conquered the Balkans and set up an empire which lasted over 500 years. The empire created different classes of people by occupation and religion, giving for example specific rights and duties to each *millet*.[2] Some of the local populations were Islamisized under Ottoman rule and this included the Albanians of Kosovo and the Moslem population of Bosnia which is Serbo-Croatian by language. The Ottoman empire, however, recognised and utilised different communities under its rule, and each had its particular authority and part to play in society. The Ottomans erratically tolerated and oppressed the Christian population (Sugar, 1977) but differential taxes for non-Moslems and the janissary[3] system were seen as particularly oppressive.

The Balkans, with the decline of the Ottomans, was contested by two other rival empires, those of Russia and Austro-Hungary. It was the Austrians who eventually annexed Bosnia in 1878. This was the great disappointment to Serbian nationalism which aspired with Russian help to create a state which included all Serbs. The Serbs, as the largest of the Slav groups, had not only fought in the service of, but also against, Turkish rule and had aspirations of nationhood and sought solidarity with the Pan Slav movements. It was discontented Bosnia Serbs who assassinated the Archduke Ferdinand in Sarajevo (on the anniversary of the symbolic and epic battle of Kosovo) and sparked off the First World War.

The defeat of the Austrian empire and Tsarist empire in that war led to the division of Eastern Europe into national states and the boundaries drawn up after the war fundamentally produced the basic political shape of Europe and the Balkans for the rest of the 20th century. It created a new state, Yugoslavia (The Kingdom of Slovenia, Croatia, and Serbia) which included areas which had long been under Austrian rule like Slovenia, areas like Bosnia which were recently under Austrian rule, independent states like Serbia who had thrown off the Ottoman rule, and independent states like Montenegro who had largely remained independent of Turkish rule. The Serbs were the largest ethnic group in a very diverse nation and the political centre was the old Serbia and its capital of Belgrade. Monarchical Yugoslavia lasted until the Second World War in which Yugoslavia was subject to invasion by the foreign forces of the Axis and also experienced a vicious civil war. During the war, the population experienced armies passing and repassing across its territory which included Germans,

Sketch Map of the Republic of the Former Federal Yugoslavia

Italians, Russians, fascist Croatians called Ustache, the Communist Partisans, the Serbian nationalist Chetniks and the NDH[4] militia forces. The horrors and atrocities of the time form a large part of the symbolic mythology of the contemporary conflict. Current massacres are explained in terms of revenge for Second World War atrocities. In 1991, and subsequently, people have been literally digging up the past by, for example, exhuming the bones of those massacred, and ceremonially reburying them.

The group which came out on top, backed by both east and west, was that of the partisans led by Tito, who created the new socialist republic in 1946. This post war Yugoslavia was a federal state consisting of six republics: Serbia, Croatia, Montenegro, Bosnia and Hercegovina, Slovenia, and Macedonia. These last two republics had their own languages recognised, in addition to Serbo Croatian, by the Federal state. Serbia had two autonomous regions characterised, in the case of Voyvodina by the Hungarian minority, and, in the case of Kosovo, by the Albanian population. The new state followed a distinctive road to socialism and did not submit to domination to Moscow, but was a leading figure in the non-aligned movement using its strategic position to balance East and West and succeeded through the 1950s and 1960s to achieve a significant level of economic growth. However, this economic development petered out in the 1970s and particularly in the 1980s, and while the population was willing to acquiesce to the dominance of the party while prosperity was growing, the economic crisis led to a political crisis and the disintegration of the Yugoslav communist party (Beloff, 1985; Singleton & Carter, 1982; Besemeres, 1977).

National rivalries were not kept entirely in check by the Partisan state; Tito felt it necessary to put tanks into Zagreb and purge the party to keep down Croatian nationalism, and the Serbian communist leader, Slobodan Milosevic, came to power on an aggressive nationalist policy. Communist Yugoslavia was a highly decentralised Federal Republic which sought to co-opt rather the destroy ethnic identity. The disintegration of the Communist party was effectively realised when the Slovenian and the Croatian parties withdrew from the Yugoslav party conference (Magas, 1993). In 1990 multi-party elections were held and the communists were voted out of power and replaced by nationalist groups in all the republics, except Serbia and Montenegro. These republics voted last and here, the renamed communist party succeeded in playing the nationalist role and retained power.

How to tell who is who in Bosnia

Historically, the primary ethnic difference in Yugoslavia, in general, and Bosnia, in particular, is related to religion. The different constituent parts of Yugoslavia evolved under different empires, the Croatians and Slovenes follow Austria in being Catholic, and Moslems of Bosnia follow Islam introduced by Turkey, and the Serbs follow the Orthodox church derived from the Eastern Roman Empire and recognised by the Turks as a *millet*. Although religion, with its association with basic values imparted through primary socialisation, is usually seen as a particularly solid and long-lasting social boundary, like all ethnic boundaries, once subject to close inspection, it becomes more problematic. Atheists claim to be Serb or Croat, and Bosnians explain that Moslems are a national group (nacionalnost) and are not the same as moslems as members of a particular faith (narodnost). Furthermore, there are communities and individuals who do not quite fit the stereotypical categories: Albanian-speakers, Catholics, Montenegrins or gypsy groups who seem able to be Moslem or Orthodox. Bosnian Moslems have had, in the past, to declare themselves as Croatian Moslems or Serb Moslems. Some Serb extremists claim that Moslems are not an ethnic group, merely Serbs who

The only way to tell the ethnic identity of these children is to know the village they come from in central Bosnia, or from the political graffiti in the background ('HDZ' is the main Croatian nationalist party).

have lost their true religion. Religion and religious symbols have come to play a key part in nationalist politics. The ruling party in Croatia advertised itself on posters displaying a map of the country with a rosary around it. Slobodan Milosevic, the Serb leader, has taken pains to be seen with the senior clerics of the Serbian Orthodox church at crucial points in his political career. The place of religion in education and in law are controversial political issues as the successor nationalist regimes have taken over from the atheist Yugoslavia.

Language also plays a significant part in national identity. In the former Yugoslavia Slovenian, Macedonian, Hungarian, and Albanian, were clearly distinctive in the sense that they are codified and nationally recognised. However, Serbo-Croatian, as the major language of that state is written in two alphabets — Roman and Cyrillic. Cyrillic is seen as Serbian usage. There are considerable dialectical differences in Serbo-Croatian and these are sometimes summarised as west and east variants called by some Croatian and Serbian respectively. So that the kind of language and the kinds of vocabulary and pronunciation people use are an important indicator of nationality. Extended use of Turkish words or phrases would be seen as indicative of Moslem ethnic affiliation (however, speakers from Bosnia whatever their origin would more frequently use such words than people from most other places in the former Yugoslavia). Such distinctions become subject to ideological elaboration as the nationalists in Croatia, Serbia, and even Bosnia claim their variant to be a distinctive language and the new Balkan nations use control of schooling and media to systematise and enforce the distinctions. Greetings and linguistic styles have reflected changes in politics. Linguistic differences have rapidly been elaborated at the symbolic level, distinctions being accentuated, and, in the war situation, mere presence of the 'other' script can be seen as treachery (Rieff, 1995:72).

In everyday social intercourse in Bosnia the usual way to determine a person's national identity is through their name. Family names are, in large measure, distinctive and this is held to be an ancestral division, although this test is far from infallible. First names are also distinctive with preferences for Moslem names such as Azra, or Suliman; the Serbian Milorad, or Mica; or Croatian, Ante, or Kata. The family patronym is seen to be important and nationalities are assumed from names. Blood lines, in terms of imputed origins of either or both parents and expressed through family names, are often called as evidence of 'national' identity. A numbers of 'modern' first-names (for example those which imitate those of western pop stars) are not clearly one nationality or the other — although some new names can also be ethnic labels (e.g. Nasser).

Most young people in Bosnia were distinguished by their jeans and trainers; the standard clothes of young people across Europe. Their ethnic origins were, in the vast majority of cases, invisible to the passer-by. Even traditional styles of costume were frequently distinctive to a particular village and therefore not always unambiguous with regard to ethnicity. However, personal styles of dress can be used as ethnic markers. Key elements of dress, now seen as traditional, become key badges of identity. Aspects of the traditional modes of dress have been adapted in the contemporary situation, and become self-proclaimed pride in national or religious origin. Although very few in number in 1992 the Moslem revivalist groups tend to take on dress styles more familiar to Western audiences through images of Iran, the male close-shaved chin-trap beard, the sombre single colour *shadour*. More typically older Moslem men would wear a beret or perhaps the traditional fez (cf. Thompson, 1992:121). The radical Serb nationalists are developing more and more flamboyant beards. This has been traditional for Orthodox priests, but nowadays someone sporting a big black bushy beard is a Serb. Indeed there was a cartoon in *Nedilija,* a Bosnian political magazine, in 1991, showing a soldier from the Yugoslav national army passing a barber's shop and, when the barber calls the soldier in for a shave, the military man feels his growing stubble and says 'I don't think I need it these days'. The moral being that the army, which at that time was still meant to be a Yugoslav army, had become dominated by Serb nationalists. Clearly certain symbols worn as part of dress — crucifixes (Croatian), fez (Moslem), women's trouser styles — are taken as indicative of ethnic identity. Aspects of physical appearance are also thought of as indicative – darker skinned and black-haired people are thought to be Moslems or gypsies. There is an important colour symbolism, which is increasingly being used in flags. Green being the Islamic colour, people who drive green cars, or wear green, are thought to be Moslem. Blue, associated with the Virgin Mary, can be associated with Croatians. The blue, red, and white of the Serbian tricolour is being increasingly used. But Fascists from all national groups seem to like black.

Place of origin in some circumstances can also be used as indicative of ethnic identity. A dangerous side-line on travel in war-torn Yugoslavia is that Yugoslav number plates indicate town of origin, and can be used to make assumptions about the ethnic nationality of the occupants (c. f. area-based telephone numbers on their cabs made taxi drivers vulnerable to sectarian attack in Belfast). The symbolic distinction between urban as opposed to peasant was commonly used in former Yugoslavia. The Croats, and in particular those from Zagreb, are seen as sophisticated/stuck-up, civilised/bourgeois compared with the folksy/ignorant, straightforward/aggressive Serbs. At the interpersonal and neighbourly level, relationships were not at all bad; indeed often very good and sociable, neighbourliness being a very developed Yugoslav institution. However, it was at the level of political and categorical ascription that the dangerous stereotyping occurred enabling people to believe the worst about a generalised 'other' with no specific names except perhaps those of their political representatives. This reflects reported patterns of inter-ethnic relations in rural Northern Ireland (Harris, R., 1972).

A further similarity with ethnic symbolism in Northern Ireland is the pairing of symbols. The symbols of ethnic identity take their meaning from a place in a structure of opposites. Dates, flags, songs and images in some sense mirror that of the 'other-side', standard in form yet opposed in symbolic content. In Northern Ireland for example, 1688 and the battle of the Boyne are contrasted with 1916 and the Easter Rising. In Bosnia the three way split complicates this dichotomous symbolic structure Thus while Serb violence against Croats can be proclaimed legitimate vengeance for Second World War atrocities by Croats against Serbs, such self-justifications do not construct a morality for violence against Moslems. For this purpose, the Battle of Kosovo in 1389 when the Turks destroyed the Serb royal heroes, has to be revived and symbolically relived.

It is worth pointing out that there are a number of potential identities for ethnic mobilisation which have not become concretised in the current Yugoslav situation. It is conceivable that there could be a Christian-Moslem divide, whereby difference within the Christian religions and the culture of the different Moslem groups are disregarded in favour of a set of religious symbols which contrast all Christians, including both Catholic and Orthodox, with all Moslems, whether they are Bosnian or Albanian. Such patterns have been found in Lebanon and a similar identification occurs in Northern Ireland where 'Protestant' covers a variety of denominations (Abdulrahim, 1990). However, this contrast has remained latent in the current situation since the boundary between Catholic and Orthodox has taken on far more symbolic potency because of its salience in distinguishing Serb from Croat – the two largest nationalities contending for control of territory in the former Yugoslavia. Certain peripheral identities like Montenegrin, Hercegovinian, or Dalmatian also do not seem to be very significant. The Montenegrin Republic was ruled by a branch of the Serbian Socialist Party loyal to the Serbian ruler Slobodan Milosevic (they lost the 1997 elections and power was still being contested on the streets in 1998). A key part of this alliance and split being related to identity or distinctiveness of Serb and Montenegrin identity.

Issues of national identity are a severe problem for the independent nation of Bosnia. There are attempts being made by some to develop a Bosnian identity with historical claims and cultural and linguistic distinctiveness. However these claims tend to be seen as justifications for the distinctiveness and political rights of Bosnian Moslems rather than uniting all those who live in Bosnia. Many of those defending Sarajevo, Tuzla and Bihac did so in the belief in a secular ideal for a Bosnian state. Since independence, liberal minded Bosnians who reject nationalist identifications, find the notion of 'Bosnian' more congenial than the previously used label of 'Yugoslav' which has been hijacked by the supporters of Greater Serbia. The European identity has been used in a variety of ways in the conflict, for example by Serbian nationalists to try to mobilise West Europe against Bosnian Moslems, and by besieged Bosnians to appeal to the alleged values of European civilisation.

The relationship between the institution of the modern state and the development of ethnic nationalism

In a previous paper contrasting ethnicity in Val d'Aosta and Kashmir I sought to demonstrate how personal identity can be related to nationalism in peripheral areas (Vincent, J. 1982). The three key points from that paper relevant to the context of Yugoslavia are firstly, oppositional ethnic identities develop at the peripheries of modern nation states; secondly the symbols of ethnic identity develop in opposition to the symbols used in state formation; and thirdly, differences develop between traditionally orientated and modernising ethnic elites.

Social groups in conflict create symbols which are matched in form but opposed in content. The symbols which come to establish ethnic identity develop in response to the state formation process. A process which peripheral social groups are a part of, but against which they seek to struggle by (re)defining themselves through symbols that contrast with those of the new nation state. Where ethnic identity is created in opposition to a dominant national identity, the symbols, which express that ethnic identity, mirror in opposition those symbols which were used to establish national identity during state formation. For example, it is possible to compare the claims made by some for national sovereignty in the mountain valleys of Valle d'Aosta in Italy and Kashmir in India. The origins of the Italian nation lie in a national movement based on language and culture. This has meant that linguistic definitions are important to Valdotain ethnicity, whereby people in the Autonomous Region of the Val d'Aosta seek to reaffirm a distinctive identity for themselves. This situation, where language forms the key basis of identity, contrasts with the situation on the Indian sub-continent where religion formed the basis of the original division of India from the moslem state of Pakistan. This has meant that those who wish to validate a Kashmiri identity with claims to political rights have tended to refer to religious symbols rather than linguistic ones. Resistance by peripheries to incorporation into dominant states affected the symbolic processes by which people dressed and presented themselves to others. Can we understand the symbols of national identity used in Bosnia in a similar way?

There is a division which can be identified between two kinds of ethnic social movement. On the one hand there is the traditional, usually rural-based, mainstream national movement whose ethnicity was 'conservative', and on the other hand the radical 'young turks' whose ethnicity was a re-emergence and reaffirmation of ethnicity amongst educated people who frequently aspired to white-collar positions. The supporters of this second kind of movement were often educated, but unemployed, people and those having difficulty in getting access to state employment as teachers or civil servants. They seek to revalue their 'cultural capital' and devalue that of others by demands for an ethnic basis for the local state. They use an appeal to ethnic nationalism to try and capture part of the state apparatus and its resources. What kinds of people and motives supported nationalist social movements in Bosnia?

Strong comparisons can be drawn between Slovenia, the Val d'Aosta and Kashmir. All three are north-west mountain valleys, peripheral to the geographical and political centres of the state, distinctive linguistically and culturally, and relatively prosperous compared to much of the rest of the country. Thus a similar analysis might fit the movements for Solvenian independence very well. There are problems, however, when we try to apply this analysis to Bosnia. In the geography of the former Yugoslavia, Bosnia was strategic and central rather than a periphery. However, Bosnia was politically and economically marginal to dominant political and economic centres in Belgrade and Zagreb. Its central location made it a strategic area of conflict between Serb and Croat territories. Further, in contrast to Slovenia's rather high degree of cultural homogeneity, in Bosnia everyone was a minority. Bosnia has both Serbs and Croats who identify themselves as co-nationals of majority populations in neighbouring republics. Bosnia's other 'national' groups carried very little weight in the politics of the former Yugoslavia. The Moslems were the republics largest single group but they did not represent an overall majority of the population. There were in addition a large number of people who came from mixed families and from yet other ethnic groups such a Romanies, Jews and Vlachs. The various populations in Bosnia were largely intermixed down to a very local level and

Gazi Husref Begova Mosque: Sarajevo

thus ethnic-based violence, even more than other parts of former Yugoslavia, has had disastrous consequences. The question of ethnic nationalism in Bosnia, as opposed to that in Slovenia, is to understand the rise of ethnic divisions which threaten not only the disintegration of the state but the continued existence of whole communities. A centre/periphery model is not adequate in these circumstances where everyone is a minority and a key part of the problem is the absence of an effective centre.

The fall from power of the communists was clearly part of a broader geopolitical movement in the whole of Eastern Europe and the Balkans. Although the hegemony of the Soviet military never extended to Yugoslavia, the east-west polarisation had the effect of stultifying political change. Elsewhere in Eastern Europe militant nationalism has revived and, in some places, this has threatened the integrity of the state. It is not at first glance obvious why a decline in communist power should lead to a revival of nationalism. The communists recognised ethnic nations and national aspirations and were careful to be seen to be even-handed between them. The South-eastern European socialist states both opposed and celebrated nationalism – it is quite clear that the regimes appealed to the legitimacy of national sentiments as a political base and in particular produced an ethnic 'key' as the basis of distributing national resources (Supek, 1989). Many of those voting nationalist are in no way extreme nationalists looking for confrontation. One of the key characteristics of many of those leaders elected to replace the communists was precisely their reputation for anti-communism, people did not trust former or disguised communists, they voted for those who had the seal of authenticity in the form of a trial and a prison sentence. However the cadres of the parties which were the first to form in opposition to the communists were nationalists and frequently supported from *émigré* groups abroad. The progressive communists, with very few exceptions, did not succeed in being elected or in retaining office.

The insight that many radical ethnics are young educated people, trying to valorise their cultural capital and claim part of the state apparatus and its jobs and resources, is also applicable to the rise of nationalism in the former Yugoslavia. In Bosnia and elsewhere in Yugoslavia, the new parties behaved like the old communist party, as patronage networks. They saw their role as fixing jobs, pensions, grants, opportunities, the blind eye of the law etc. Indeed the Bosnian interior ministry went on strike briefly due to the level of political interference from the three nationalist parties who shared government. The new political elite does not operate a western concept of civil society but takes the model of its powers implicitly from the previous regime. This is understandable in the absence of a democratic political culture and of a widely acceptable ideological framework for political competition. The language of ethnicity or nationalism reflects a system of thought which is closed, circular and rigid. The ethnic conspiracy explanation for personal troubles always works and can seldom be discredited. In the current climate of violence, terror, and misinformation, the 'ethnic conspiracy' explanation for all problems reigns unchallenged and works in the political favour of extreme nationalism.

Ethnic identities are reinforced in situations of patronage-based politics (cf. Carter, 1974) in contrast to radical politics where efficient performance and commitment to the new social order are the prime motives for political recruitment. In Yugoslavia politics was seen as a route for personal social mobility. As the new post-war elites rigidified and in the absence of a general commitment to a system of social transformation; primary social identities – kinship and ethnicity – became more important. Faced with any of the many problems in making organisations work that beset life in modern bureaucratic societies, finding a job, getting a pension, obtaining permission to build a house – how does one find out what is permissible, find the right forms and submit them? The belief in the ethnic conspiracy answers these questions. You find the right contact through kin and community after all – ' they help their own' – people believe that the only way to get things done is personal contact. This principle, applied systematically, becomes ethnic favouritism. In concrete terms people maximise their opportunities; they pursue both official and unofficial solutions to their dilemmas. They do it the official way – fill in forms, write letters of application, etc. – but they also do it the unofficial way – ring up people who they know who might have information or influence, use personal networks to offer inducements and ask favours. If the application works, even if it was legitimate and fitted the official criteria and would have been granted anyway, the ethnic conspiracy is confirmed. If the application fails, the ethnic conspiracy also explains the situation in that the contacts used were not right, the jealousy of the 'others' got in the way and did 'us' down. To reinforce this situation, when it is looked at from the alternative ethnicity, this application and its outcome are also explicable in terms of ethnic conspiracy. The successful application was ethnic favouritism, the failure was because the application was not valid anyway and it is only because it was refused that the person is aggrieved and has an ethnic chip on their shoulder. From the point of view of the bureaucrats and officials doing the administration, people think ethnic advantage is being given, however objectively they do their job. They find that such personal service is expected and will find it very difficult not to confirm this expectation, at least in outward appearance, to those soliciting favours. In other words, whatever happens in these kinds of cases, it appears to the general public, applicants, potential applicants and observers, that the most consistent explanation of events is ethnic favouritism.

In those areas which are ethnically homogeneous, either all Serb or all Croat or overwhelmingly Moslem, the patronage basis of politics meant that second ethnic parties polled well (e.g. the MBO the second Moslem national party, the SPO the non-communist Serb nationalists, and smaller Croatian parties). They form rival patronage cliques within a single communal group. The patronage element in Bosnian politics is also expressed in the original willingness of all three dominant nationalist parties elected in Bosnia in 1991 to share government together, prior to the Serb military invasion, even though their political appeal and symbolic definition of themselves is structured around opposition to each other. Without sharing power they could not get patronage to dispense. The constitutional framework of self-managing Yugoslavia separated elected legislature from professional executive at every level including federal and republican governments. Thus economic policy was never discussed as a political issue but rather presented as a technical matter, and none of the Bosnian nationalist parties has a developed or distinctive economic programme. Politics is therefore seen as access to power and influence, and so people vote for those they know, those who are most likely to do them the right favours, i.e. 'us' not 'them'. Patronage politics in Bosnia becomes ethnic politics in a multi-party situation. Nationalist politicians, unable to deliver the economic goods and dispense patronage, resort to the ethnic conspiracy to explain their failure, and try and keep their supporters loyal by raising the level of ethnic conflict. Of course, such a system is inherently unstable and spirals out of control.

Catholic Cathedral: Sarajevo

The Bosnian economy as it developed under the former Federal Yugoslavia had a major contradiction between the need for integration and the need for autarchy. It was, on the one hand, dependent on close ties with Europe, particularly Germany, in terms of labour migration which is its major export. Bosnia simply cannot survive without repatriated deutchmarks from the *Gastarbeiters*. In addition, the tourist industry depended on free movement of people and a level of integration with the prosperous areas of Europe which provide the tourists. On the other hand, the industries of Bosnia are large 'social' enterprises, often located for political and strategic rather than economic reasons, and which depended on highly protected markets. Exposing these industries to integration into wider markets created a state of chronic collapse whereby many of these enterprises were unable to pay their workers. They included steel, metalwork, car and truck production, and also chemicals. They tended to be in the inefficient capital goods sector created during the drive for autarchic industrialisation. The political nature of the decisions to locate and develop industrial enterprises reinforce the link between the political and economic crises. Local workers have tended not to support the communists or the left but look to ethnic parties to save their jobs. The nationalist parties in Bosnia tended to find greater support in the rural areas, the urban populace having a greater awareness of the benefits of wider integration. Those areas which were most resistant to nationalist politics were the most industrially advanced in Sarajevo and Tuzla. The strategic dispersal of arms and munitions manufacture across Bosnia had a significant effect on the course of the war in Bosnia and the ability of isolated populations to resist.

The economic crisis throughout former Yugoslavia deepened rapidly and dramatically through the 1980s. The successor governments rapidly ran out of resources with which to reward supporters, and resorted to ever more extreme nationalism to blame other ethnic groups for their economic plight. Every nationality in the former Yugoslavia claims to be oppressed. The census in the last year of the former Yugoslavia took on a very political aspect. In this enumeration, and in all forms of bureaucratic identification people are being forced to identify themselves with one of the three major groups in Bosnia. The proportions enumerated as belonging to each group form the ethnic 'key', which affects job opportunities and access to many kinds of economic resources by determining how many from each group should be employed in an institution. For example, the officially required proportions of nationalities in the police, in the media, in universities etc. can control people's chances of work and promotion. The more it is believed that ethnic identification is necessary for economic success, the more likely that in fact it will be. In the negotiations which attempted to find a political solution in Bosnia, there have been bizarre attempts to carve up all the institutions of civil society into ethnic slices, bits of the television, part of the university, some of the police force. The proposals for cantonisation have less to do with the practicalities of running a multi-ethnic society than the need for a supply of patronage goods. There was an inevitable progression, patronage politics became nationalist politics. Ethnic particularism became secessionist politics. Those areas like Bosnia with a complex ethnic mix then became the victims.

The Yugoslav state was essentially the Partisan state, established by the military victory of the partisans over their rivals. The state which they created was socialist in name, and had highly decentralised characteristics and entrenched privileges for the partisans and those loyal to them. It was the party which made the over-complicated bureaucratised 'self-management' system work. Without that central control it was impossible to make the Yugoslav constitution work. Hence the demise of the communist party was a bigger threat to the continuity of the state in Yugoslavia than it was in say Hungary, Poland or Bulgaria. There are no non-communist unifying symbols of Yugoslavia – the Yugoslav flag has a red star in it, nobody waves the flag without the red star. The key symbol of the pre-war state, the monarchy, is seen as Serbian. The army as the last bastion of the Partisan power-base tried to set itself up as the Yugoslav People's Army but, in practice, it was discredited, because it was both communist dominated and Serbian dominated. There were no democratic elections at the Federal level following those at local republic level and hence there was a chronic lack of legitimacy for Federal institutions (Thompson, 1992: 104). It left the JNA as an army with no political accountability. In the absence of national collectivity and symbols, it would have taken a form of imperial rule to keep Yugoslavia together. The imperium of the Yugoslav communist party has gone. The imperial rule which many Yugoslavs aspired to was that of the European Common Market. Their economy was dominated by it; they saw it, particularly Germany, as a consumerist utopia. Most Bosnians wish to be Europeans, and feel bitter that Europe failed to take decisive action to stop the aggression.

Rather than saying ethnicity is based in cultural tradition, it might be more appropriate to say cultural tradition is the message an aspiring ethnic group needs to convey — 'that we are people with a valuable tradition'. Tradition should be seen as something which is not simply based on the social origin of the group, it is rather the particular selection of history which symbolises the message that that group wants to convey about itself. Thus to say 'we' reject the communists is to reject their victory in 1946, and to use symbols from that era follows from that logic. Many of the permanent overseas Yugoslavs have adopted ethnic nationalist symbols in their new countries, and tend to be a source of resources for militants. But the 'we' that lost to the Communists were a pretty unwholesome lot of warlords and fascists, i.e., the Chetniks and Ustache of current demonology. It has been disastrous for the people of Bosnia that the use of these symbols to oppose Communist rule gives a degree of power and legitimacy to them. It is possible to conclude that the foundation of the Partisan state during the Second World War has set the framework for the current conflict in Yugoslavia. It is the Second World War which provides the symbols of antagonism, the Ustache with fascist symbols, the Chetniks with skull and crossbones, the hats and uniforms, the bones of the martyrs disinterred and reburied religiously (cf. Ramet, 1992: 254). It is precisely the overthrow of the Partisan state that has led to the use of Ustache and Chetnik and other symbols rather than any other repertoire of symbols and identities available from different historical epochs.

The point to conclude on is that ethnic conflict is not inevitable. Bosnia was a potential model of cultural pluralism and not an inevitable tragedy which could only be concluded in violence. The Germans and the French fought three wars and exchanged territory by violence, and yet in contemporary Europe they are firm allies at a national level and history does not get in the way of commercial or other forms of interpersonal relations between them. The conflicts in contemporary Yugoslavia, contrary to much media simplification and to many local definitions of the situation, are not simply conflicts, partially suppressed by years of communism, only to break out again when the party collapses. Rather the flags, hats, songs, etc. are newly vitalised symbols utilised by protagonists to deal with the disintegration of the state. It is the circumstances and symbols involved in the creation of the state which lead to the symbols of ethnic opposition to that state. However, with the disintegration of the state these symbols come to play leading roles in the politics of the succession. In order to understand why certain symbols, such as an insignia painted on the side of a tank, can move people to acts of great heroism and of great inhumanity, a history of the symbol is a necessary but not sufficient explanation. A fuller explanation requires an appreciation of how historical symbols acquire a range of meanings salient to contemporary situations. The symbols, becoming resanctified in the current conflicts over the creation of the successor states in the Balkans, will themselves play a role in whatever political processes evolve in those states. The need for a man in contemporary Bosnia to grow a beard or shave his head, in order to achieve a pride in appearance, stems not only from history of symbols but also the specifics of the political and economic crisis which led to the disintegration of the former Yugoslavia.

References

Abdulrahim, Dima (1990) *From Lebanon to West Berlin*. Ph.D. University of Exeter.

Barth, Fredrik (Ed.) (1969) *Ethnic Groups and Boundaries*. Boston: Little Brown and Co.

Beloff, N. (1985) *Tito's Flawed Legacy*. London: Gollancz.

Besemeres, John F. (1977) 'The demographic factor in inter-ethnic relations in Yugoslavia', *South Eastern Europe* 4 (1): 1-31.

Carter, A. (1974) *Elite Politics in Rural India*. Cambridge: Cambridge University Press.

Cohen, A. (Ed.) (1974) *Urban Ethnicity*. ASA Monograph No.12 London: Tavistock.

Coles, John W. (1985) 'Culture and economy in peripheral Europe ', *Ethnologia Europea* 15 (1): 3-26.

Grillo, R.D. (Ed.) (1980) *'Nation' and 'State' in Europe*. London: Academic Press.

Gutman, Roy (1993) *A Witness of Genocide*, Shaftesbury: Element Books..

Harris, Rosemary (1972) *Prejudice and Tolerance in Ulster: A Study of Neighbours and 'Strangers' in a Border Community*. Manchester: Manchester University Press.

Magas, Branka (1993) *The Destruction of Yugoslavia*. London: Verso.

Ramet, Sabrina P. (1992) *Nationalism and Federalism in Yugoslavia 1962-1991*. Bloomington: Indiana University Press,

Rex, J. and D. Mason (1986) *Theories of Race and Ethnic Relations*. Cambridge: Cambridge University Press.

Rieff, David (1995) *Slaughterhouse: Bosnia and the Failure of the West*. Vintage: London.

Ringer, B.B. and E.R. Lawless (1989) *Race, Ethnicity, and Society*. New York: Routledge.

Singleton, Fred and Bernard Carter, (1982) *The Economy of Yugoslavia*. London: Croom Helm.

Singleton, Fred (1985) *A Short History of the Yugoslav Peoples*. Cambridge : Cambridge University Press.

Smith, Anthony D. (1981) T*he Ethnic Revival*. Cambridge: Cambridge University Press.

Sugar, Peter F. (1977) *South Eastern Europe under Ottoman Rule 1354-1804*. Seattle: University of Washington Press.

Supek, Olga. (1989) 'Etnos i Cultura', *Migracijsketeme* 5 (2-3): 145-154.

Thompson, Mark (1992) *A Paper House: The Ending of Yugoslavia*. London: Vintage.

Vincent, J. (1982) 'Differentiation and resistance: ethnicity in Valle D'Aosta and Kashmir', *Ethnic and Racial Studies* 5: 313-325.

Wallman, Sandra (1978) 'The boundaries of 'race': Processes of ethnicity in England.', *Man* 13 (2): 200-217.

Wolf, Eric Robert (1959) *Sons of the Shaking Earth*. Chicago: University of Chicago Press.

Notes

1   The situation has changed so rapidly that perhaps it is necessary to specify that this chapter was initially drafted during nine months fieldwork in Bosnia in 1991, a first draft completed in Britain in December 1991 and updated a number of times subsequently. Thanks, but no responsibility for the contents of this chapter, must go to the British Academy and the Bosnia and Hercegovina Academy of Sciences who funded my exchange visit from January to June 1991.

2   The millet system was the way in which the Ottomans organised governmental life around divisions of their subject into religious communities. Each millet kept its own religious hierarchy, law, courts, schools and welfare system, and were accorded specific rights and duties. There were three dominant non-Muslim religious groups — Orthodox, Armenian and Jewish.

3   The Ottomans took a levy in boys from the non-Moslem population and turned them into an elite of warriors and administrators called janissaries.

4   Nezavisna Drzava Hrvatska. Independent Croatian State – a puppet state allied to the Germans (in Bosnia my elderly informants told me their local forces were largely Moslem in composition).

'Those blue remembered hills...':
National Identity in English Music
(1900–1930)

Fiona Clampin

Defining the national in art has always been a contentious issue, particularly in music, which is believed by some to be free from political, social and cultural associations because of its 'abstract' nature. Musicology as a discipline has often chosen to ignore the implications of the label 'national music' of which we speak so complacently. To ask what the term 'English music' might signify, for example, would raise a number of awkward questions as to the nature of national identity, the intentions of the composer, the reception profile of the works and the status and role of music itself. At the beginning of the 20th century composers in Britain were particularly anxious to create a sense of national identity in music; the extent to which they achieved this has gone largely unquestioned and therefore popular images continue to circulate concerning the expression of 'Englishness' in the music of composers such as Vaughan Williams, Holst, Delius and Elgar, despite the foreign influences present in their work. Attempts to place the music of this period in a political and ideological context have proved anathema to those who would rather music inhabited an artistic realm essentially removed from 'real' life. Musicology has, unfortunately, been slow to embrace movements in literary and cultural theory, and especially in the study of early 20th century English music the ideology of the period has tended to obscure the complex issue of national identity. This chapter aims to redress that balance to a certain extent by examining the motivation behind the desire for 'national' music, uncovering some of its myths and exploring its wider implications.

At the close of the 19th century English music was in the doldrums. Composers were considered to be suffering from an overdose of Teutonic music which had dominated concert programmes in England for decades. England, with its many choral societies, seemed to exist on a diet of the oratorios of Handel and Mendelssohn. This situation was responsible, it was generally believed, for stifling all sense of originality in the nation's composers and hence they were unable to write music which expressed their own experience and culture, being based entirely on models from abroad. Although the influential teachers Parry and Stanford, both rooted in the Germanic tradition and ardent admirers of Brahms, attempted to change this situation by encouraging younger composers to find a new path more suitable to the English character, their own compositions on the whole still displayed the hallmarks of all the great German composers they revered. Recognition of music as an academic discipline and as a respectable career was also at an all-time low, although this was gradually beginning to change. Yet to the foreigner the state of English music was encapsulated in the notorious phrase 'das Land ohne Musik' which haunted generations of English composers towards the end of the 19th century. When Sterndale Bennett was introduced in Germany as an English composer, he was met with the response 'an English composer? No composer at all!' Music was for many something that we imported from abroad along with the performers, despite the fact that the practice of amateur music-making went on unabated. It was felt that England, unlike other nations, lacked a native musical voice. English composers at the beginning of the 20th century had grown up with a knowledge of German music which continued to dominate concert programmes, and modern French and Russian works were appearing more frequently, thanks to the untiring efforts of the conductor Henry Wood. English composers were exposed to all these different types of music, and this new musical language influenced their works to varying degrees. Vaughan Williams, the leading musical figure in England throughout the first half of this century, was keen for composers to 'express their nationality' in their music. Yet in attempting this, the so-called 'national' music of Vaughan Williams and his contemporaries sometimes revealed a variety of stylistic influences whose origins could often be traced to foreign sources. Elgar's music, seen by many to be the epitome of Englishness is, in the eyes of one critic, 'a composite of the influence of such diverse figures as Massenet, Bizet, Brahms, Wagner and Strauss'.[1] If Grieg and Dvorák had succeeded in composing a 'national music', why shouldn't English composers follow their example? The idea of representing the nation in music was therefore strongly encouraged in the early years of this century and this extract from a letter to the *Musical Herald* in 1915 exemplifies the prevailing attitude:

> This lack of national element in our own music cannot be denied, and the reason is that our composers, with few exceptions, have been content to build upon and even imitate the work of various foreign composers and schools as each one came into prominence. [...] I feel sure all [our composers] would be only too thankful could they write music distinctly British in idiom and character, but it cannot be denied that most of our modern music is the fruit of a foreign tree. [...] I do not think it wise for a creative artist to have to twist his tongue into manners or idioms of speech foreign to his nature. [...] Should the national spirit have so influenced his temperament as to be a characteristic unconsciously reflected in his music and not artificially dragged in, then we shall hail him as a truly British composer.[2]

The lack of English composers able to rival Brahms was a source of great shame, so the attitude quoted above proved a spur for the new generation of English composers, including Ralph Vaughan Williams and Gustav Holst. In fact they had already decided some while before Captain Cyril Jenkins informed the *Musical Herald* of the sorry state of English music that it was time to restore to the nation

the musical heritage which was the birthright of all English people. Here was a great opportunity to compose music which was not based on a Germanic idiom but music which was built on the achievements of our ancestors and therefore truly 'national'. This is clear in such works as Vaughan Williams's *Fantasia on a Theme by Thomas Tallis* for string orchestra and Peter Warlock's song *Sleep*. In these two pieces there is a conscious attempt to emulate a musical language of the 16th and 17th centuries respectively. This was myth-making in action. By linking a contemporary style with the music of their English ancestors, Vaughan Williams, Howells, Warlock and their contemporaries hoped to find a solution to the popular misconception that the English had no indigenous musical culture. One solution they adopted – and it was a fruitful one – was to create a sense of national identity in music through the use of history, often employing an archaic phraseology and using the ancient church modes rather than a major or minor tonality. This gave their works an immediate sense of the past which was distinct from the music being written on the Continent.

At the beginning of the 20th century music was an important part of the creation of Englishness which was seen as so necessary to confirm Britain's privileged place in the world. This formed part of the prevailing artistic tendency, as architects such as Pugin and many artists looked back to the past in order to connect in some way with their ancestors and feel they were part of a national continuum. In fact, other European countries responded in a similar way, rediscovering a sense of identity when the main threat to national individuality, Germany, was seeking to widen its frontiers, both physically and culturally. This self-conscious link with the music of their ancestors could not fail to succeed in raising the level of national consciousness. Cloaked in the mantle of history and therefore unquestionable, the music of composers such as Vaughan Williams and Holst was considered English as never before. This raised awareness of the importance of historians and musicologists as self-styled keepers of a national culture and emphasised their fundamental role in the rediscovery of Britain's long-lost musical treasures, thereby securing their place in history.

Folksong was another means of signalling music's national credentials for composers in the early 20th century. All over Europe folk melodies, folk inflections and the rhythms of 'traditional' music found their way into symphonies and string quartets, imbuing works with 'local colour'. In France the meridional composer Déodat de Séverac advised his friend Joseph Canteloube (best known for his *Chants d'Auvergne*): 'Faites comme moi, mon vieux! chantez votre pays, votre terre!'.[3] Canteloube and many others like him carried out field-work, writing down folksongs performed to them by members of the rural community, eventually incorporating these melodies into their own compositions or publishing them in harmonised versions for use in schools.

For many people the English folksong movement is exemplified in the work of Cecil Sharp. He was one of a number of collectors who ventured into rural England to note down traditional songs. Unfortunately many of his misconceptions of rural communities and their culture have influenced a large number of collective notions as to what constitutes Englishness. These ideas have been used as significant political tools for similar unifying aims by such radically different figures as William Morris, who imagined a rural England as a place where a sense of community was prominent in people's lives, to former Prime Minister John Major, whose more recent evocations of warm beer and cricket on the village green relate to a mythical past prior to the Industrial Revolution and, at best, a small section of the English landscape. Nevertheless this is something which forms a significant part of the collective imagination. In *English Folk Songs: Some Conclusions* Sharp called for a return to the values folksong supposedly represented which perpetuated the myth of rural England, of 'the good old days', a life before industry and commercialism. Sharp never bothered to chart the development of urban musical culture, as the city, in his view, was synonymous with evil, change and modernity. Folksong, however, was a product of the traditional, more authentic way of life because it had followed its own path, used its own musical system of modes (distinct from the development of Western art music) and handed down the beliefs of a race. It was for this reason that folksong was perceived as the true voice of the nation and therefore it became part of the search for national identity which occupied English composers at the turn of the century.

While claiming to have exorcised the Teutonic ghosts from their music in the name of a new national school of composition based on folksong and Tudor music, an increasing awareness of modern French music could be heard in the works of Vaughan Williams, Holst and their contemporaries. This reveals an underlying problem: the acceptance of this music as quintessentially 'English' must therefore be called into question. To do this we must begin by defining our terminology and probing these issues of national identity and nationhood, which are far more complex than we would normally allow, before their place in music can be assessed.

National identity is a fundamental means of self-definition. In our day-to-day social situations our nationality forms part of our subconscious, but once we come into contact with people who are not of our own nationality, or if we travel to a foreign country, this part of our identity is thrown sharply into relief. It is this assumption of difference which is an essential process of any definition of the 'national'. Any identity begins by establishing difference, since 'to simply exist, by and for oneself, is an impossibility'.[4] This is one of the central tenets of semiotic theory, which insists that identification and meaning are referential, rather than being located in 'some notional, causal or essentialist, connection between signifier and signified'.[5] The degree of difference may be debatable, but the meaning of 'English' is constructed through the assumption of, for example, 'non-French' or even 'anti-French', as history has proved on many occasions.

This awareness of an 'Other' has always been a fundamental element in the construction of any national identity. Whenever we conceive of ourselves, others and therefore cultural products as 'English', we believe that what we have just described as nationality is fixed and unquestionable; culture becomes moulded as specific to the nation. This assumption is an important process in defining national

identity, as, although we will never meet all our fellow nationals, we can assume
they exist in what the historian Benedict Anderson calls 'an imagined political
community'.[6] This community has boundaries which, although physical in some
senses, are largely imagined and often arbitrary. The imaginary element makes
nations as tangible entities notoriously hard to define, but this is where ideology
plays its part, giving meaning to a nation. Historians are divided on the point as to
the importance of ideology in forming a sense of nationhood: some argue that ideas
about the nation are imposed by a dominant class, whereas others believe that the
feeling for one's fellow nationals is a natural creation originating in a desire for
community. This cohesion may surface when the nation is mobilised, perhaps by an
external threat such as war or by a moment of victory such as England winning the
World Cup. Although identity is created and constructed it may not necessarily be
false, as there is a constant agreement on the existence, if not on the definition, of
the nation as an entity. In this narcissistic fashion we desire to see ourselves
reflected in the nation, but nationhood also arises out of a wish to make sense of
our world, to have our place in it legitimised.

What is certain is that whatever way nationhood is created for whatever ends, it
is invested with a sense of history, of continuity and naturalness which make its
status as fact ostensibly unquestionable. David Morley and Kevin Robins make this
clear:

> Powerful institutions function to select particular values from the past and to mobilise
> them in contemporary practices. Through such mechanisms of cultural reproduction, a
> particular version of the collective memory and thus a particular sense of national and
> cultural identity, is produced.[7]

National identity, masquerading under a cloak of immutability, is a child of its
time. Although certain notions of Englishness undoubtedly linger on (such as the
common view of the national character as reserved and restrained), others have
faded away and some have taken on a new aspect.

Yet it is all too easy to forget that the significance of being English has changed
over the years. The pride in the Empire has limited appeal in contemporary society
and evocations of its legacy today are likely to be ironic. It is no longer tenable, if it
ever was, to assume Britain's superiority and exceptional status in the world, but
the days when 25 percent of the world was under British rule saw a version of
Englishness which rejoiced in the fact that Britain had brought civilisation to the
'savage' peoples of the globe. Many believed that Britain had been chosen to
conduct a divine mission and this was justification enough for British control.
Music was not slow to realise its potential reinforcement of this idea, and therefore
any music which waved an explicitly 'English' banner would help to bolster the
country's flagging sense of national identity. While the words of *Land of Hope and
Glory* 'God make thee mighty' are explicit, Elgar's tune, with its characteristic
marking of *nobilmente*, literally embodies the sentiments expressed in the text. The
slow four-time march suggests the erect posture of the heroic soldier and by
association lends the music a very 'masculine' character. The harmony moves

sharpwards through the use of secondary dominants, thus creating a sense of expansiveness which reflected the widening of Britain's frontiers.

While the 'wider still and wider' vision of the Empire was part of the national consciousness in Elgar's lifetime, today's notions of Englishness often voice its decline. This is found most notably in evocations of England's former glory and beautiful landscapes, as if calling on this collective culture could somehow soften the blow of our loss of face as a world power. The Last Night of the Proms, far from being the expression of Imperial values, is for many people an opportunity to have an enjoyable evening, and the singing of *Jerusalem* and *Land of Hope and Glory* is, on the whole, a make-believe. These changing attitudes to our national culture should therefore make us aware of the pitfalls of a complacent approach, assuming that 'Englishness' is somehow immutable and even definable in concrete terms. To speak of a 'national' culture may be no more than a superficial consensus and can often be exclusive. Rupert Brooke makes this explicit in his poem *The Old Vicarage, Grantchester* (1915) where the vision of the returning soldier (albeit ironic) offers a vision of England remote from a woman's experience:

> God! I will pack, and take a train,
> And get me to England once again!
> For England's the one land, I know,
> Where men with Splendid hearts may go;
> And Cambridgeshire, of all England,
> The shire for Men who Understand.

With its reference to Cambridge the poem underlines the durability of England's image by calling on a collective memory of English symbols and traditions. Yet these may need to be invented and history refashioned. These then take on new significance as symbols of continuity which the nation takes for granted. However many traditions have been shown to be of recent coinage. Much of the ceremony associated with the monarchy has only emerged in this century, but its swift transformation into a symbol of national pride, strength and antiquity is quite astonishing.[8] Roland Barthes found similar mythologising interesting in the way in which manufactured traditions and rituals assumed an immutable and natural character, fooling us into believing that these things had always existed: 'Semiology has taught us that myth has the task of giving an historical intention a natural justification, and making contingency appear eternal'.[9] The example of *Land of Hope and Glory* is particularly relevant here, as this song was by no means present at the inception of the Proms. Although the piece was often played during the festival (and it must be remembered that Binyon's words were added some time after its composition), it was the conductor Malcolm Sargent who standardised the Last Night format with *Land of Hope and Glory* in the 1950s. The transparency of a national history, a set of traditions and many so-called 'national' cultural products is therefore clear, but this has not in any way inhibited their effect.

This confusion of nature with history cited by Barthes in *Mythologies* can be seen in the mythologising process which surrounds not only the re-invention of history but also in evocations of England's countryside, and again music has become implicated in that process. It is believed that the true England can be found in these backwaters, untouched by pernicious modernisation, a place where 'traditional values' are still important. This idea has been remarkably pervasive over the years and is associated with a sense of nostalgia. Stanley Baldwin's vision of an England where people could escape from radical change, where you could hear 'the corncrake on a dewy morning, the sound of the scythe against the whetstone, and the sight of a plough team coming over the brow of a hill, the sight that has been seen in England since England was a land, [...] for centuries the one eternal sight of England'[10] has its counterpart in the familiar images of the Malvern Hills used to sell recordings of Elgar's music, thereby creating a permanent association between music of this period and the English landscape. Given that folksong was believed to be located only in the country, Vaughan Williams's use of folksong in his music invited a connection with the English countryside, prompting Peter Warlock to suggest that *A Pastoral Symphony* was 'rather too much like a cow looking over a gate' (although the symphony did not in fact quote any folksongs). In response to these ideas Vaughan Williams was later to stress that the work was inspired by the countryside around Ecoives in France where he was stationed during the war, and despite his comment, in a letter of 1938 to Ursula Wood (his future wife), that 'it's not really lambkins frisking at all'[11] it was to no avail. A contemporary review by Rupert O. Erlebach of *A Pastoral Symphony* did not describe its musical style however or attempt an analysis of the work, content rather with detailing:

> A Gloucestershire village with its little river, spanned by many diminutive bridges. The cottages and old church are built of the yellow-grey Cotswold stone which contrasts sharply with the vivid green hills, rising close over the valley to the sky-line, undulated with cornricks, hedges, and many trees.[12]

George Bernard Shaw, in response to the familiar lyrical claims to evoke rural England in music, ridiculed this idea by remarking that 'Grieg's music does not remind me of Norway because I have never been there'. This raises the inevitable question of a geography of English music of this period. There is a sense of place perhaps in certain works of Vaughan Williams and his contemporaries but this is something which they made a conscious choice to valorise. Ivor Gurney asked his friend Howells that he 'sing of Western things. Show us Tintern and the sunset across the Malverns and Welsh hills'.[13] The association of nostalgia and pastoralism as expressions of Englishness has also been strengthened by the fondness of these English composers for the poetry of A. E. Housman, rooted in Shropshire. This idea of the pastoral school has been effective in that it tapped a seam of myth that was already prevalent in society. Keith J. Stringer notes that invented traditions 'were most successful when they built on sentiments that were already present. Elite ideas may thus have evolved partly in response to messages from below'.[14] The Arcadian image and its self-conscious expression of Englishness is, even today, still a powerful symbol in contemporary society. To claim that this 'geography' of art is irrelevant in musical terms would be to ignore a significant element in the reception of English music, as Carl Dahlhaus notes that 'a musical fact is not something pieced together from precise, unambiguous components but the result of the categorical formation of an acoustic substratum, a formation which presupposes or includes aesthetic and ideological elements as well as structural and syntactical factors'.[15] Yet to neglect the 'French' features in a work such as Vaughan Williams's song cycle *On Wenlock Edge*, merely to use the music as an example of the expression of a specifically English identity, would be equally questionable and dangerously myopic.

Vaughan Williams constantly stressed the importance of the English composer using his surroundings, of drawing on his native culture and traditions instead of looking to other countries for inspiration. Only then, he claimed, could an authentic 'national' music exist: 'all the composers of this renaissance from Parry to Britten, different and often antagonistic as their aims are, have this in common – that they realise that vital art must grow in its own soil and be nurtured by its own rain and sunshine'.[16] This is somewhat ironic since Vaughan Williams himself felt the need to go abroad to study with other composers, first to Bruch in Germany and then Ravel in Paris (1907–1908), as he believed his style to be 'lumpy and stodgy' and 'too Teuton'.[17] This was probably due to the teaching at the Royal College, where Stanford was known for his worship of Brahms. The immediate effects of Ravel's teaching can be heard in early works of Vaughan Williams such as the *String Quartet in G minor* (1909) and the song cycle *On Wenlock Edge* (1910) through the use of non-diatonic harmonies and what Vaughan Williams himself termed 'atmospheric effects', but the influence of modern French music also permeates later works such as *A London Symphony* (1914), whose opening takes its cue from Debussy's *La Mer*, and the scoring of *A Pastoral Symphony* (1922) which owes much to Ravel. Holst's music on the other hand, a product of English teaching and culture, showed a debt to Wagner in his early works (e.g. *Sita*) and then some Debussy (the orchestration in *The Planets* is one instance, 'Neptune' in particular with the use of a wordless female chorus; Debussy had used this effect in 'Sirènes' from his orchestral *Nocturnes*). He eventually evolved a more individual style inspired by his study of Oriental philosophy and religion.

French music was only one of a number of foreign influences on English music at the turn of the century, but it was also one of the most seductive and profound. Vaughan Williams did not escape from the 'French fever', as he called it, which gripped England around 1908, and caused some to express concern that imitating modern French composers such as Debussy and Ravel was merely a substitution for Teutonic music and would not further the quest for an 'English' school of composition. Yet it was largely a result of years of German cultural imperialism that England welcomed art from other countries in a united effort to define themselves as distinct from the Hun. France too had embraced anything which came from the Wagnerian shrine of Bayreuth and many composers thought it about time to assert a resolutely French national identity in music which did not involve aping Wagner. Like Vaughan Williams, Debussy looked back to France's golden age of the 17th century and tried to instil those qualities of clarity and *légèreté* he found in the music of Couperin and Rameau into his own compositions, which he perceived as integral parts of the French character.

This new musical language baffled English audiences initially who were used to the clear tonal structure and formal outline of the German classics. In much the same way that the Impressionist painters had confounded critics who attempted to explain the new style with an unwieldy and anachronistic terminology, Debussy's music emphasised the need for a new critical vocabulary. Discussion of subjects and development sections which served to guide the listener through a performance of Brahms for example had to be dispensed with in Debussy's case, leaving many with a sense of disorientation. To dismiss this music out of hand was however a common reaction to something which critics could not understand. Charges of vagueness and lack of form were frequent, even in sympathetic writers. Ravel's *String Quartet* was described by the *Musical Times* as 'music chiefly remarkable for vagueness of significance, incoherence and weird harmonic eccentricities'.[18] It was difficult for the more conservative critics to appreciate the debt which Debussy and Ravel owed to their predecessors. There were many who could not perceive the solid technique behind the new harmonies, largely because they were trained to judge tonal progression in terms of preparation and resolution. The fact that Wagner had delayed the resolution of a chord throughout the whole of *Tristan und Isolde* did not seem to bother them.

Another crucial factor entered the equation regarding the reception of French music in England: its perceived Frenchness. This was intimately connected to the sensibility and interests of an age which had witnessed the flourishing of the Bohemian artists who took their cue from Parisian culture. Figures such as Arthur Symons, W. B. Yeats, Oscar Wilde, Ernest Dowson and William Rothenstein pursued Pater's dictum of 'art for art's sake' with great zeal in the pages of such journals as the *Yellow Book* and the *Savoy*. Many of them were well-acquainted with the leading literary figures in France and brought much of the new poetry and novels to the attention of the English public. Translations of Zola's novels and Laclos' *Les Liaisons Dangereuses* established France as the home of art and a particular brand at that – one which was decadent, modernist and concerned only with sensuous experience. French art became synonymous with French life and hence a view of France was created in the English mind which owed more to received ideas than it did to actual fact. It was very easy to tar all French art forms with the same brush, precisely because they were French, foreign, and therefore exotic in some way. This was certainly the case with articles about French music, in which early critics tended to group together d'Indy and Debussy as representatives of the modern school, a concept which today is hard to understand in the light of Debussy's subsequent influence on 20th century music compared to that of d'Indy. This is even more unforgivable, given that by the time English critics turned their attention to discussions of Debussy and his music, he had long since evolved a personal style which bore little resemblance to the preceding generation of French composers such as Saint-Saëns. But 'France' meant certain clearly defined things to English critics which it was possible to call upon without much true critical observation; it connoted a series of reactions from which few were willing to stray.

However distorted that image of French culture might be, it would be used extensively as a yardstick to measure the perceived Frenchness of the music of Debussy and Ravel. An English review of the premiere of Debussy's opera *Pelléas et Mélisande* left its readers in no doubt as to the writer's views on modern French music: 'an important event, another step downwards in the evolution of the musical theories and the musical taste of our age happened on April 30 last'.[19] The majority of critics found Debussy's music 'vague', 'atmospheric' and above all artificial, traits which were often lent to French art in general. Debussy's style was so recondite, in the opinion of the writer Ernest Newman, that it eventually lost its way, and the continued quest for originality ended in mannerism. Given the English mistrust of intellectuals (of which France had plenty), it was easy to extend the argument and suggest that Debussy's music was cerebral, devoid of all emotion. Debates raged as to whether the French composer was a mere tangential moment in the development of Western art music or something far more profound. The public however was quick to acknowledge the sensuous beauty of this music, and repeat performances of the *Prélude à l'après-midi d'un faune* followed its premiere in 1904. The first English performance of *Pelléas et Mélisande* in 1909 was also a great success and hence positive Debussy appreciation increased.

With the advent of war and with anti-German feeling running high, criticism of modern French music showed that in general (with notable exceptions) people had come to recognise the achievement of Debussy and Ravel and that they were certainly more familiar with their music. Ravel, first hailed as an *enfant terrible*, was soon identified as distinct from Debussy. Whether it was his innate classicism or the fact that Debussy had prepared the ground in a certain sense is hard to tell, but the English public warmed more quickly to his musical style. The composer D. K. Sorabji was rapturous in his praise for Ravel's *Trois Poèmes de Stéphane Mallarmé* in 1915: 'nowhere is that super-subtlety, electric sensitiveness and airy delicacy so typical of M. Ravel shown more fully nor more intensely than in these wondrous songs'.[20] These were positive attributes which not so long ago would have been derided for their vagueness and artifice. The war had brought change to society's mores, and with it more interest in modern French music, aided by the dearth of performances of German music.

Yet it was at this point in particular that the question of national music reared its ugly head once more. The writer and critic Edwin Evans recalled that 'a wit of the day said that the only chance a British composer had of hearing one of his works twice was the exceptional good fortune of a performance at the Albert Hall, where there was an echo'.[21] Composers felt that if this neglect of the country's own music was allowed to continue, French music would prove to be yet another intoxicating influence from which English music would never recover. Yet their fears were ungrounded, as the influence of Debussy and Ravel was a step down the road towards self-realisation. Although some of the composers under discussion voiced their concern, many of those same composers followed Continental developments with interest, even if this did not, on the whole, extend to slavish imitation. A work such as Rebecca Clarke's *Sonata for Viola and Piano* (1919) reveals a knowledge and enthusiasm for the work of the modern French school, adding a subtlety and a passion not hitherto present in English music. The echoes of Debussy and Ravel which can be heard in such works reveal that their music was an element in the developing artistic consciousness of the young English composer. With the signing of the *Entente Cordiale* in 1904 the English climate had been favourable to French culture for some time and this wave of interest gave composers greater opportunity to hear and learn these new works from across the Channel. English music did not exist in a vacuum; it was a meeting ground for a variety of different styles from both home and abroad.

So why has musicology been so reluctant to acknowledge the presence of foreign elements in early 20th century English music? Musicologists have attempted to highlight the 'national' features of the music in the context of the Tudor and pastoral revival at the expense of the 'imported' elements which form part of the musical fabric, clinging to the 19th century notion that music is an expression of the nation and the composer therefore typical of their race. The unfortunate outcome of this attitude and its concomitant methodology is a view of English music as parochial and anti-modernist (because ostensibly it looks back to the past), which ignores to an alarming degree the stylistic tensions prevalent in this period, elements which contribute to the creation of any identity. Nikolaus Pevsner in *The Englishness of English Art* (1956) insisted that English art was to be found in apparently irreconcilable opposites – the rational and the irrational, the flowing line and the Perpendicular. He argued that the essential attitude towards the subject was the same. Musicologists, however, have attempted to explain Englishness through something intrinsic to music which only a Vaughan Williams or an Elgar could produce, rather than defining identity in relation to other types of national music, considering its ideological context and the selective process involved in any definition of Englishness; perhaps this is because they are proud of our 'unique' position as a nation of islanders. Yet music, by its very nature, here invokes a large number of thorny issues which are outside the scope of this chapter, but do need to be considered. Is national identity important to every composer, and if it is, to what extent does a composer achieve the expression of Englishness in music? John Ireland (whose fondness for Debussy and Ravel can be heard in his piano music) claimed 'I've never been conscious of my music being excessively English. It is true, my past is in this country and traditions I was brought up on were English, but all that only affects you unconsciously'.[22] Is music able, in a non-representational way, to convey a sense of national identity? If so, is it the subject matter (such as the use of a folksong) or something in the notes themselves which creates extra-musical images, a hot potato with which Igor Stravinsky took issue.

Writers and musicologists who have referred to the Englishness of Elgar, Vaughan Williams and their contemporaries have been curiously reluctant to define what it is that leads them to this conclusion, and hence their arguments rarely stand up to close scrutiny. The music of Delius for example, ignored by many in the early 20th century because the composer was 'tainted with cosmopolitanism' (he spent most of his life in France), was eventually championed by such luminaries as Sir Thomas Beecham, and its 'English' credentials were highlighted. Delius himself, however, indulged in vitriolic letters when it came to England and English music. A work such as *Summer Evening*, although highly individual, uses a musical vocabulary common to late Romanticism with its lush scoring and shifting harmonies which feature so often in the music of Wagner, yet there are other passages which seem to echo the sound world of Debussy, particularly in the use of horns. In spite of this, Delius is, for many, synonymous with Englishness. Cecil Gray, a fellow composer and writer on music, drew on all the available myths which have been shown to foster a sense of national identity in his appreciation of Delius, claiming that *Brigg Fair* evoked 'the atmosphere of an early summer morning in the English country, with its suggestion of a faint mist veiling the horizon, and the fragrant scent of the dawn in the air!' He went on to link Delius with historical figures, noting that 'this very sweetness and sensuousness is perhaps the most noteworthy characteristic of English art'[23] and those who did not agree with this view were dismissing Shakespeare, Dowland, Herrick and others as representatives of the English character. The composer Peter Warlock was similarly appreciative of Delius's use of folksong, in sharp contrast with his derisory comments concerning Vaughan Williams. England claimed Delius for a national composer, yet Robert Stradling suggests that Delius effected a notable change of direction in works such as *Brigg Fair* which is 'otherwise unaccountable',[24] unless he intended to make his music more 'English' in order to increase his popularity.

The term 'English' music carries with it, unfortunately, a whole host of connotations which are likely to influence the listener's reception of a work. Think of Elgar and images spring quickly to the mind of rolling hills and we like to imagine that the music reminds us of 'old England', of a distant memory of Imperial values when people rallied together as one nation. Elgar's ceremonial music perhaps creates this association because the monarchy is such a powerful symbol in English society. Yet this is precisely the point: label your work *Crown Imperial* (William Walton) or *A Pastoral Symphony* (Vaughan Williams) and you have already prescribed a pattern of reception in your audience. The listener imagines the music to follow a certain trajectory, and will at any rate be happy in the knowledge that what they have just heard, written by an English composer in the early part of the 20th century, is a genuine expression of a specific national identity because this is what they have been led to expect.

Can we say then that English music exists? The identity asserted by the composers under discussion was a self-conscious one whose basis was the expression of a particular nationality, but as we have seen, elements of a national character undergo constant fluctuation and redefinition, being closely linked to economic, social and political factors. Yet English music of the early 20th century continues its association in the popular imagination with the expression of a national identity, but this is perhaps a result of selection. Our diet of English music ignores parts of the repertoire which would greatly alter the present view of Englishness in music: Vaughan Williams's song cycle *On Wenlock Edge*, Rebecca Clarke's *Sonata for Viola and Piano* and Howells's string quartet *In Gloucestershire* are just some of those works which display a marked influence of Debussy and Ravel, but concert programmes in the 1990s have tended to privilege music perceived as quintessentially 'English'. With regard to Vaughan Williams this means the *Fantasia on 'Greensleeves'*, the *Fantasia on a Theme by Thomas Tallis* and perhaps the occasional symphony. It has been shown however that what 'English' is generally taken to mean in music is far from certain and also that Englishness is by no means a notion which is uniform or historically constant. Alain Frogley calls for a reassessment of Vaughan Williams 'whose critical reception so often remains mired in misconceived notions of Pastoralism, Nationalism, and other blanket clichés that only thinly conceal raw nerves in the national self-image',[25] so that instead of considering English music as a representative of a monolithic national identity, it might be more useful to consider English music in terms of polarities, realising that different and at times self-contradictory ideas are needed to form a picture of national music at any one time.

Is it therefore this amalgam of French (and other) influences which becomes transmuted into a set of characteristics or a style that one can define ultimately as English? Or are we rather hearing the individual voice of each composer and confusing, to use Pevsner's distinction, the spirit of the age with the expression of national character? How would one identify purely English music or even attempt to define it without referring to other types of 'national' music, and furthermore could that decision be taken by people who are far too involved in English culture? Is it even possible to conceive of a style that one could not attribute in part to a variety of sources? This type of question becomes caught in an ever-increasing spiral as Dahlhaus asks 'do individual characteristics proceed out of the national substance, or is the concept of what is national formed by generalisation on the basis of individual characteristics?'.[26] Has not 'English' music been decided for us? It is clear that early 20th century English music formed a part of the 're-packaging' of English music to meet a demand for a national style, and it is this involvement in ideology which is worthy of study rather than attempting to seek Englishness in, say, the use of the flattened seventh. Myths take on a substance of their own. The reasons why the desire to express the nation in music was so great have been touched upon in this chapter; this and the other questions posed above deserve closer attention in the future. The repertoire mentioned here could easily be broadened to approach the music, not in terms of superficial comparisons but, as the aim has been in this study, to locate English music within the context of the issue of national identity.

Bibliography

Anderson, Benedict (1991) *Imagined Communities: Reflections on the Origin and Spread of Nationalism*. (Revised edition) London: Verso.
Barthes, Roland (1972) *Mythologies*. (Trans. Annette Lavers) London: Cape.

Bjørn, Claus, Alexander Grant and Keith J. Stringer (eds) (1994) *Nations, Nationalism and Patriotism in the European Past*. Copenhagen: Academic.

Boyes, Georgina (1993) *The Imagined Village: Culture, Ideology and the English Folk Revival*. Music and Society. Manchester: Manchester University Press.

Campos, Christophe (1965) *The View of France: From Arnold to Bloomsbury*. London: Oxford University Press.

Colley, Linda 'Britishness and Englishness: An Argument.' *Journal of British Studies* 31 (1992): 309-329.

Colls, Robert and Philip Dodd (eds) (1986) *Englishness: Politics and Culture 1880–1920*. London: Croom Helm.

Crossley, Ceri and Ian Small (eds) (1988) *Studies in Anglo-French Cultural Relations: Imagining France*. Basingstoke: Macmillan.

Dahlhaus, Carl (1980) *Between Romanticism and Modernism: Four Studies in the Music of the Later Nineteenth Century*. (Trans. Mary Whittall) Berkeley: University of California Press.

Foreman, Lewis (1987) *From Parry to Britten: British Music in Letters 1900–1945*. London: Batsford.

Frogley, Alain 'H. G. Wells and Vaughan Williams's A London Symphony: Politics and Culture in fin-de-siècle England.' *Sundry Sorts of Music Books: Essays on the British Library Collections*. Edited by Chris Banks, Arthur Searle and Malcolm Turner. London: British Library, 1993. 299-308.

Giles, Judy and Tim Middleton (eds) (1995) *Englishness 1900–1950: An Introductory Sourcebook on National Identity*. London: Routledge.

Grant, Alexander and Keith J. Stringer (eds) (1995) *Uniting the Kingdom? The Making of British History*. London: Routledge.

Gray, Cecil (1924) *A Survey of Contemporary Music*. London: Oxford University Press.

Hobsbawm, Eric, and Terence Ranger (eds) (1989) *The Invention of Tradition*. Cambridge: Cambridge University Press.

Howes, Frank (1966) *The English Musical Renaissance*. London: Secker.

Marsh, Jan (1982) *Back To The Land: The Pastoral Impulse in England, from 1880 to 1914*. London: Quartet.

Norris, Christopher (ed) (1989) *Music and the Politics of Culture*. London: Lawrence.

Orwell, George (1982) *The Lion and the Unicorn: Socialism and the English Genius*. Searchlight. London: Penguin. Also (1941) London: Secker.

Pevsner, Nikolaus (1993) *The Englishness of English Art*. London: Penguin.

Rich, Paul 'Victorian Values: The Quest for Englishness.' *History Today* 37 (1987): 24-30.

Said, Edward W. (1993) *Culture and Imperialism*. London: Chatto.

Samuel, Raphael (ed) (1989) *Patriotism: The Making and Unmaking of British National Identity*. 3 vols. History Workshop Series. London: Routledge.

Stradling, Robert, and Meirion Hughes (1993) *The English Musical Renaissance 1860–1940: Construction and Deconstruction*. London: Routledge.

Sykes, Richard 'The Evolution of Englishness in the English Folksong Revival, 1890–1914.' *Folk Music Journal* 6 (1993): 446-490.

Vaughan Williams, Ralph (1986) *National Music and Other Essays*. Edited by Michael Kennedy. Second edition 1963; Oxford: Oxford University Press.

Wiener, Martin J. (1992) *English Culture and the Decline of the Industrial Spirit, 1850–1980*. London: Penguin.

Notes

1   Michael Kennedy, foreword, *National Music and Other Essays*, by Ralph Vaughan Williams, 2nd ed. Oxford: Oxford University Press, 1987, pp. vii-viii.

2   Capt. Cyril Jenkins, 'To the *Musical Herald*', September 1915, *From Parry to Britten: British Music in Letters 1900–1945*, ed. Lewis Foreman. London: Batsford, 1987, pp. 77-78.

3   Qtd. in Françoise Cougniaud-Raginel, *Canteloube: Chantre de la terre*. Beziers: Société de Musicologie de Languedoc, 1988, p. 60.

4   Sean Cubitt, 'Introduction: Over the Borderlines', *Screen* 30 (4), 1989, p. 4.

5   Cubitt, p. 2.

6   Benedict Anderson, *Imagined Communities: Reflections on the Origin and Spread of Nationalism* London: Verso, 1991, p. 6.

7   David Morley and Kevin Robins, 'Spaces of Identity: Communications Technologies and the Reconfiguration of Europe', *Screen* 30 (4), 1989, pp. 10-34.

8   David Cannadine demonstrates that the state opening of Parliament as practised by Edward VII and attendants in full regalia, (considered to be an age-old tradition) was in fact 'something which Victoria had not done for forty years'. 'The Context, Performance and Meaning of Ritual: The British Monarchy and the 'Invention of Tradition', c. 1820–1977', *The Invention of Tradition*, ed. Eric Hobsbawm and Terence Ranger, Past and Present Publications, Cambridge: Cambridge University Press, 1983, p. 136.

9   Roland Barthes, *Mythologies*, trans. Annette Lavers. London: Cape, 1972, p. 142.

10 'England is the Country and the Country is England'. qtd. in *Englishness 1900–1950: An Introductory Sourcebook on National Identity*, ed. Judy Giles and Tim Middleton. London: Routledge, 1995, p. 101.

11 Qtd. in Ursula Vaughan Williams, *R. V. W.: A Biography of Ralph Vaughan Williams*, Oxford Lives, 1964; Oxford: Oxford University Press, 1988, p. 121.

12 Rupert O. Erlebach, 'Vaughan Williams and his Three Symphonies', *Monthly Musical Record* 52, 1922, p. 151.

13 Ivor Gurney, 'To Herbert Howells', undated, qtd. in Christopher Palmer, *Herbert Howells - A Centenary Celebration*. London: Thames, 1992, p. 46.

14 Keith J. Stringer, 'Social and Political Communities in European History: Some Reflections on Recent Studies', *Nations, Nationalism and Patriotism in the European Past*, ed. Claus Bjørn, Alexander Grant, and Keith J. Stringer. Copenhagen: Academic Press, 1994, p. 28.

15 Carl Dahlhaus, *Between Romanticism and Modernism: Four Studies in Music of the Later Nineteenth Century*, trans. Mary Whittall. Berkeley: University of California Press, 1980, pp. 85-86.

16 Ralph Vaughan Williams, 'A Minim's Rest', *National Music and Other Essays*, 2nd ed. 1934; Oxford: Oxford University Press, 1987, p. 168.

17 Ralph Vaughan Williams, 'A Musical Autobiography', *National Music and Other Essays*, 2nd ed. 1950; Oxford: Oxford University Press, 1987, pp.187-191.

18 'Modern French Music', review of String Quartet by Ravel, Parisian Quartet, La Société des Concerts Français, Leighton House, Kensington, London, 6 Dec. 1907, *Musical Times* 49, 1908, p. 40.

19 S. Marchesi, 'A New Lyric Drama at Paris', review of *Pelléas et Mélisande*, cond. André Messager, Opéra Comique, Paris, 30 April 1902, *Monthly Musical Record* 32, 1902, p. 107.

20 D. K. Sorabji, 'Trois Poèmes de Stéphane Mallarmé', *Musical Standard* 5, 1915, p. 196.

21 Edwin Evans, 'Cock-a-hoop', *Time and Tide* 5 Dec. 1931

22 John Ireland, interview with Murray Schafer, *British Composers in Interview*. London: Faber, 1963, p. 31.

23 Cecil Gray, *A Survey of Contemporary Music*. London: Oxford University Press, 1924, pp. 73-74.

24 Robert Stradling, 'On Shearing the Black Sheep in Spring: The Repatriation of Frederick Delius', *Music and the Politics of Culture*, ed. Christopher Norris. London: Lawrence, 1989, p. 90.

25 Alain Frogley, 'I. G. Wells and Vaughan Williams's *A London Symphony*: Politics and Culture in fin-de-siècle England', *Sundry Sorts of Music Books: Essays on the British Library Collections*, ed. Chris Banks, Arthur Searle, and Malcolm Turner. London: British Library, 1993, p. 305.

26 Carl Dahlhaus, *Between Romanticism and Modernism: Four Studies in Music of the Later Nineteenth Century*, trans. Mary Whittall. Berkeley: University of California Press, 1980, p. 82.

Theatre and Nation in Austria:

The Vagaries of History

W. E. Yates

The Austrians love to celebrate anniversaries and jubilees. The passing of 100 years since a playwright's death, 125 years since a musician's birth, 150 years since the founding of a theatre – any such occasion is likely to be commemorated in lavish exhibitions, colourful postage-stamps, and ambitious conferences, to say nothing of specially named new pastries. 1991 was a bumper year – 200 hundred years since the death of Mozart and the birth of Grillparzer. Preparations are already in hand for the 200th anniversary of the birth of Nestroy in 2001. The biggest celebrations of all were in 1996, when the whole country had a millennium to celebrate – not a thousand years of its continuous existence as a political entity, but a thousand years since the first recorded use of the name 'Ostarrichi'. Devotees of exhibitions, postage-stamps, and conferences were not disappointed – the history and the very character of Austria were documented, commemorated, and debated. The 'identity' of Austria became the topic of the year.

It is not mere chance than recent celebrations have featured Mozart, Grillparzer, and Nestroy, the great national masters of opera, tragedy, and comedy respectively. There can be no country in Europe in which theatre has so central a place in the national consciousness, for historical reasons that will be addressed below. One of the 'millennial' conferences about the 'identity' of Austria was precisely on theatre – the meeting of the international Grillparzer-Forum held in Vienna in November 1995 had as its theme 'Theater auf Österreich-Suche' ['Theatre in search of Austria']. It concentrated on the establishment of the image of Austria in the theatre and on the function of the theatre as a vehicle both for mythopœic expression of that image and for critical subversion of the public myth, as in the work of such playwrights as Ödön von Horváth during the First Republic and Thomas Bernhard during the Second Republic.

That it was so natural for theatre as an institution to be associated with the very identity of the nation – and that national 'identity' can be a subject of such intense interest – needs to be explained historically, at the level both of political history and of theatre history.

For the fact that despite the millennial context the 'identity' of Austria was not – and is not – something that can simply be taken for granted is a direct consequence of the political changes that have convulsed central Europe in the last 150 years. Nothing has been less permanent on the map of Europe than the boundaries within

German-speaking Europe. 1804 is a convenient place to pick up the story; that is the year in which Franz I renounced the title of Holy Roman Emperor which the Habsburgs, with their principal seat in Vienna, had held since the 15th century. In the post-Napoleonic period Metternich, the Chancellor of Austria, was one of the driving forces behind the systematic suppression of separatist nationalism which helped to shape the political stagnation of the so-called 'Biedermeier' period between the end of the Napoleonic age and the revolution of 1848: writing in 1839, Grillparzer defined the whole policy of his government as being directed at only two aims – the repression of liberalism and the maintenance of the *status quo*.[1] By 1848, however, pan-German sympathies were on the rise. Like the other German states Austria sent delegates to the National Assembly in Frankfurt (even if the Austrian delegation to the preliminary *Vorparlament* in March, who included a prominent playwright, Grillparzer's friend Eduard von Bauernfeld, missed taking part by arriving too late); but military defeat by Prussia in the summer of 1866 was followed by the exclusion of Austria from the German Confederation. When the Habsburg Empire was transformed into the Dual Monarchy in February 1867, with Franz Joseph filling the twin functions of Emperor of Austria and King of Hungary, the multinational character of the empire was under threat, while at the same time its German-speakers were excluded from the German nation that would be united for the first time, under Prussian leadership, in 1871. The result was the beginning of an authentic crisis of national identity. Writers conscious of belonging to the same culture as Goethe defined themselves resolutely as 'German'. One of many statements of this kind is a defiant epigrammatic poem written by Grillparzer in 1867: he had been born a German, he wrote, and nothing could take away what he had written in German.[2] Politically, however, there was resentful suspicion of the power of the new Germany. Even in the First World War, when the two countries fought side by side, a writer such as Hugo von Hofmannsthal, a traditionalist Austrian patriot – one of his biggest pre-war successes (1911) had been the libretto for *Der Rosenkavalier*, set in the Vienna of Empress Maria Theresia – was concerned to define what he called the 'idea of Austria' explicitly by contrast with 'German' characteristics. The differences were partly historically based, taking account both of the dominant position of the Roman Catholic Church in Austria after the Counter-Reformation and also of the ethnic and cultural diversity of the Dual Monarchy. But Hofmannsthal's crudest summary of supposed national characters, published as a newspaper article in 1917, is hardly more than a list of clichés – the Prussians efficient, driven by will-power and authority, the Austrians humane, individualistic, characterised by self-irony and a tendency to 'play-acting' ('Schauspielerei').[3]

In his political views during the war Hofmannsthal was influenced not least by an old friend and fellow-writer, Leopold von Andrian, who was a professional diplomat trained in the staunchly pro-Habsburg Foreign Office. With hindsight the disintegration of the Dual Monarchy in 1918 looks inevitable, but at the time it caught a nation largely unprepared. Even so experienced an observer as Henry Wickham Steed, who had been the Vienna correspondent of *The Times* for 11 years, confidently asserted as late as 1913 that there was no 'sufficient reason' why the

Habsburg monarchy should not 'retain its rightful place in the European community'.[4] The effect on a dramatist such as Hofmannsthal of what he saw simply as the collapse of Austria after the war was a sense that the very basis of his work had been undermined.[5] The newly-established republic wanted to call itself 'German Austria' (Deutsch-Österreich), and envisaged being an integral part of republican Germany; when this development was forbidden by the treaties of Versailles and Saint-Germain-en-Laye, the new state, a rump republic of under 7 million inhabitants by comparison with the 52 million inhabitants of the Dual Monarchy, and shorn of a large part of its natural and industrial resources, was widely perceived as being not economically viable. Still worse was to come – civil war in February 1934, followed by an attempted Nazi *putsch* and the assassination of the Chancellor, Engelbert Dollfuss, in July, and the eventual engulfing of Austria by Hitler's Germany in 1938. It re-emerged under allied occupation in 1945, but was not restored to full political independence until 1955. In less than 100 years, a series of political events had altered the constitution, size, allegiance, and status of the country so often and so radically as to make its 'identity' genuinely problematic.

Successive events in the developments briefly outlined above left their mark in the theatre. In the patriotic euphoria that followed the Congress of Vienna and the final defeat of Napoleon, for example, the popular dramatist Adolf Bäuerle enjoyed a considerable success with a spectacular comedy *Wien, Paris, London und Constantinopel* (première 1823, Theater in der Leopoldstadt) in which three discontented Viennese craftsmen are taught by magic to appreciate the virtues of their native city by comparison with the other great capitals: 'Preist das Ausland, wo es zu preisen ist, aber zieht es nicht muthwillig dem heimischen Boden vor. Ihr sollt wieder eure Vaterstadt erblicken. Sonnt euch in der Nähe *des Pallastes, der des Österreichers Liebstes in sich vereint!*' ['Give foreign parts the praise they are due, but do not give them arbitrary precedence over your homeland. You shall see your native city again: bask beside the palace that contains all that is dearest to

Figure 1. *Adolf Bäuerle*, Komisches Theater, *Vol. 6, Pest: Hartleben 1826, p. 143.*

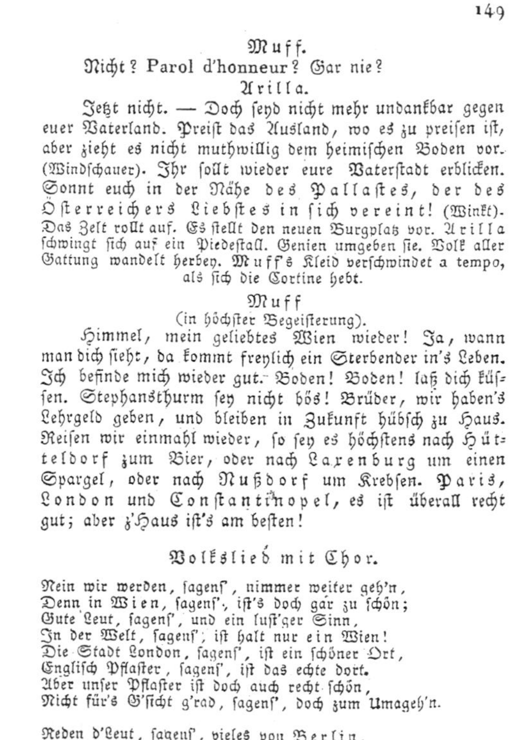

¹⁴⁹

Muff.
Nicht? Parol d'honneur? Gar nie?
Urilla.
Jetzt nicht. — Doch seyd nicht mehr undankbar gegen euer Vaterland. Preist das Ausland, wo es zu preisen ist, aber zieht es nicht muthwillig dem heimischen Boden vor. (Windschauer). Ihr sollt wieder eure Vaterstadt erblicken. Sonnt euch in der Nähe des Pallastes, der des Österreichers Liebstes in sich vereint! (Winkt). Das Zelt rollt auf. Es stellt den neuen Burgplatz vor. Urilla schwingt sich auf ein Piedestall. Genien umgeben sie. Volk aller Gattung wandelt herbey. Muff's Kleid verschwindet a tempo, als sich die Cortine hebt.

Muff
(in höchster Begeisterung).
Himmel, mein geliebtes Wien wieder! Ja, wann man dich sieht, da kommt freylich ein Sterbender in's Leben. Ich befinde mich wieder gut. Boden! Boden! laß dich küssen. Stephansthurm sey nicht bös! Brüder, wir haben's Lehrgeld geben, und bleiben in Zukunft hübsch zu Haus. Reisen wir einmahl wieder, so sey es höchstens nach Hütteldorf zum Bier, oder nach Laxenburg um einen Spargel, oder nach Nußdorf um Krebsen. Paris, London und Constantinopel, es ist überall recht gut; aber z'Haus ist's am besten!

Volkslied mit Chor.
Nein wir werden, sagens', nimmer weiter geh'n,
Denn in Wien, sagens', ist's doch gar zu schön;
Gute Leut, sagens', und ein lustger Sinn,
In der Welt, sagens', ist halt nur ein Wien!
Die Stadt London, sagens', ist ein schöner Ort,
Englisch Pflaster, sagens', ist das echte dort.
Aber unser Pflaster ist doch auch recht schön,
Nicht für's G'sicht g'rad, sagens', doch zum Umageh'n.

Reden d'Leut, sagens', vieles von Berlin,
Zeigens' die schönsten Städt' da beym Müller *) drin —

*) Müller's Kunstgallerie, worin Enslens optische Zimmerreise aufgestellt war.

Figure 2. Der Kobold. Herausgerissene Blätter aus seinem Album, 2. Heft, 8. Lfg., Vienna: Höfelich 1847, p. 57.

every Austrian!'].[6] At this point the stage is transformed to represent the newly-completed square outside the Imperial Palace, and the repentant craftsmen exclaim in loyalist delight. In the 1840s, rising hopes of the emergence of an enlightened united Germany led to various demonstrations of pan-German feeling in Vienna. In the court theatre in Vienna, the Burgtheater, Bauernfeld enjoyed one of his biggest box-office successes in 1844 with a historical drama treating the theme of German unity, *Ein deutscher Krieger* ['A German Warrior'], which is set at the end of the Thirty Years War. In February 1847 the Theater an der Wien staged a re-working by Meyerbeer of his opera *Ein Feldlager in Schlesien* ['An Encampment in Silesia'] – which had originally been composed for the re-opening of the Berlin Opera three years earlier – under the title *Vielka*, with Jenny Lind in the title role. With a libretto specially rewritten by one of the most popular German playwrights of the day, Charlotte-Birch-Pfeiffer,[7] it was perceived as being imbued with a nationalist spirit, but still created such a run on the box-office that a whole issue of the satirical magazine *Der Kobold* ['The Imp'], edited by a minor local dramatist, Friedrich Kaiser, was devoted to cartoons on the '*Vielka* fever', showing the pavements outside the theatre as having been transformed into a veritable battleground and caricaturing situations such as a fiancée turning against her betrothed in favour of a rival suitor who was in possession of tickets. In April 1848, a month after the outbreak of revolution, a drama by Heinrich Laube, *Die Karlsschüler* ['Karl Eugen's Pupils'], which centres on the first performance of Schiller's *Die Räuber* ['The Robbers'] and until the revolution had been banned in Austria, was performed in the Burgtheater, with applause for every mention of Schiller's name and also of the ideas of liberty and justice. It is no coincidence that when the first barricades went up in the streets of Vienna in May 1848 one of the most impressive was erected directly in front of the Burgtheater itself. Seventy years later, after the collapse of the monarchy in 1918, one of the most significant responses was the foundation of the Salzburg Festival, first held in 1920 and centring on opera and spoken drama – before the end of the war the principal inspirational genius of the Festival, Max Reinhardt, was already planning that it must be based on 'autochthonic art',[8] and subsequently its programme was systematically expounded by Hofmannsthal as a token of the vitality of a recognisably Austrian (or 'Austro-Bavarian') cultural tradition rooted in the Baroque period but embracing an artistic cosmopolitanism in the spirit of the multinational perspectives associated with the Dual Monarchy. Twenty years after that, after the *Anschluss*, one of the strategic steps taken by Nazi Germany to underline the integration of Austria in the Third Reich was to move the *Reichstheaterfestwoche*, a prestigious annual festival of theatre, to Vienna that summer, while the programme of the Salzburg Festival was swiftly 'Aryanised' to conform to Nazi policy, with the annual opening show, Reinhardt's production of Hofmannsthal's *Jedermann* ['Everyman'] in front of the Cathedral, replaced by an indoor production of a play by a North German dramatist, Heinrich von Kleist. And in 1955, when the treaty restoring Austria's independence was finally signed, the event was marked by a production in the newly-reopened Burgtheater of the most famous of all dramas based on Austrian history, Grillparzer's *König Ottokars Glück und Ende* ['The Rise and Fall of King Ottokar'], which is based on the ambition of the Bohemian King Ottokar II for the imperial crown, his defeat by Rudolf I of Habsburg in the 1270s, the election of Rudolf as 'German king', head of the Holy Roman Empire, and the establishment of Habsburg rule in Austria.

Figure 3. *The Barricade on the Michaelerplatz, May 1848, by Vinzenz Katzler. From Heinrich Reschauer and Moritz Smets,* Das Jahr 1848. Geschichte der Wiener Revolution, *2 vols, Vienna: Waldheim 1872, II, 285.*

   The distinctive centrality of theatre in Austrian life is related historically to the fact that Vienna was for a long time the only metropolitan centre in German-speaking Europe. (It was not overtaken in size by Berlin until the mid 19th century.) In the country districts from the late Middle Ages onwards there was also a tradition of folk drama, mainly deriving from Passion plays and Christmas plays; these forms flourished especially in the Tyrol and south-eastern Austria, including the Burgenland. But it was Vienna that was the dominant theatrical centre. The Habsburg court mounted some of the most spectacular festive productions of the Baroque age, culminating in 1668 in a celebrated production of Cesti's opera *Il pomo d'oro* ['The Golden Apple'] as part of the festivities associated with the marriage of

the Emperor Leopold I at the end of 1666. In the late 18th century, the operatic culture of the court theatres contributed to Mozart's excited enthusiasm for Vienna where, as he wrote to his sister on 4 July 1781, the theatre became his 'sole entertainment'. But the theatrical life was by no means confined to the court. Vienna had long been a centre for troupes of touring players, who had performed popular entertainments combining heroic drama on classical subjects with comedy centring on the traditional figure of Hanswurst. From about 1710 one of these troupes had a permanent theatre, and when the reforms introduced in 1776 by the great enlightened Emperor Joseph II made it possible for a number of commercial theatres to be built outside the old city walls, a vigorous tradition of indigenous entertainment was established. The oldest of the new playhouses, the Theater in der Leopoldstadt, came to enjoy the reputation, still recorded in Murray's *Handbook for Travellers in Southern Germany* as late as 1837, of being 'the

Figure 4. *Joseph II: unsigned print published by Menard & Desenne, Paris.*

true national theatre of Austria'. One of the features of the popular comedy of the commercial theatres in the first half of the 19th century, including particularly the works of Nestroy, is how frequently theatre itself serves as a dramatic subject – an artful reversal of the metaphor of the world as a stage that reflects the central importance of the institution in the cultural consciousness of the audience.

Vienna was also the centre for a network of provincial theatres throughout the old monarchy, many of them in towns that are now no longer German-speaking. The last issues of the annual *Neuer Bühnen-Almanach* published before the First World War record full seasons of at least six months of German theatre not only in Prague (which had two German theatres as against three Czech theatres), Pilsen, Reichenberg, and Teplitz-Schönau in Bohemia but also in Brünn, Iglau, Mährisch-Ostrau, and Olmütz (all still predominantly German-speaking when along with the rest of Moravia they were lost to the new republic of Czechoslovakia in 1918); Teschen and Troppau in Austrian Silesia (now Opava in the Czech Republic and Cieszyn in southern Poland respectively); Pressburg (Bratislava, in Slovakia); Laibach and Marburg an der Drau (Ljubljana and Maribor, in Slovenia); Czernowitz and Lemberg (Chernivtsi and Lviv, in the Ukraine).

It goes without saying that the main cities and towns still in Austria all have flourishing civic theatres. The country's second city, Graz, has a playhouse (Schauspielhaus) going back to the 18th century, and an opera house built in 1899. Other provincial capitals with a history of theatres since the 18th century, though in every case with various rebuildings since then, are Linz, Innsbruck, Salzburg, and Klagenfurt. The civic theatre (Stadttheater) in St. Pölten was founded in 1820. Other towns with historically significant theatres include Wiener Neustadt (a foundation dating from 1794) Villach (1887), and Baden (1908). Together with a huge array of smaller theatres, especially in Graz, it is an impressive network in a country whose population still numbers under 8 million. In Vienna after the Second World War, when both the Opera House and the Burgtheater were badly damaged (the Opera House by bombing in March 1945, the Burgtheater by fire a month later), their rebuilding became an act of the first priority, a signal of re-establishing the whole cultural heritage of Austria. It was completed in time for both houses to be reopened in 1955, the year of the Austrian State Treaty. The Salzburg Festival too was regenerated – Hofmannsthal's *Jedermann* was restored to its central place in the programme in 1946, with Max Reinhardt's wife, Helene Thimig, appearing again in the role of Faith that she had last played in 1937. New summer festivals were also established in Vienna, Bregenz, and Mörbisch on the Neusiedlersee, the latter specialising in operetta.

At every level theatre counts on and receives generous subsidy from public funds. The cultural department of the City of Vienna alone had a budget for 1998 of

Figure 5. *Opera House (Staatsoper)*

2,090 million Schilling (over £100 million); the subsidy even for the city-owned theatres specialising in musicals, which almost anywhere else would be expected to pay their way, ran to 217 million Schilling (c. £11 million). In the prestige state theatres, the proportions of the running cost borne out of takings ranged in 1995 from 47.29 per cent in the Opera House to a mere 13.09 per cent in the Burgtheater and its sister house, the Akademietheater.[9]

One historical consequence of the special prominence and prestige enjoyed by theatre, especially in Vienna, was that when censorship was in force, as it was from the late 18th century until after the First World War, the stage was subjected to particularly watchful scrutiny. The Baconian principle that 'the minds of men are more open to impressions and affections when many are gathered together than when they are alone', which informed censorship of the stage in Shakespearian England, was also an established orthodoxy in Vienna, spelt out in 1795 by a long-serving censor, Franz Karl Hägelin, in a lengthy memorandum summarising the principles of the censor's practice.[10] Reading books and tracts of political import was a minority taste; attending the theatre, especially the commercial theatres, was open to an audience drawn from a broad social spectrum. Consequently no plays could pass the censor that belittled either the ruling dynasty or the institution of monarchy or that portrayed political rebellion. Hägelin, writing shortly after the French Revolution, noted that the very terms 'liberty' and 'equality' must be avoided. The censors were wary not just of plays with political subjects – including almost any aspect of Austrian history – but also of any kind of *double entendre* that might be taken as referring either to a ruler or to a specific public institution or event. The best-known example of the consequences of this anxious defence of the state is the delayed première of Grillparzer's historical drama *König Ottokars Glück und Ende*. The text was submitted for approval in November 1823, but the police censorship office reported that it was politically unsuitable, and it was not performed until February 1825. The reason was basically that the action of the play involved tensions within the various components of the multinational empire. Yet it was a familiar subject – the play celebrates the establishment of the Habsburg dynasty, and is impeccably loyalist, ending with cries of 'Habsburg für immer!' ['Habsburg forever!']. (This ending was cut in the 1955 production, but was rightly restored in the most recent production, in 1991.) The text also contains in Act Three a long eulogy of Austria by a minor character, Ottokar von Horneck, which has become a classic patriotic set piece, essential in every production.

Conscious perception of theatrical activity as an essential characteristic of Austria developed only following the political changes of the late 1860s and early 1870s and the formal separation of Germany and Austria as distinct 'nations'. When the Emperor Joseph II declared the Burgtheater a 'national theatre' in 1776, it was in an Enlightenment spirit, building up a German-speaking theatre of a kind that might rival the Comédie Française in standing and repertoire, for the advancement of culture and the improvement of taste. Similarly the attempted establishment, in contrast to the Italian operatic style, of a 'Nationalsingspiel' in 1778 – an initiative that led among other things to the commissioning of Mozart's *Die Entführung aus dem Serail* – was not conceived as a nationalistic step except in the sense of cultural nationalism, an attempt at cultural improvement. How different the climate was a 100 years later can be seen in the reception of Grillparzer, who died in 1872. In many ways the natural heir of Weimar classicism, he defined his artistic and cultural aim in one of his epigrams – first drafted in 1844 and variously reused in subsequent years – as being 'to stand where Schiller and Goethe stood'.[11] Dying just a year after the creation of the united German empire, he was inevitably enthroned in Austria as the great national classic, and condemned outside Austria to being regarded as nothing but an Austrian national classic. [12]

A different kind of consequence can be seen in early 20th century interpretations of Nestroy. Both as actor and as dramatist Nestroy dominated the commercial stage in Vienna for a quarter of a century from the early 1830s onwards. On the occasion of the 50th anniversary of his death in 1912 the satirist Karl Kraus argued the case for recognising him as the 'greatest satirical philosopher' in the German language.[13] But the leading Nestroy scholar of the time, Otto Rommel, placed his emphasis much more on Nestroy's place within the history of Viennese popular theatre, which he presented as a unique tradition. In fact Nestroy drew the plots of a large proportion of his plays from French sources (something for which conservative Viennese reviewers criticised him sharply); he also drew material from works by playwrights in London (Poole, Oxenford, Boucicault) and in Berlin. He adapted his material freely, transforming it into specifically Viennese comedy. But to stress the uniqueness of local theatrical tradition, as conservative critics did even in his own time, was to deflect attention from the internationalisation that was under way in the commercial theatre: in their organisation, in their repertory, and in the changing composition of their public, the suburban theatres in Nestroy's Vienna had striking similarities to the equivalent commercial theatres in mid 19th century London and Paris. The connections in the theatrical life of the three cities did not escape Grillparzer when he visited France and England in 1836, recording his impressions in a fascinating diary.[14]

What misleads commentators into assuming that Viennese theatre tradition is entirely *sui generis* is the use of dialect. This has certainly prevented international appreciation of Nestroy's stature, for while the language spoken by his characters is not a realistic reproduction of dialect, his satirical effects depend on playing with contrasting linguistic registers, including dialect. Visitors from other German-speaking states such as Saxony, who had to have all the jokes explained to them, provided the satirist with a sitting target.[15] Moreover, even 'serious' dramatists from Grillparzer onwards tend to use a much more natural non-literary idiom than their north German counterparts. In 1828, at the height of his powers and reputation, Grillparzer described himself in a diary note as 'ein dorischer Dichter' ['a Doric poet'], who did not give a fig for formal correctness and spoke the language of his native country.[16] The language of northern German sounds stiff and unnatural to Austrian ears, by comparison with the various dialects and regional varieties of German spoken in Austria. One consequence of this is that dramatic dialogue lends itself to contrasting things Austrian and things German. The commercial theatres nurtured an extremely lively tradition of parody, in which the artifice of pretentious high drama was exposed by being contrasted with the naturalness of dialect in a more or less overtly Viennese setting. The sceptical attitude recurrently adopted is exemplified by a figure in Nestroy's late play *Umsonst* ['In vain'] (1857), an actor who is trying to learn by heart rhetorical passages in Schiller's *Die Räuber*: 'So redt gar kein Mensch' ['No-one actually talks like that'].[17] Nestroy's output includes classic parodies both of Hebbel's early prose drama *Judith* and of two Wagner operas, *Tannhäuser* and *Lohengrin*. The political potential of the contrast between German and Austrian was even exploited by Hofmannsthal in the most polished of all society comedies in German, Hofmannsthal's *Der Schwierige* ['Hard to Please'] (1921), which is set towards or just after the end of the First World War. It is most often interpreted as a comic reworking of the so-called 'language crisis' of the early 20th century, and Hofmannsthal himself noted at an early stage of writing its affinity with his famous 'Chandos letter' of 1902.[18] But what the workings of the plot turn on is the rivalry of two aristocrats, one an old-world Viennese, the other a pushful North German, for the affections of two young Viennese countesses and the hand of one of them. At a *soirée* on which the second act turns, the North German makes clear his view that the seductive charmers to be found in the Viennese salon are figures of the past, totally cut off from 'the real world in which the intellectual crises of the century are decided'. His routing by the ultra-charming Viennese central character functions as a suggestive metaphor, a projection of political wishful thinking about the balance of power in the post-war world.

There is a much-quoted passage in the memoirs of one of Hofmannsthal's younger contemporaries, the novelist Stefan Zweig, in which he recalls that what the Viennese middle class around the turn of the century looked for when they opened their daily papers was news not of political events or parliamentary debates but of what was on in the theatre.[19] The passage is often rightly cited as evidence of the naively – and dangerously – apolitical character of the intellectual climate before 1914. It may also remind us, however, of the extent to which the theatre had long functioned as a substitute for overt politics, so that it was precisely there that political instincts found their outlet. Half a century earlier, in the decade or so leading up to the 1848 Revolution, when there was no democratic involvement in government and when overt discussion of political issues, not just in print but even in the coffee-houses, was proscribed, an ideological battle between liberals and conservatives was fought out in a sustained press debate about the character of Viennese popular comedy, whether it should be satirical or sentimentally improving, and whether local forms should be defended against the incursion of material from Paris. Even in the 20th century the passions which in other countries enliven practical politics have tended in Vienna to be directed at the politics of the Opera House. This is shown, for instance, in the temper of debate during the years when Mahler was director around the turn of the century, or again when Karajan was director in the 1960s. More recently, the controversial reign of Claus Peymann as director of the Burgtheater since 1986 – due to end in 1999 – has been debated not only in terms of the defence or endangering of Austrian tradition in the repertory of the national theatre but also and more significantly along party lines; in a country governed by a Grand Coalition, no other issue has so polarised left and right as Peymann's modernising of the Burgtheater programme. And in no event has that division of opinion been sharper than in reactions to his 1988 production of Thomas Bernhard's drama *Heldenplatz*, in which the whole political character of Austria is brought into question. The play is set at the time of the *Anschluss* and its title is taken from the name of the square outside the Imperial Palace in Vienna, where Hitler was received by cheering crowds after his invasion of Austria. The production, the classic example of 'theatre in search of Austria', was timed to coincide with a characteristic Austrian celebration of a round number, in this case the centenary of the present Burgtheater building, and so to function as a deliberately controversial counter to the patriotic celebration that had informed the production of *König Ottokars Glück und Ende* for the reopening in 1955.

The entry of Austria into the European Union, which took place at the beginning of 1995, is only one further unsettling factor. It has evoked opportunist nationalist rumblings from the right-wing opposition, but multinationalism is a less revolutionary idea than in Britain; there are no equivalents in Austria to the little Englanders who take pride in the historical isolation of offshore islands. The debate about the 'Euro' is also bound to excite less strong feelings than in the UK – after all, in the last century and a half Austria has worked its way through a succession of currencies, the Gulden, the Krone, the Schilling (introduced after the hyperinflation of 1921-22 and named, ironically, to evoke the rock-solid security associated with sterling), the German Mark after the *Anschluss*, and the Schilling again. Moves to closer political integration within the European Union even hold out the prospect of diffusing the longest-standing political discontent in Austria, the partition of the Tyrol imposed by the much-resented treaty of Saint-Germain-en-Laye. Nevertheless the threat of being dominated by German neighbours to the west and north may give cause for continuing nervousness about the preservation of a separate national 'identity'; both in safeguarding that cultural identity and in attracting money-spinning tourism, on which the health of the economy heavily depends, it is a safe bet that a central role is bound to be played by the theatre, especially the Staatsoper in Vienna and productions at the Salzburg Festival.

Bibliography

Fuhrich, Edda and Gisela Prossnitz (eds) (1990) *Die Salzburger Festspiele. Ihre Geschichte in Daten, Zeitzeugnissen und Bildern*, Vol. 1: *1920-1945*, Salzburg: Residenz.

Gregor, Joseph (1948) *Geschichte des österreichischen Theaters. Von seinen Ursprüngen bis zum Ende der Ersten Republik*. Vienna: Donau-Verlag.

Haider-Pregler, Hilde 'Die Wiener "Nationalschaubühne" (1776-1794): Idee und Institution' in: Roland Krebs and Jean-Marie Valentin (eds), *Théâtre, nation & société en Allemagne au XVIIIᵉ siècle*. Nancy: Presses universitaires de Nancy, 1990, pp. 167-192.

Hein, Jürgen 'Die Bühne als Welt. Bild und Rolle des Theaters im Werk Johann Nestroys' *Neue Zürcher Zeitung* 9-10 April 1983 (no. 82), pp. 81-82.

Das Wiener Volkstheater, 3 (1997) neubearbeitete Aufl.. Darmstadt: Wissenschaftliche Buchgesellschaft.

Heydemann, Klaus 'Unser Grillparzer. Beobachtungen zur Grillparzer-Rezeption in Österreich 1945-1955' in Sieglinde Klettenhammer (ed) (1992) *Zwischen Weimar und Wien: Grillparzer – ein Innsbrucker Symposion*

(Innsbrucker Beiträge zur Kulturwissenschaft, Germanistische Reihe, 45), Innsbruck: Institut für Germanistik, pp. 223-239.

von Hofmannsthal, Hugo *Festspiele in Salzburg*, 3 (1980) Aufl., Frankfurt a.M.: S. Fischer, 1952.

Hüttner, Johann 'Theatre Censorship in Metternich's Vienna', *Theatre Quarterly* 10, no. 37, pp. 61-69.

Jelavich, Barbara (1987) *Modern Austria: Empire and Republic, 1815-1986.* Cambridge: Cambridge University Press.

Kleindel, Walter (1995) *Österreich. Daten zur Geschichte und Kultur.* 4th edition edited and revised by Isabella Ackerl and Günter K. Kodek. Vienna and Heidelberg: Ueberreuter.

Lothar, Rudolph (1934) *Das Wiener Burgtheater. Ein Wahrzeichen österreichischer Kunst und Kultur.* Vienna: Augartenverlag.

Schmidt, Leopold (1962) *Das deutsche Volksschauspiel. Ein Handbuch.* Berlin: Erich Schmidt.

Schmidt-Dengler, Wendelin 'The Ideology of the Salzburg Festival' in Ritchie Robertson and Edward Timms (eds) (1993) *Theatre and Performance in Austria: From Mozart to Jelinek* (Austrian Studies 4). Edinburgh: Edinburgh University Press, pp. 171-176.

Yates, W. E. (1992) *Schnitzler, Hofmannsthal, and the Austrian Theatre.* New Haven and London: Yale University Press (pp. 201-217 on Salzburg).

– (1996) *Theatre in Vienna: A Critical History, 1776-1995.* Cambridge: Cambridge University Press (pp. 25-48 on censorship).

Notes

1   Franz Grillparzer, *Sämtliche Werke*, hist.-krit. Ausgabe, ed. August Sauer and Reinhold Backmann, 42 vols, Vienna: Gerlach & Wiedling and Schroll, 1909-48, Vol. I.13 (*Prosaschriften*, I), p. 176.
2   Grillparzer, *Sämtliche Werke*, Vol. I.12/i, p. 341; see note, Vol. I.12/ii, p. 422.
3   Hugo von Hofmannsthal, *Prosa III* (*Gesammelte Werke in Einzelausgaben*, ed. Herbert Steiner), Frankfurt a.M.: S. Fischer, 1952, pp. 407-409.
4   Henry Wickham Steed. *The Hapsburg Monarchy*, London: Constable, 1913, p. ix.
5   Hugo von Hofmannsthal – Josef Redlich, *Briefwechsel*, ed. Helga Fussgänger, Frankfurt a.M.: S. Fischer, 1971, p. 116: letter of 28 November 1928.
6   Adolf Bäuerle, *Komisches Theater*, Vol. 6, Pest: Hartleben, 1826, p. 143.
7   See Birgit Pargner, 'Zwischen Tränen und Kommerz. Das Rührtheater Charlotte Birch-Pfeiffers (1800-1868) in seiner künstlerischen und kommerziellen Verwertung. Quellenforschung am Handschriften-Nachlass', dissertation, University of Munich, 1997, p. 199.
8   Letter to Ferdinand Künzelmann, 21 July 1918. Quoted by Oskar Holl, 'Dokumente zur Entstehung der Salzburger Festspiele': Unveröffentlichtes aus der Korrespondenz der Gründer', *Maske und Kothurn*, 13 (1967), pp. 148-180 (p. 177).
9   Figures from: *Wiener Zeitung*, 14 April 1997, and *Die Presse*, 22 November 1997.
10 Carl Glossy, 'Zur Geschichte der Wiener Theatercensur. I', *Jahrbuch der Grillparzer-Gesellschaft*, 7 (1897), pp. 238-340 (pp. 298-340).
11 Grillparzer, *Sämtliche Werke*, Vol. I.11/i, p. 172.
12 See Ian F. Roe, *Franz Grillparzer: A Century of Criticism*, Columbia, SC: Camden House, 1995, pp. 2-3.
13 *Die Fackel* 345/346, 31 March 1912, p. 40.
14 Grillparzer, *Sämtliche Werke*, Vol. II.10, pp. 1-126.
15 Johann Nestroy, *Sämtliche Werke*, hist.-krit. Ausgabe, ed. Jürgen Hein, Johann Hüttner, Walter Obermaier and W. Edgar Yates, Vienna: Jugend & Volk and Deuticke, 1977 ff., *Stücke 22* (1996), p. 36: *Die beiden Herrn Söhne* [1845], II,9.
16 Grillparzer, *Sämtliche Werke*, Vol. II.8, p. 296.
17 Johann Nestroy, *Sämtliche Werke*, hist.-krit. Ausgabe, *Stücke 35*, ed. Peter Branscombe (1998), p. 37: *Umsonst* I, 15.
18 Hugo von Hofmannsthal, *Sämtliche Werke*, hist.-krit. Ausgabe, ed. Rudolf Hirsch *et al.*, Frankfurt a.M.: S. Fischer, 1975ff., Vol. XII, *Dramen 10*, ed. Martin Stern *et al.* (1993), p. 223.
19 Stefan Zweig, *Die Welt von gestern. Erinnerungen eines Europäers*, London: Hamish Hamilton; Stockholm: Bermann Fischer, 1941, p. 22.

Questions of National Cinema[1]

Susan Hayward

The purpose of this chapter is to set out issues and to propose mappings of a national cinema. In particular the discussion will bear in mind the crucial question – what does cinema as a cultural artefact tell us about national identity in terms of the problematics of the very concept of the national? Whilst the issues raised and the mapppings suggested are of a quite universal order within the Western world, specific reference in this chapter, in terms of a national cinema, will be made to that of France, arguably the birthplace of cinema.

Introduction

Throughout history there has been a constant interaction between social organisation and culture. Film is no exception. By definition culture is a term which refers both to the material production (artefacts) and to symbolic production (the aesthetic). In both instances, culture functions as the record and reflection of social history and the social process — however, as we shall go on to make clear this is not a unidirectional reflection. Concepts of nation and national identity are also bound up in this socio-cultural functioning. It is the synergy between socio-political organisation and culture that is the basis of political culture whereby, in Marxist terms, the productive base (material production) finds its reflection in the non-productive superstructure (the aesthetic). In other words, political culture — which Raymond Williams usefully delimits on a five-point map as industry, democracy, class, art and culture — is a signifying process which unceasingly reflects socio-political change. For example, the standardisation of the French language and education over the whole of France during the 19th century was both a national and socio-cultural hegemonising process but it was and still is a process that is always consonant with the socio-political moment. In this context, education both endorses the nation's view of itself and works to update that vision. Political culture, in this respect, becomes the process whereby myths are created about a nation's various and particular institutions. Once again the notion of cultural reflexiveness is in evidence here because those same institutions must sustain and perpetuate those myths which have been created to explain them. Thus, political culture affirms what it reflects, and is affirmed by what it reflects.

To date, Marxist theory on culture has predominantly stressed this unidirectional relationship between base and superstructure and it is not difficult to point to the problematics inherent in this limited definition. Viewed in this light, culture becomes a series of discourses which have become solidified into truth (culture affirms the social and therefore the political and economic relations).

However, certain neo-Marxists (Gramsci, Althusser and Marcuse in particular) have argued that the superstructure can react back on to its determining base and that culture can function to subvert these discourses by opposing the affirmative character of culture. By refusing the Marxist notion of transparence, culture displays its radical potential effectiveness to innovate. This negative culture can react back through a subversion of codes (including aesthetic conventions), thus creating a two-directional relationship between base and superstructure. According to this view, when subverting political cultural convention, culture brings into question the ideological nature of cultural signs and renders institutional mythologies unstable. Thus, for example, the Surrealist and Dada movements, or avant-garde cinema, are concrete manifestations of this negative culture. Conversely, when culture upholds the affirmative function of political culture, it serves to reinforce and even naturalise those same institutional mythologies (so, for example, bourgeois theatre/melodrama, mainstream cinema). As we shall go on to explain, cinema as a cultural artefact practices both these functions (it can be subversive, negative or conversely, affirmative).

In the light of the description of this synergy what can we say about cinema and its function as a cultural artefact in relation to the national and the social? Concepts of nation and national identity, when they are perceived in terms of socio-political processes and the cultural articulations of these processes, inevitably mean that the culture speaks the national and the national speaks the culture. In other words, within the specific context addressed here, film functions as a cultural articulation of a nation and even if it subverts it, it still addresses and reflects it, albeit negatively and oppositionally (the concept of the national is still present). In so doing, cinema-as-film textualises the nation and subsequently constructs a series of relations around the concepts, first, of state and citizen, then of state, citizen and other (and so on). In this way, cinema — a 'national cinema' — is ineluctably 'reduced' to a series of enunciations that reverberate around two fundamental concepts: identity (state and citizen) and difference (state/citizen and other).

Concepts of a nation

The concept 'nation' is notoriously difficult to define despite the fact that as a term it has such common currency. It has almost tautological proportions – 'it's there because it's there'. Indeed, it is teleological in purpose – the idea of nation promotes the notion of nationhood which in turn plays a vital role in maintaining social order. Already it is not difficult to perceive that the concepts of nation bring it very close to myth — an 'imagined political community' as Benedict Anderson puts it (1990: 15).

To understand why it is there (even though as 'myth' there is no 'there'), we need to understand how it got there — what put it there. Both Anderson and Fredric Jameson (1986) point to the function of cultural artefacts in this context and to how they serve to put 'nation' into and onto the mental map and also to maintain it there. According to Anderson and Anthony Birch (1989) the concept of nation-ness and the emergence of nationalism as an ideology, in a global sense, came about

Napoléon vu par Abel Gance, Abel Gance, 1927:
'The virtuosos of silent cinema'
National Film Archive London

as a consequence of the French Enlightenment and Revolution. There are three major reasons why this was so. First, early theories of the nation-state emerged, in part, in response to how France was viewed from outside, particularly by German intellectuals who, at the beginning of the 19th century, felt strong resentment towards the French for both cultural and military reasons. It was at this time that Herder coined the term *nationalismus* as a reaction to the French Enlightenment's advocacy of the principle of universalism. Universalism, although based in assumptions of equality, has inherent within it political cultural empire-building (as a concept of good government for civilization to adopt). The concept of nation and nationalism in its first sense then becomes a concept mobilised in relation to, and as a counter-reaction against, universalism. It is an oppositional concept, therefore, for nation is based in an assumption of difference — because differentness is its starting point.

The concept of 'nation' is always already an imagined concept. A second reason for its imagining was the role it played in fulfilling a sense of loss/lack. In this second instance, nation as a concept came to replace what had been removed. That is, social and political cultures produced a meaning ('nation') to be put where there was now a lack of one. How is this so? The French Enlightenment and Revolution put an end to religious modes of thought symbolically through the execution of the Monarch (the divinely-ordained ruler). The earlier meaning of monarchy (the divinely-ordained) and fatality (the will of God) had been emptied out of its significance. What was now required was 'a secular transformation of fatality into continuity, contingency into meaning' (Anderson, 1990:19). And few things were 'better suited to this end than an idea of nation' (ibid.) Nation, then, becomes in this context a secular transformation of religion and divine monarchy into a sovereign state (the state is sovereign now not the monarch). Viewed in this light, the concept of nation becomes rooted in the idea of continuity (and not difference as it does in its first imagining). Thus nation becomes closely aligned with the idea of history. The nation as its imagined history.

A third level (at least) of meaning of 'nation' is the concept of nation as identity. The point here is that nation had to be imagined to give people a secure sense of identity. It had to be imagined as the 'other' in relation to the 'rule by empire-building' cultures. In this respect, nation becomes an imagined unified collectivity whose whole *raison d'être* lies in its imagined otherness. This third 'definition',

Le Jour se lève, Marcel Carné, 1939:
'Exemplary studio practices of the 1930s'
National Film Archive London

implicitly, does not embrace the same notion of the assumption of difference since it is based on the idea of unified identity (as one).

If problems arise in defining nation, therefore, it is surely because of its imagined (often seemingly contradictory) status. It is that which makes it such a slippery concept. It is not hard to see that any attempt to fix a cultural artefact within a concept of 'nationalness' is going to be equally problematic. How can such a concrete substance as a cultural artefact (cinema in this instance) be said to speak for, and be spoken to, by an imagined concept (for such 'nation' is)? We see the problem before us. What follows are not answers but mappings for what we might mean by a national cinema or need to consider when attempting to conceptualise a national cinema.

Concepts of a national cinema

The 19th century was the first age of nationalism. It seems more than appropriate that cinema was born (in 1895) in that age of nationalism. But it must be added that it was also born at a time which was the age of the *fin-de-sièclisme*. Two very distinct modalities and mentalities. The first reflecting the rapid ascendancy in national individualism, the second the decadence and ruin mobilised by the implicit narcissism of such a nationalism. A hybrid product (art and technology) born at the interface of these two moments, cinema becomes inscribed, therefore, with a series of paradoxes – ascendancy and decline on the one hand and, on the other, nationalism and narcissism. This was also an age which witnessed the birth of psychoanalysis, with all the resonances of questions of identity which that term connotes and which, as we have explained, is a central concern of nationhood as well. It is significant too that in France (the birthplace of cinema) histories of the cinema were being written as early as 1900 and that by the early 1900s film theory was already an arena of debate. Equally significant is that by the 1920s calls were being made for a truly national cinema as a defence against the American hegemony as far as its film industry was concerned (e.g. Hollywood). All of this tells us that cinema was perceived very early as a national cultural artefact. As such it mirrors or is a projection of nationalist discourses and their own investment in historicism and narcissism.

In the writing of a national cinema there are two fundamental yet crucial axes of reflection to be considered. First, how is the national enunciated? In other words, what are the texts and what meanings do they mobilise? Second, how to enunciate the national? That is, what typologies must be traced into a cartography of the national? Or, expressed more simply, what is there, what does it mean and how do we write its meaning?

Let us start with the first axis of reflection. Essentially with regard to the cinema as a national institution, there are three modes of enunciation – the films themselves, the written discourses which surround them and, finally, the archival institutes in which they are housed and displayed. This triad in turn generates the question of which cinema are we addressing, for there is not one cinema but several. Here the concern is not just with the art and popular cinemas, but with mainstream and peripheral cinemas. And what do we say about their shifts? For the cinema — though a stable concept — is not a constant entity. It changes. The cinema of the centre changes in its identity depending on who is canonising it as central (audiences and critics). It changes with the exigencies of the political-social context (censorship). It changes through the optic of history as well (censorship and critics). Furthermore, cinemas of the periphery come into the centre and push those at the centre out. By way of illustration, let me refer to the example of a 1930s Renoir film *La Règle du jeu* (1939). During the 1930s, Jean Renoir had a number of highly successful films, two of which just predated this one: *La Grande Illusion* (1937), and *La Bête humaine* (1938) (both Jean Gabin vehicles it has to be said, which might explain their huge popularity). If not mainstream, Renoir was certainly very popular during this period and so his work was central to the industry's production practices. He did not, however, remain at the centre for long. *La Règle du jeu* was hated by audiences who booed and caused general mayhem in the film theatres. Critics were none too partial to the film either. They saw in its depiction of the effects of class boundaries and abuses of social hierarchies of power a very pessimistic vision of France as it faced the ineluctability of war with Germany. The film was panned by critcis and audiences alike. Worse still, once war was declared against Germany it was banned. So this film was doubly on the periphery – hated and banned. Only subsequently, in the 1950s, was the film restored to its full version and shortly thereafter consecrated by critical opinion as one of the great masterpieces of French cinema. The decried became canonical.

Thus, in relation to films themselves, the first line of enquiry becomes which films should constitute the corpus of a national cinema? As we can see this is almost impossible to answer. Clearly popular cinema which is the majority of cinema produced (as opposed to art cinema) has to be central to any investigation as does audience consumption. And it has to be seen in relation to the cinemas of the periphery. But what does this actually mean? French cinema, since the advent of sound in 1930 produces 100 feature films per year — a daunting prospect for examination. Co-productions with other nations (particularly Italy) cloud this figure — do they get considered as a national product if the percentage factor of money invested says they are French? Much of early pre-sound cinema is inaccessible (either it is too fragile, or it has been lost forever) and no detailed statistics on production practices and audience attendance were kept in France until the mid-1930s. Thus other sources, such as contemporary accounts (e.g. *Cinémagazine, Pathé Journal*) and scholarly researched texts by film historians have to serve as partial guidelines for establishing what constituted France's national cinema in the first third of its existence/history. Clearly gaps emerge and imprecision risks slipping in — and, too, convenient recourse to historicism.

This point brings us to the second mode of enunciation, that of the written discourses. Many discourses surround a nation's cinema. But which cinemas do they mobilise and which do they leave unspoken? Where France is concerned there are three discursive modalities which re-present the cinema as an institution – historical, critical and state discourses. Historical documentation includes histories of the indigenous cinema, pamphlets published by unions and other sectors representing the film industry (e.g. technicians and actors) and memoirs of the industry's industrialists (such as Pathé and Gaumont). The critical discourses range from film criticism to film history. Finally, state discourses include such texts as ministerial decrees, documentation on state intervention, publications emanating from the Centre national de la cinématographie (CNC), and the official statistics on

Casque d'or, Jacques Becker, 1952:
'Cinéma de qualité? or cinéma d'auteur'
National Film Archive London

all aspects of cinematic practice. Although state discourses may appear to be a closed text and of little interpretative value, in that they provide records of legislative measures and figures, their impact on cinematic production and style (and record of same) has been and still is quite considerable.

All three written discursive modalities, therefore, have served to shape the nation's cinema history and caused things to happen to films and trends in cinema in general. But in that they inevitably privilege a certain type of cinema (whether for political, critical or historical reasons), these discourses are not free from the problematics of historicism either. So, film movements get imagined (Poetic Realism and the New Wave for example), directors lionised, and films canonised at the expense of a larger body of film production whose social and aesthetic value and high audience appeal have been overlooked or inadequately represented.

The third mode of enunciation of a national cinema, archival institutions, such as the Cinémathèque, create similar problems since in their role as conservators of the culture, they also act as monuments to cinema. Although it is clear that they perform a vital function in keeping the cultural heritage alive, nonetheless they simultaneously act as agents of petrification of that heritage (e.g. this is it, this is the heritage). This then generates a further set of problems because the question now becomes, which films are in a fit state to be screened? Which ones have been privileged over others that are waiting to be restored? Preservation of the culture means, therefore, that a museumification takes place which mobilises a very specific construction of the cultural.

None of these modes of enunciation are, then, without their problems. And part of the writing of a national cinema must be to expose those problems; to show how the construction of a national cinema in and of itself is a problematisation of national culture and therefore of the national.

If we now turn to the second axis of reflection, how to enunciate the 'national' of a national cinema, we need to consider that cinema itself contributes to the construction of the concept of the national and, thereby, to the myth of the 'national' in a national cinema. Traditionally, the national of a cinema is defined in terms of its difference from other cinemas of other nations (see the first concept of 'nation as difference'). This has come primarily to mean its difference from Hollywood. This definition exposes the essentialising effect of 'national as difference' — of defining a nation's culture in reference to a dominant other: in this context — there is Hollywood cinema and then the rest. Certainly, Hollywood has been empire-building since 1914 but national cinemas other than Hollywood must also be seen as points of reference. Also it suggests that there is only one national cinema particular to any nation state — a collective unified cinema (say for argument's sake a Frenchness of French cinema) — when patently this cannot be the case. Nationhood as hegemonic is after all an imagined conceptualisation of the nation (see the third concept of 'nation as unity').

It is true, however, that there are moments in history when a nation's cinema feels compelled to represent itself as a 'real national cinema', as one that resists its own indigenous political culture and the dominant practices of an empire-building film industry (such as Hollywood). And one is reminded here of the Latin American countries' cinema nôvo of the 1970s which was a resistance against both the capitalist practices of their own nation-states and the homogenising effect of American film practices. These moments tend to be short-lived and they do not preclude mainstream cinema from being produced by the indigenous film industry.

National cinemas, as we have explained, may be based in difference and unity. However, because there is no single national cinema but rather a plurality of cinemas that make up the national product, national cinemas are also based in the concept of pluralism (something nationalism tries hard to conceal incidentally). Thus to go down the route (of difference and unity) exclusively is too limiting and other ways have to be found to resolve how to enunciate a national cinema. One such way is to talk about national cinema in terms of a set of typologies. Notionally, there are six discernible typologies and whilst the way in which the 'national' can be enunciated through them may remain constant, clearly what the term national signifies will change according to social, economic and political mutations and pressures. The six typologies are as follows:

1   narratives
2   genres
3   codes and conventions
4   gesturality and morphology
5   the star as sign
6   cinema of the centre and cinema of the periphery

1. Narratives

In a very useful study on national fictions, Graeme Turner (1986) makes the point that a country's narratives are produced by the indigenous culture and these narratives serve a reflexive role in that a culture uses them in order to understand its own signification and meaning. Narratives are a nation's way of making sense to itself. Nations may and do have narratives in common but the specificity of their articulation is determined by the particular culture. For example, Beauty and the Beast was originally a Greek myth in Western culture, but it refers to an earlier Indian myth — both versions were to do with sexual awakening. In more contemporary times, this tale was re-written as a moral fable advocating marriage of reason.

It is in its specificity, therefore, that a filmic narrative can be perceived as a reflection of the nation. This reflexivity can occur in two ways (at least), neither one of which excludes the other. First, the filmic narrative can be based on a literary adaptation of an indigenous text. Second, the filmic narrative can confront the spectator with an explicit or implicit construction of the nation. In the first instance, when film transposes a literary text it offers up a double nation-narration – that of the novel/play-as-a-national-artefact and its own filmic text (as a national product). Literature is up on screen becoming national heritage (we go to see our books, our culture). In the second instance of explicit and implicit textual constructions of the

Touchez pas au grisbi, Jacques Becker, 1954:
'The American film noir *comes to Paris'*
BFI Stills, Posters and Designs

nation, explicit textual constructions refer to those films which set out to signify the nation by constructing moments in a nation's history. They are propagandistic in their narratives, thus they are explicit. Implicit textual constructions of the nation refer to those films which are closer to the idea of reflecting the dominant ideology of a nation (so they will reflect the prevailing institutions of their time of production, as for example, white middle-class values of marriage, social mobility, and so on). The nation is implicitly present and the films still fulfil an ideological purpose.

2. Genres

Grand epics are not France's style on the whole. There are filmic modalities that are specific to a particular nation and, in France's case, the dominant generic mode is, first, comedy (50 per cent of production), and, second, the thriller (25 per cent of production). There are reasons why this should be the case. To read generic modes of a nation's cinematic output is to infer how the nation speaks to and of its citizenry, how the cultural artefact problematises the nation and shows the nation as troubled, problematised in its sense of itself. Genres do address the question of

Brigitte Bardot:
'The star-system à la française'
BFI Stills, Posters and Designs

identity, and implicitly, national identity. Thrillers are in part a release of certain pathologies tied into a sense of a lack of identity. Comedies are forceful plays with fixed identities and question the notions of stereotypes, whilst also reinforcing them, to a lesser or greater degree. They also directly address notions of (in this context) Frenchness by displaying them. Genres change over time and that evolution can be seen to reflect changes in the social and political environment. Genres, as a social, even national, comment, reflect back on the society in which they are played out — so there is a cross-fertilisation between the nation's image of itself and the imaging of the nation. An example would be the impact of Bardot's films of the 1950s on France's notion of herself as a new nation, a *nouvelle vague*. It was in Roger Vadim's hugely successful 1956 film *Et Dieu créa la femme* that Bardot became the embodiment of the new generation of French youth. The youth class — in the form of Brigitte Bardot in all sorts of alluring attire — emerged as a new social class, pouting, exercising sexual freedom and defying patriarchal order. This new image of France, which Bardot created in her films, then spread back into the cinema of the late 1950s. Producers wanted more work by young directors and stars (like Vadim and Bardot) and were willing to invest in a whole new generation of young filmmakers. This was one of the major contributing factors to the birth of the so-called Nouvelle Vague cinema (1958-64).

3. Codes and conventions

It is important here to think in terms of both the mode of production and the iconography of the image. A product, emanating from the French film industry, remains intrinsically French from the point of view of labour and production practices. Legislation and union practices affect the product just as much as the traditions of production. French production practices tend to favour the medium-budget film as opposed to the blockbuster film, which Hollywood mostly favours. The actual financial state of the industry at any one time necessarily impacts upon the production practices. Thus, when the major companies are experiencing financial difficulties, they tend to retrench and this allows for independent companies to come to the fore in greater numbers with their small-to-medium budget films (this occurred in the 1930s, the late 1950s, and is happening again now in the 1990s). These moments tend to be heralded as new waves or golden ages in French cinema, precisely because there is a more distinct artisanal look to the film and because the film tends to be produced by a close-knit group of technicians, actors and filmmakers.

Essentially, a national cinema has several modes of production — and these production practices in turn have their effect upon the final product. Thus there is no single French cinema. There is also the thorny problem of co-productions. With a totally French-produced film, the filmmaker has what are called the *droits d'auteur*, which means that s/he has the ultimate say on the final cut of the film. With co-productions, that question becomes blurred as does ownership — is anything under 50 per cent French-produced likely to be French? There is only an economic answer really. In terms of where the money goes from audience revenue, each country investing receives the percentage value of its input (thus a Franco-Italian film with a 60-40 per cent share means France receives 60 per cent, Italy 40 per cent).

With regard to the iconography of the image, there are two questions to be addressed. How does the representation of the nation (through the image) carve up and/or construct the nation? And what problematics does this representation engender? In other words, what is represented and what is left out? Who or what remains invisible? As can be seen, the iconography of the image generates a series of binary paradigms of which the very first is absence/presence. Thus, for example, in the cinema of the 1950s there is not a single mention of the Algerian crisis (blocked as it was by censorship); nor is there any visibilisation of the immigrant labour-force that came to France from North Africa. Conversely, in certain films of that same period there are specific visual representations of the American influence on French culture (cars, drugs, whisky, etc.) and in the thriller genre the evil gangsters (as opposed to good French gangsters) are almost without exception foreign (Italian, Hispanic, and so on). The effect of this precise duopoly based in binary oppositions is to make possible a homogenised and conciliatory myth of the national context. Nation in this imaged context becomes both continuity and discourses of othering (which as our discussion of the concepts of nation made clear are the two other meanings that discourses of nationness put in place).

4. Gesturality and morphology

What separates one nation's clusters of stars from anothers? The answer lies in the gesturality and the morphology of the body. Gestures, words, intonations, attitudes, postures — all of these separate one cluster from another, thus affirming the plurality of the cultures. Indeed, it could be argued that the gestural codes, even more so than the narrative codes, are deeply rooted in a nation's culture. Thus, when analysing the nation's cinema, traditions of performance must also be brought into consideration as a further marker of differentiation and specificity. As always, though, there are problems with this typology. What happens to 'cultured others' within a description of national cinemas? What do we say about a second generation French Arab actor and his or her gesturality and morphology? Where does that fit into the notion of nation? Nation as post-colonial? The answer is not a simple one.

5. The star as sign

Sign of the indigenous cultural codes, institutional metonymy and site of the class war in its national specificity, the signification of the star 'naturally' changes according to the social, economic and political environment of the time. Thus the Jean Gabin of the 1930s becomes the Jean-Paul Belmondo of the 1960s and, then, the Gérard Depardieu of the 1980s — three very different types of 'proletarian' heroes (and one might add some more 'real/authentic' than others). In addition, spectators impose on their stars their own expectations. The stars become the mediators between the real and the imaginary and come to signify as signs for the contemporary. They are the nation's point in time. How we read them and how we read the audience's reception of them tells us a great deal about the popular culture scene of any given time and, too, the central concerns of a nation's sense of self (such as questions of sexuality to name but one obvious one).

6. Cinema of the centre and cinema of the periphery

Implicit in this typology is the notion of a hierarchy centre/periphery and this needs to be read within the double context of product and production practices. There are essentially three antagons – Hollywood/'other'; standardised equipment/production and narrational specificities; central indigenous cinema/peripheral indigenous cinema. These antagons require further explanation. The first is a self-evident one to a degree. Hollywood is the epicentre in the West because it is the major producer and exporter of films and because all other cinemas of the Western world define their difference in relation to this dominant cinematic culture, against which they cannot compete either on the economic, or the production, level. But that first antagon (Hollywood/other) generates a secondary one of 'other'/'other' — since within other cinemas there are again those that dominate either internally or as export products over other cinemas. Thus, for example, French cinema dominates British cinema within France, but, in a good year, Britain exports (pro-rata) more film products than the French. We can already see that the curious thing about centres and peripheries is that, as we progress down the chain of antagons, that which was on the periphery eventually becomes central.

If we now consider the second antagon of standardised equipment and its homogenising effect on cinema we can observe a similar slippage in terms of centres and peripheries. At first the standardised equipment can be said to have a global homogenising effect on cinema and so is the centre. For example, a majority of films presently are widescreen with dolby surround sound. However, cinema does not just standardise, it also particularises. The technology may be uniform, but national specificities will emerge, through editing style for example, or in the way a narrative is shot. The peripheral production practices of the indigenous cinema operate outside of technology; so once again the peripheral becomes central through its practice.

A Bout de Souffle, Jean-Luc Godard, 1959:
'The French New-Wave - A new cinema'
National Film Archive London

As to the third antagon, what was peripheral according to the first antagon, indigenous cinema, now becomes central for the following reasons. Since the indigenous industry, in this instance French cinema, cannot compete with Hollywood, it tends to invest in what constitutes (in relation to Hollywood) the periphery. That is, it invests largely in a cinema for French audiences — not a cinema with export in mind. So the peripheral becomes central thanks to this investment. This production for a safe home market leads unwittingly to a construction on the part of the industry of a French national cinema. This cinema is made by those who are at the centre of the culture, that is the major French production and distribution companies (or the independents, depending on the economic climate). And it is made almost exclusively for a home market.

These companies are not the only bodies that currently control the 'look' of France's cinema. This centre now includes television channels which, although they

Diva, Jean-Jacques Beineix, 1980:
'The new Cinéma des jeunes'
BFI Stills, Posters and Designs

invest in films, nonetheless perceive these films' ultimate destination as the
television screen. This particular cinema of the centre impacts considerably on what
is seen — and the tendency is to repeat safe formulas and use the same directors. In
this respect, cinema normalises and functions very similarly to the centre of the
second antagon (the homogenisation effect of standardised equipment). Nor, by this
logic, does the peripheral cinema of this third set of antagons escape the centre.
That cinema (be it *avant-garde*, *auteur*, or of some minority) can get co-opted into the
cinema of the centre — the cinema of the centre essentially pastiches that of the
periphery (taking ideas from the peripheral cinema). But it is also the case that a
hierarchy exists within this so-called cinema of the periphery. Thus, for example,
regional cinema is seen as less central than *auteur* cinema; *Beur* cinema as less
central than regional cinema; lesbian and gay cinema as less central than *Beur*
cinema; and so on.

   This typology helps to make the point that there is no single cinema that is the
national cinema, but several. It thereby puts an end to the dangers of historicism
which identify a national cinema with specific movements or directors and

suggests, rather, that there is a flux, slippage even, between the various cinemas which constitutes the nation's cinema. This typology also makes clear that Hollywood does not need to be seen as the 'other', the threatening dominant empire-building force, but as one cinema amongst others with which national cinemas can be in cross-fertilising discussion. Finally, this typology suggests that discourses around a national cinema no longer need address cinema in an exclusive way, such as for example, defining it as the work of pioneers alone, or indeed, as an ideological institution. These are some of the discourses but they are just some, amongst so many others.

Conclusion

To what extent and how does cinema reflect the texture of society at a national level? It follows from the previous section that the cinemas that make up a national cinema reflect both from within, and without, the hegemonic social sphere (centre and periphery). It is equally clear, from the above that film narration calls upon the available discourses and myths of its own culture. Clearly, these cultural, nationalistic myths are not pure and simple reflections of history. They are a transformation of history. Thus, they work to construct a specific way of perceiving the nation. Cinema, whether it is of the centre or the periphery, is no exception to this nation-construction. And the question becomes, what myths does a national cinema put in place, and what are the consequences? Without being too reductionist, the point to be made is that the cinemas of the centre and the periphery represent these myths in radically opposing and opposite ways. The former, in its reconstruction provides hegemonic transparence. The latter challenges, even deconstructs, that transparence and hegemony. In any event, given that cinema is an industry and, therefore, an affair of capital, it is evident that the cinema of the centre will dominate the other in its myth-making practices. However, there is within this dynamic a degree of unfixity and so we can say that a national cinema is historically fluctuating. Just as the cultural specificity of a nation changes over the course of history, so too do its artefacts, including cinema. It changes because the signification of the term 'national' changes according to political social and economic pressures and mutations. Just as the state of the nation changes in time, according to its position in the world, so too does its cinema.

Bibliography

Anderson, B. (1990) *Imagined Communities: Reflections on the Origin and Spread of Nationalism*. London: Verso (first published: 1983).

Birch, A.H. (1989) *Nationalism and National Integration*. London: Unwin Hyman.

Jameson, F. (1986) *The Political Unconscious Narrative as a Socially Symbolic Act*. London: Routledge.

Turner, G. (1986) *National Fictions*. Sydney: Allen and Unwin.

Note

1. This chapter is an updated and reworked version of my introductory chapter to Hayward, S. (1993) *French National Cinema*. London & New York: Routledge.

National Identity, European Identity and the Euro

Carole B. Burgoyne and David A. Routh

Introduction

Whether they like it or not, the citizens of Europe are already engaged in the process leading to Economic and Monetary Union (EMU) and the European single currency. To many, the process appears like that of a train accelerating into an unknown future, along tracks that are still being laid. It matters little whether one is 'aboard' at the first station or not – all of us in Europe will be affected by this major economic and social change. Recall the Europe-wide impact of German interest rates at the time of the reunification of East and West Germany. One of the goals of the project is to achieve greater economic stability in Europe, and some hope that it will also lead to an enhanced sense of European identity and closer political integration (Dedman, 1996; 1998). Others doubt very much that this will be achieved, and feel that, given the deep differences in economic culture within Europe, monetary union was 'always a reckless project' (Dahrendorf, 1998). Governments have their own agendas for Europe; but what are the implications for ordinary people? Will a European identity be possible, or will it pose too great a threat to national identity? To what extent, for example, does a British identity depend upon the familiar symbol of the Pound, with all that the latter implies about our imperial history, our past strength as a trading nation, and our present status as a financial centre? Are the effects of the single currency likely to be the same for all Britons, or will these differ depending upon whether one is, for example, English or Scottish? In short, what kinds of national identity do people possess at present, and how might this change as a result of EMU and the Euro? These are some of the questions that we shall address in this chapter.

In attempting to shed light on these questions, we take a psychological perspective, drawing upon the literature on social and national identity (e.g. Breakwell and Lyons, 1996) with illustrations from recent empirical studies. We make use of two principal sources of data – the European Commission's general public opinion surveys (Eurobarometer) and a fifteen-country study[1], in which we were the United Kingdom participants (Burgoyne and Routh, 1998). The latter relate primarily to the 15 Member States of the European Union, viz., *Austria, Belgium, Denmark, Finland, France, Germany, Greece, Ireland, Italy, Luxembourg, Holland, Portugal, Spain, Sweden* and the *United Kingdom*.

Some preliminaries

Most ordinary citizens feel very much in the dark about what their governments are doing about EMU. So, in order to facilitate later discussion and understanding, let us consider the present position of EMU and how the process will unfold in the next few years. Under the terms of the 1992 Treaty on European Union (EU) – the so-called 'Maastricht Treaty' – Member States subscribed to important provisions for developing economic and monetary union and the introduction of a single European currency - now called the 'Euro'. Most European Union members were committed to adopting the Euro, if and when they met the necessary economic convergence criteria. There were two exceptions to this – under 'opt-out' clauses, the Maastricht Treaty permitted the United Kingdom and Denmark to decide at a later date whether they wish to be considered for admission. Despite the fact that several earlier attempts to launch EMU failed (Dedman, 1996, 1998), at present, many politicians, business men and commentators believe that EMU will go ahead on time.

Table 1 provides a brief summary of the three stages of EMU, and Table 2 presents a more detailed timetable for the remaining phases of the process. For further information, there are several excellent and comprehensive introductions to the European Union and EMU (Bainbridge & Teasdale, 1997; Reuters, 1997).

In the last year or two, government officials and business people have been engaged in making preparations for EMU and its associated problems, often with unseemly haste. As indicated earlier, these are no less urgent for the EMU "outs" than they are for the 'ins' (Fishburn, 1997; Currie, 1998a). For example, the United

Stage 1	1957	Treaty of Rome established the European Economic Community (EEC); calls for increased economic cooperation and creation of a single currency
	1979	Creation of European Monetary System (EMS) European currency unit (ECU) and Exchange Rate Mechanism (ERM).
	1992	The Treaty on European Union or 'Maastricht Treaty': economic, political and legal framework for single market, EMU, and single currency (came into force Nov. 1993).
Stage 2	1994	Setting up of European Monetary Institute (EMI) as prelude to European Central Bank (ECB).
Stage 3	1999	Introduction of single currency (euro) and setting up of European System of Central Banks (ESCB)

Table 1. The 3 stages of EMU

1998	(May). EU political leaders decided which countries were qualified to launch monetary union, using 1997 economic data analysed by the European Council (EC) and Council of Ministers (ECOFIN) and 'convergence criteria' as yardsticks.
	ECOFIN leglislation to confirm ECB's mandate and appointment of ECB's governing board and other details
1999	1st January. Irrevocable fixing of exchange rates between the euro and currencies of participating countries, and between the old currencies.
	The old Ecu 'basket of currencies' replaced at rate of 1 Ecu = 1 euro
	Businesses to choose to use the temporary denominations of euro or denominations of old currencies.
	The ESCB to use euro only for operations in money market and foreign exchanges
	In the absence of euro banknotes and coins, all cash transactions in national notes and coins
2002	By 1st January at the latest, euro notes and coins become the legal tender and national currencies withdrawn. Dual circulation of national and euro banknotes and coins to cease by 1st July; old national currencies cease to be legal tender

Table 2. The euro timetable

Kingdom Government decided that an abbreviated version of Currie's (1997) *The pros and cons of EMU* should be given the widest possible circulation (see also Currie 1998b for a resumé). Moreover, a torrent of analyses, guides and commentaries have appeared in *The Economist* (1997a; 1997b; 1998) and other quality publications, such as *The Financial Times*. The World Wide Web has also become replete with websites associated with governments, political parties and commercial agencies, each proffering briefings and advice for supporters, opponents, and clients alike.

What of the ordinary citizen who may be oblivious to such developments, or who may lack easy access to such resources? Recent opinion polls may be showing that the tide of public opinion is turning in favour of the Euro in some European Union countries. However, a recent cover story in *The European* (27 November 1997) suggests that, although the introduction of the Euro is imminent, many Europeans remain incredibly ignorant about it. In order to combat this, considerable sums of EC money are being made available to various European

Union governments and advertising agencies (to cover TV, press and poster advertising) in an effort to market the euro. In France, each household has received a 'factual' brochure entitled *L'euro et moi*, and in Italy, the Finance Ministry has teamed up with Walt Disney, to produce a children's magazine called *Topolino* (Mickey Mouse) extolling the virtues of having a single currency. However, whilst it is essential that ordinary citizens should be informed about the changes, simply bombarding them with propaganda from advertising and educational initiatives may be ineffective, or even counter-productive, unless there is a better understanding of how the public feel about losing their national currency, and the extent to which this might have an impact upon their sense of national identity. For some, it may be possible to accommodate their national identity within an enlarged, European identity. For others, the very idea of a European identity might pose an unacceptable threat to their sense of nationhood, and this might lead to a rejection of the currency that embodies this threat.

A psychological analysis of Social, National and European Identities

It is well-established in psychology that individual self-categorisation can be many-layered, including personal, social, national and supra-national sources of identity, with the salience of these identities depending upon the social context (cf. Tajfel, 1974; Tajfel and Turner, 1986). For example, someone may be a keen supporter of their local football team, and thus be opposed to teams from other parts of England, but may switch their allegiance to the national team in an international contest such as the World Cup, regardless of the origin of the individual players. A sporting event which pitted Europe against the rest of the world would no doubt make one's European identity salient in a similar way.

A number of writers have pointed out that both the concepts of 'nation' and 'Europe' are contested categories (Hutchinson and Smith, 1994). Individual nations are not 'natural' or 'given' categories, but exist as social constructions, that is, they are constantly undergoing revision and reconstruction. Smith (1991: 14) defines a nation as 'a named human population sharing an historic territory, common myths and historical memories, a mass, public culture, a common economy and common legal rights and duties for all members.' However, one important point to bear in mind when considering national identity is that what constitutes the 'nation' may be recognised and represented in different ways by different segments of the population. Indeed, although the terms 'nation' and 'state' are often treated as though they were synonymous, the idea of 'nation' as an 'imagined community' (Anderson, 1991, reprinted in Hutchinson and Smith, 1994) which can transcend both time and space, can be contrasted with that of 'state' as an organisation which 'controls the principal means of coercion within a given territory' (Tilly, 1975, reprinted in Hutchinson and Smith, 1994). For example, in the case of Britain, England has (historically) enjoyed a clearer identity as a nation within the territorial state of the United Kingdom when compared with Scotland, Wales, and Northern Ireland (Dowds & Young, 1996). Moreover, identity at the national level may be derived from a whole range of different sources – cultural, historical, social, and economic, and the emphasis on one or other of these may differ from country to country. According to Jenkins and Sofos (1996: 3), 'Britishness' has been a somewhat elusive concept, more cultural in flavour than political, with a symbolism related to a 'narrow and sentimental vision of 'Home-Counties' Englishness'. This stands in marked contrast to the French national identity, which has been much more political and oriented towards such matters as the legitimacy of the state.

People's attachment to their 'nation' may therefore be expressed in a variety of different types of nationalism, with the potential for corresponding differences in their beliefs about Europe.

We should not forget that Europe, too, is a multidimensional concept, which exists as a social and political community, as well as a geographical entity within specific boundaries (Hopkins & Reicher, 1996). Europe has been described as the birthplace of the concept of the nation-state, yet it has been subject to major upheavals and changes throughout its history, not least in the late 20th century. The addition of new Member States and shifting levels of power within Europe as a whole are likely to have implications for one's sense of what it is to be European. Moreover, as the context of comparison changes, the stereotyping of one's own nation and that of others is likely to change in content (Hopkins, Regan & Abell, 1997). For example, what it means to be British may differ depending upon whether the comparison is made with just those in Western Europe, or with a wider European community which could include members of the former Soviet bloc. Changes of a different order have also had an impact on the concepts of nation and national sovereignty, such as the loss of economic independence associated with the post-Cold War globalization of the market economy (Jenkins & Sofos, 1996, p. 1).

The implication of all these potential sources of identification is that people may be able to 'customise' their social identities in many ways and at a variety of different levels. It is also possible for these identities to be in conflict. Thus Hewstone (1986) found that British students perceived a conflict between their national and European loyalties. There has been relatively little research on the ways in which national and European identities might interact, but work by Cinnirella (1997) throws some light on this. Since the European Union has often been represented (in United Kingdom political debates and the media) as a threat to British national sovereignty, a European identity may be perceived at the same level of abstraction as that of national identity, and thus conflict with it. In contrast, the Italians tend to experience their European identity at the international level of abstraction, and so have little problem in incorporating their national identity within it. Cinnirella (1997) found no differences between British and Italian respondents in the strength of national identity, but the Italians exhibited a much stronger sense of European identity than their British counterparts. Also, unlike the Italians, the British saw the two identities as incompatible.

A number of investigators have made a useful distinction between different types of attachment to the nation. For example, Cinnirella (1996) suggests that people may tend towards either a 'sentimental' orientation with an adherence to national symbols, culture, etc., or an 'instrumental' orientation which is more concerned with gains and losses, ideas of citizenship, and levels of satisfaction with political organisation and public services. In his 1997 study, he showed that Italians had a rather low opinion of their nation's political or economic systems, but were very proud of their rich cultural and historical legacies. In contrast, whilst the British also thought highly of their culture and history, they were very proud of their democratic system and their civic identity. A similar distinction between utilitarian and historical/cultural elements has been observed in attitudes towards Europe. A study by Hilton *et al.* (1996) in Britain, France and Germany showed that although perceptions of the utilitarian costs and benefits of European unification could predict attitudes in all three countries, representations of history (such as the causes of Hitler's rise to power) also played a role in France and Britain, but not in Germany. Similarly, attitudes in the UK towards the Euro differ depending on whether attachment is cultural or instrumental (Routh and Burgoyne, 1998).

It is not difficult to imagine that, if one's national identity were seen as deficient in some important respect, then closer links with Europe might provide a more acceptable alternative. The findings of Dowds and Young (1996) in the United Kingdom suggest that those with a relatively weak emotional attachment to the nation-state (as could be the case for the Catholic population in Northern Ireland) may find it easier to take on a supranational identity. These authors found that Britons could be categorised into four groups on the dimensions of 'exclusiveness' (a tendency towards protectionism and xenophobia) and 'national sentiment' (pride in national heritage and culture). The first of these groups, Supranationalists, were low on both dimensions and had little sense of national identity; Patriots were low in exclusiveness but high in national sentiment; Belligerents were high in exclusiveness and low in national sentiment, and John Bulls were high on both dimensions. Whereas the first two groups tended to be better-educated and more libertarian, the latter two groups were less well-educated and held more authoritarian views. The salience of European integration as an issue was the same for all four groups, but only the Supranationalists felt that there should be closer ties with Europe and were in favour of a single currency, though both they and the Patriots held positive views about European membership. In contrast, the Belligerents and John Bulls were opposed to closer links with the rest of Europe. The significance of these distinctions is that they serve to remind us that a favourable attitude towards the European Union may coexist with an unfavourable attitude towards the euro. Moreover, the type of attachment orientation to one's nation may determine the extent to which the loss of the national currency might pose a threat to national identity.

Expressions of National and European identity

The studies mentioned in the preceding section provide some insights about which subgroups in Britain are likely to favour closer links with Europe, but what is the general level of attachment to Europe, both in Britain and the rest of Europe? In

Britain, attitudes towards the European Union have become more ambivalent, and by the time of the negotiations leading up to the Maastricht Treaty in 1992, Britain was becoming increasingly isolated *vis-a-vis* the other eleven. Newspapers which supported the John Major government cited the concepts of national sovereignty, national identity, and democracy as justification for opposing EMU, and the United Kingdom government emerged from the Maastricht negotiations with an 'opt-out' clause on the single currency (Verkuyten, 1996). But what do the general public feel about these matters?

Although based upon aggregate data in each country, (and bearing in mind the caveats about subgroup differences in national identity outlined above) some findings from the *Eurobarometer* 46 (1997), fielded in October-November 1996, can shed light on this. One of the questions asked respondents whether 'in the near future' they saw themselves in terms of their 'nationality only', as 'nationality and European', 'European and nationality' or 'European only'. In Europe as a whole, 51 per cent saw themselves as 'European' to some extent, the same proportion as had done so two years earlier, but the remainder felt less attachment to Europe, with an increase in those who expressed only a national identity. In all countries, those who felt mainly or wholly European were in the minority, ranging from only 5 per cent in Greece to 27 per cent in Luxembourg. Not surprisingly, there was a strong association between seeing one's country's membership of the European Union as 'a good thing' and perceiving oneself as European, with male, younger, and better-educated respondents more inclined towards a pro-European view. Those on the left of the political spectrum were also more in favour of European Union than those on the right.

Figure 1[2] scales the extent to which people in different countries tended to see themselves in terms of either a national or European identity, with those saying 'nationality only' towards the bottom of the figure, and those expressing a 'European only' identity shown towards the top. It accounted for 68.6 per cent of the variance in the data.

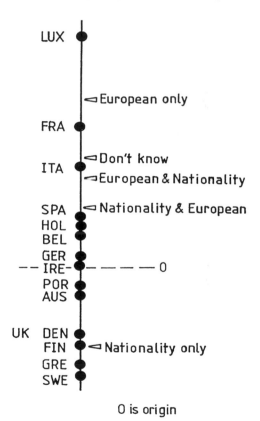

Figure 1. The perception of identity in the near future in terms of nationality or Europeanness (derived from Eurobarometer 46, Table 4.1, p. B44).

Abbreviated names of the countries are shown to the left of the axis, corresponding to the various locations on the scale. Luxembourg showed the greatest tendency towards using the 'European only' response (perhaps because of the high number of EC non-nationals in that country), and this is some distance away from France, the next most 'European' country (though this concerned only a small proportion of responses in the latter). To the middle we find a cluster of countries which felt that they had only their own nationality, including Sweden, Greece, Finland, Denmark and the United Kingdom. The remaining countries are located between these two extremes, indicating that their populations identified both with their own nationality and that of Europe to varying degrees.

Thus, it seems that, although the European Union has been in existence for many years, a European identity remains a somewhat tenuous concept, with relatively few citizens across the European Union seeing themselves in these terms. How much of a difference is the introduction of the Euro likely to make?

Money, currency, and the Euro

What does a change of currency mean for ordinary people? Does it matter if the Pound in their pockets becomes the Euro instead? After all, isn't it just a matter of substituting one means of exchange for another? Well, it is true that money serves a number of economic functions (e.g. besides acting as a medium of exchange, money also serves as a standard and store of value, and a unit of account). It can also be defined in a number of ways such as *fiat* money (currency), 'narrow money' (a combination of hard deposits and demand deposits) and 'near' money (money which pays interest to the owner (Lewis *et al.*, 1995). However, this approach gives us only a partial picture. When we broaden the perspective to consider money as a social and psychological phenomenon, we encounter meanings associated with its various sources, forms and uses. For example, the source of money often has consequences for how it is perceived and used, as indicated by the terms 'dirty money', and 'blood-money'. There are many non-economic constraints on the various uses of money; for example, in our society, money is considered in some contexts to be unsuitable as a gift, and the use of money within the family is often gender-linked (Burgoyne, 1990; 1991; Burgoyne & Routh, 1991; 1995). Since sources often hypothecate uses, this can sometimes lead to the creation of 'special purpose monies' such as housekeeping money within the domestic economy (cf. Zelizer, 1994). There are even 'independent economies' such as the 'Local Exchange and Trading Systems' (LETS) where people use an alternative means of payment to exchange goods and services and no actual currency changes hands (though the units of these alternative currencies, with names like 'Creds' (in Crediton, near Exeter), are often based on the standard unit of value in the national currency). Of course, many forms of 'official' money also exist; each country has its own notes and coins, and historically, objects of many different kinds including large stones, shells, tea-bricks, and animals, have served some of the functions of money.

Thus, neither 'money' nor 'currency' can be regarded solely as an economic matter, and neither are they synonymous. The coins in our pockets typically have two different faces, one bearing symbols of the state and its authority (in Britain, the Queen's head) and the other carrying information about the exchange value of the coin in economic transactions. Thus, in introducing the Euro, we are not simply replacing one form of money with another, but something quite different and more elusive. Money can be regarded as a commodity, something that we use on a day-to-day basis. But the money that we use in everyday transactions derives its power from that of the national currency, which is in turn partly a function of the power of the state and a symbol of national sovereignty.

Viewed in this way, as a pervasive feature of everyday life and imbued with all sorts of symbolic meanings, the adoption of a single currency across Europe seems more cataclysmic than a simple change of money, and the effects are not easy to predict. However, there have been other currency changes in recent history (albeit on a smaller scale), such as the conversion to decimalisation in Britain in 1971 and the switch in 1983 from the Pound note to the Pound coin. Can we learn anything from these changes about the potential consequences for national identity?

Decimalisation proved to be a major event in Britain (Moore, 1973; Bruce, 1989). One of the major decisions prior to 1971 concerned the unit of the currency; should it be based on the pound or the 10 shillings system? Some argued that, since the pound was used in a third of the world's trade as the major unit of currency, its removal would affect many people other than the British. Interestingly, the British media and public at large were far from convinced by this argument (Moore, 1973). The British public fiercely challenged the Pound system (Bank of England, 1996), having a much stronger preference for a 10 shilling scheme, on the grounds that it appeared to offer greater protection against price increases, a matter of huge concern at the time. Keeping the shilling scheme would also permit retention of the 'tanner' as a 5p piece and the half-crown as 25p, and offer a greater degree of resemblance between old and new amounts. Since the coins could be recognised more easily, and the new denominations used more simply in everyday shopping, the newspapers described it as the 'Housewife's Choice' (Moore, 1973). Despite this, in 1971, a decimal system was adopted in which one Pound was now equivalent to one hundred pence (instead of the old 20 shillings or 240 pence). For present purposes, it is of interest to note that the public were much more concerned about understanding the currency and guarding against potential price rises than any threats to their national identity over the loss of the Pound. Also, the changeover was relatively straightforward, though elderly people can still be heard to refer to prices in the 'old' money today.

Another important event in Britain was the introduction of the Pound coin in April 1983, followed by the demonetisation of the Pound note in December of that year. This gave rise to some problems of circulation with reports that it had 'all but disappeared a month after being launched' (*The Mail on Sunday*, 22 May 1983; Webley *et al.*, 1983). In December, *The Guardian* (17 December 1983) reported that the Treasury had delayed phasing out the Pound note because 'of the psychological impact of such a move' with 'Ministers also fear[ing] reverberations on the Government's popularity because of an emotional attachment to the tradition of the

£1 note'. Speculation suggested that the public were 'boycotting' it for two reasons, because it represented a devaluation of sterling, and it had implications for the British sense of national identity. However, though these may have had some effect, other factors were also restricting the circulation of the coin. The Royal Mint stated that the coins were being collected, having 'replaced the sixpence as the traditional piggy bank coin' (*The Guardian*, 17 February 1983), and people objected to the size and weight of the coin, which made it easier to lose and spend than a note (Hussein, 1985). Since the coin seemed smaller and less valuable than a note, *The Daily Mail* initiated a campaign against what they described as the 'toytown coins'[3] (6 September 1983). In studies carried out by Hussein (1985), only a tiny minority objected to the Pound coin on the basis of a loss of tradition.

These findings might suggest that anxieties about resistance to the Euro on symbolic grounds are misplaced, since these aspects of the currency appear to have little meaning in Britain, and hence, few implications for national identity. However, this would be premature. We have to remember that, despite the changes outlined above, the major defining features of the currency remained in place initially, such as the Pound itself, the 'florin', and the sixpenny piece (though the values of the coins changed, and these have since been replaced by new coinage). In other words, there was some continuity of the currency as a vehicle for meaning. In contrast, public acceptance and trust are likely to be undermined to a much greater extent in the case of the Euro where all aspects of the currency will change – its physical appearance, its name, its value, and its various denominations. Moreover, there will be few, if any, aspects of 'associability' from the old money to the new.

A further consequence of the move to the Euro is that the same symbol will have to carry identity at two different levels – national and European. This might be difficult, when we consider that there is no supranational body that corresponds to that of the nation-state when it comes to authorising and legitimising the currency. Rather than a national government which issues the currency and gives it its authority, the European Union is not a single political entity; instead, it relies for its success upon the cooperation of a collection of nation-states. There have been other 'single currencies' in the past (for example, in the Graeco-Roman empire) but these usually arose as a consequence of conquest which forced a common identity on all those that fell within the empire. In the case of the Euro, there is an attempt to operate this process in reverse; in other words, to create a common sense of belonging from the use of a common currency. Moreover, some impact may be anticipated on the concept of the nation, when the national government becomes little more than an intermediary between the ECB and the ordinary citizen.

Although there has been intense debate at the political level in a number of the Member States, rather less attention has been paid to the views of ordinary people. What do they feel about the Euro? Again the *Eurobarometer* 46 (p. 33 et seq.) can provide some baseline data. The findings for Europe as a whole indicate a general increase in levels of support with 51 per cent in favour, and 33 per cent against the introduction of a single currency. Again, men were more positive than women, and the trends for age and education were the same as for attitudes towards the European Union in general. Support for the single currency was related to education and occupation; higher amongst self-employed people, those in management, and other white-collar occupations, and higher in those who were continuing in education. The lowest scores were observed amongst those lower down the occupational hierarchy, housepersons and manual workers. Turning to the individual countries, Figure 2 shows that Italians were the most enthusiastic about the single currency, with more than 7 in 10 in favour, closely followed by Spain, Ireland, Luxembourg and Greece. At the other end of the scale, Denmark, the United Kingdom, Sweden, and Finland were most against the single currency, with Austria, and Germany, France, Portugal, Belgium, and Holland occupying the middle ground between these extremes. Figure 2 accounted for 74.2 per cent of the variance in the data.

Comparing Figures 1 and 2, we can see that those countries in which people feel most European (Luxembourg, France, Italy) also tend to be in favour of the single currency, and some of those who feel most attached to their own national identity (Sweden, Denmark, the UK and Finland) come out as being most strongly against the Euro. However, Greek respondents, who are also strongly attached to their own nationality, are very much in favour of the single currency, perhaps because they anticipate the economic benefits of closer links with Europe.

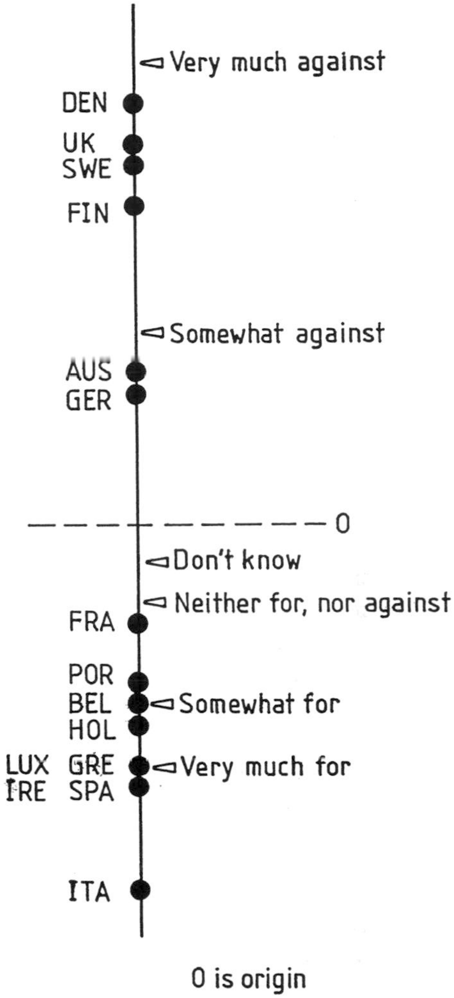

Figure 2. The extent to which people are for or against a single European currency in all EU countries (derived from Eurobarometer 46, Table 3.13, p. B36).

We can amplify these findings from the Eurobarometer with some results of our preliminary analyses on data drawn from the 'Psychology of the European Monetary Union' project. This survey, carried out by a team of researchers in the 15 European Member States in 1997, attempted to go beyond the surveys carried out by the Eurobarometer to explore some of the relationships between beliefs and attitudes towards the European Union, EMU, and the single currency (Muller-Peters, Pepermans, & Kiell, 1998). Amongst the other concepts investigated in this study were the following – expectations at the macro- and micro-economic level, pride in national symbols and institutions, important values, perceptions of justice, and social representations.

One of the problems that the single currency will have to cope with is the extent to which people are attached to their own national currency as a symbol of national identity. We can only take a broad-brush approach here to look at aggregate differences between countries, but this may help to identify those countries where more work is needed to make the Euro acceptable. How proud are people of the national currency?

Figure 3 shows the countries plotted along a dimension of 'pride in the national currency', and accounted for 86 per cent of the variance in the data. We can see that the country which feels the least pride in its currency is Italy. Some distance away, but still towards the negative pole we find Greece, with France and Spain occupying a neutral position and the remainder of the 15 countries clustered towards the positive end of the scale. Those countries with

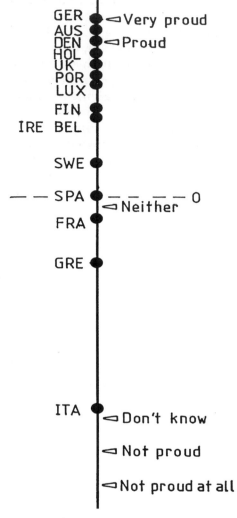

Figure 3. Pride in national currency in EU countries (The Psychology of EMU, *1998*).

the greatest pride in their currency are Germany and Austria, with Denmark, Holland, Portugal and the United Kingdom close behind. It is not altogether surprising to find Germany and Italy at opposite poles, given the strength of their respective currencies, but this suggests that Germans may find it less easy to relinquish the Mark than the French their Franc. Italy, on the other hand has the least pride in its currency, and, not surprisingly, is the most in favour of the Euro. Three countries who feel somewhat neutral about their currency are also very much in favour of the Euro, namely, Greece, France, and Spain. However, there are some countries who feel proud of their own currency, and yet are still in favour of adopting the Euro, e.g., Luxembourg, and Holland. In contrast, Denmark and the United Kingdom both exhibit a high level of pride in their own currency and are least in favour of giving it up for the Euro.

The findings so far suggest that, for some countries, their own currency is a very important symbol of what it means to be a nation. We explored this by looking at responses to the following statement: *'A country which does not have its own currency is not a true country'*. Here, the picture is a little more complicated, and we need two dimensions to see what is going on. (The horizontal dimension accounted for 68.5 per cent of the variance, whilst the vertical dimension accommodated another 20 per cent). If we look at the top left section of Figure 4,[4] we find a cluster of countries closely associated

◇ Response
● NATION
O Origin

Figure 4. Belief that without its own currency a country cannot be a true country (The Psychology of EMU, 1998).

with the 'disagree' and 'strongly disagree' responses, namely France, Spain, Ireland, Belgium, Holland and Luxembourg, indicating that they saw the national currency as relatively unimportant for national identity. Looking across to the right-hand side, we find those countries in which people tended to feel that the national currency was very important for their sense of nationhood – Germany, the United Kingdom, Denmark, Finland, Austria and Sweden (though Austria, Denmark and the United Kingdom also had a high proportion of people taking the opposite view). Towards the lower left area of the figure, Portugal and Italy are found to be associated with the 'neither' and 'don't know' responses, whilst Greece, towards the centre of the plot is not strongly associated with any of the responses.

From the results of these analyses, we can see that there is enormous variation in the way that individual countries regard their European identity, their attitudes towards the Euro, their sense of pride in the national currency, and the extent to which the latter is seen as important for their sense of nationhood. This suggests that, if governments wish to persuade their citizens that adopting the Euro is a good thing, they will have to tailor their message to suit their own populations. We can summarise some of these differences as follows:

- tending to be in favour of the Euro: Luxembourg, France, Italy, Spain, Holland, Belgium, Ireland, Portugal, and Greece. Of these, only Italy and Spain feel a lack of pride in their currency, and none regards their currency as an important symbol of nationhood;
- tending to be against the Euro: Austria, Germany, the United Kingdom, Denmark, Finland, and Sweden. All except Sweden expressed considerable pride in their currency, and most agreed to some extent that a country without its own currency was not a 'true' country. All of these countries saw themselves mainly in terms of a national, rather than a European identity.

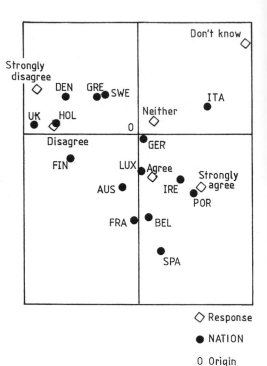

Figure 5. Belief that a single European currency will make us feel more European (The Psychology of EMU, 1998).

In the first group, only the citizens of Luxembourg, France, and Italy feel very European. However, the findings suggest that the populations in this group of countries may be more prepared to make the transition to the Euro, seeing this as less of a threat to their national identity than those in second group. For the latter, things are very different. All expressed pride in their currency, and two (Germany and the United Kingdom) regarded it as essential for a sense of their national identity. Although Austrians and Danes also exhibited pride in their currency, there was less consensus about this as a symbol of nationhood. If they wish to convert their currencies to the Euro, the findings suggest that the governments in this group of countries face a considerable challenge in terms of persuading their populations that this will be a good thing. Attachment to Europe is somewhat low, and the loss of the national currency may be felt much more keenly as a loss of national identity.

Of course, some believe that simply having a common currency may help to make individuals feel a greater sense of belonging to Europe. How far do the citizens of Europe agree with the statement that '*A single currency will make us feel more European*'? Figure 5 shows the results for this item. Again, the picture is not simple, and we need two dimensions to represent the similarities and differences between countries (with 71.2 per cent of the variance explained by the horizontal dimension and 18.1 per cent by the vertical). There were few in any country who agreed strongly with this statement, but those with the most substantial numbers showing a measure of agreement are found in the lower right portion of the figure – Ireland, France, Belgium, Spain, and Portugal. Looking towards the upper left-hand section of the plot, we find those who disagreed (some strongly) that the Euro would have this effect.   These were found in larger numbers in Denmark, (where, at the time of the survey, people already knew that they would not be participating in the Euro), Sweden, Holland, Finland, Greece, and the United Kingdom. Italy is again associated with the neutral and 'don't know' responses. Thus, with the exception of Holland, where people already identify quite strongly with Europe, it seems that those countries which feel least European do not anticipate that the single currency will achieve its political goal of promoting a greater sense of European identity.

Clearly, there are many factors pertinent to understanding national identity which would take us beyond the scope of the present chapter. For example, there have been several cross-national studies of the values held by organisational employees. With the caveat that these studies used aggregate data, it has been possible to distinguish nations on such dimensions as individualism-collectivism, power distance, egalitarian commitment, uncertainty avoidance, etc. (Hofstede, 1980, 1983). But more recent work by Smith, Dugan & Trompenaars (1996), which included most of the European Union countries, suggests a particularly interesting reinterpretation of certain of Hofstede's findings in a way that relates to aspects of identity. They found evidence for dimensions relating to the continuity of group membership (loyalty versus utilitarian involvement) and towards the obligations of social relationships (conservatism versus egalitarian commitment).

Conclusion

There has been a tendency in some of the literature on the European Union to assume that a favourable attitude towards Europe indicates a sense of European identity, but this is clearly not always the case. One can be pro-Europe for instrumental and economic reasons, without feeling any sense of cultural or political identification with the other peoples of the region. It is also possible, as shown by the recent articles by Lord Owen, to be deeply committed to the European Community, and, at the same time, adamantly opposed to the single currency. Lord Owen believes that joining the single currency would represent a 'quantum leap in the pooling of sovereignty', since the loss of economic sovereignty associated with the adoption of the single currency, would inevitably mean a loss of political sovereignty as well (Owen, 1998). The Euro cannot be 'coralled' within economic boundaries. In his view, the single currency will mean federalism, something that has always been on the agenda of the Continental Europeans. Owen points out that, in order to work successfully, the single currency will require a much wider integration of fiscal, political and social policy, which 'raises profound questions of democratic control and accountability' (Lloyd, 1998). 'Most people' he says 'accept that change [in the nation-state] is inevitable, but while they may not be able to define the nature of the state in which they want to live, they know they will recognise when that state no longer exists' (Owen, 1998).

The precise ways in which people's sense of national identity will be affected by EMU is at present very unclear. However, any such changes have to be seen in the context of increased globalization, the porosity of national boundaries, and the changes that have already been set in train by other developments, such as the influx of foreign nationals and the increased participation of women in public life. 'Europe is simultaneously undergoing a process of centralisation and fragmentation' (Schlesinger, 1992, reprinted in Hutchinson and Smith, 1994), and the nation-state is being both undermined and made more salient by the process of integration within Europe. This carries a risk of xenophobia and conflict as the darker side of nationalism starts to rear its head in some quarters, since 'national sentiments are still deeply entrenched, and . . . will not be transcended simply by a refusal to acknowledge them' (Jenkins and Sofos, 1996). Indeed, Dahrendorf (1998) believes that the Euro will divide Europe more deeply than anything else has done in recent history: 'There is no logic of history to suggest a political union in Europe brought about by some mysterious *force des choses,* more particularly, *des choses monetaires'.* It is still far from clear what 'Europeanness' actually means. Some argue that it will have to be conceptualized mainly in cultural terms, but that this is more likely to reflect the views of the 'intelligentsia' rather than the ordinary citizen (Schlesinger, 1992). One thing is clear, however, in the face of so many uncertainties about Europe, the debate about closer economic, political and social integration is likely to continue well into the future.

References

Anderson, B. (1991) *Imagined communities* (revised edition). London: Verso. Reprinted in J. Hutchinson and A.D. Smith, (eds) (1994) *Nationalism.* Oxford: Oxford University Press.

Bainbridge, T. and A. Teasdale (1997) *The Penguin companion to the European Union.* London: Penguin.

Bank of England Museum (1996) *All Change: 25th Anniversary of Decimal Currency in Britain.* London: The Governor and Company of the Bank of England and the Royal Mint.

Breakwell, G.M. and E. Lyons (eds) (1996) *Changing European Identities: Social Psychological Analyses of Social Change.* Oxford: Butterworth-Heineman.

Bruce, V. (1989) 'Human Factors in the design of coins'. 1989 C.S. Myers Lecture *The Psychologist: Bulletin of the British Psychological Society* 12, 524-527.

Burgoyne, C.B. (1991) *The Meanings of Money.* Bath University: Unpublished Doctoral Thesis.

Burgoyne, C.B. (1990) 'Money in Marriage: How Patterns of Allocation both Reflect and Conceal Power'. *The Sociological Review,* 38, 634-665.

Burgoyne, C.B. and D.A. Routh (1991) 'Constraints on the Use of Money as a Gift at Christmas: The Role of Status and Intimacy'. *Journal of Economic Psychology* 12, 47-69.

Burgoyne, C.B. and D.A. Routh (eds) (1995) 'Personal and Household Finances'. Special Issue of *Journal of Economic Psychology* 16, 355-540.

Burgoyne, C.B. and D.A. Routh (1998) 'The psychology of the European Monetary Union in the UK: "No S.E.C. please, we're British"' in A. Muller-Peters, R. Pepermans, and G. Kiell, (eds), *The psychology of the European Monetary Union: A cross-national study of attitudes towards the euro.* Report submitted to the European Commission, DG X: Brussels.

Cinnirella, M. (1996) 'A Social Identity Perspective on European Integration'. Chapter 16 in G.M. Breakwell and E. Lyons (eds) *Changing European Identities: Social Psychological Analyses of Social Change.* Oxford: Butterworth-Heineman.

Cinnirella, M. (1997) 'Towards a European identity? Interactions between the national and European social identities manifested by university students in Britain and Italy'. *British Journal of Social Psychology* 36, 19-31.

Currie, D. (1997) *The pros and cons of EMU*. London: The Economist Intelligence Unit.

Currie, D. (1998a) *Will the euro work?: The ins and outs of EMU*. London: The Economist Intelligence Unit.

Currie, D. (1998b) 'Economic and Monetary Union: Prospects, problems and opportunities' in M. Fraser (ed) *Britain in Europe*. London: Strategems Publishing Ltd., pp. 98-100.

Dahrendorf, R. (1998) 'Disunited by a common currency'. *New Statesman,* 20 February, 32-33.

Dedman, M.J. (1996) *The Origins and Development of the European Union 1945-95: A history of European Integration.* London: Routledge.

Dedman, M.J. (1998) 'EMU: The First Time Around'. *History Today* 48(1), 5-7.

Dowds, L. and K. Young (1996) 'National Identity'. Chapter 7 in R. Jowell, J. Curtice, A. Park, L. Brook and K. Thomson (eds) *British Social Attitudes: the 13th Report*. Aldershot: Dartmouth Publishing Co. Ltd.

Eurobarometer Report Number 46 (1997) Brussels: European Commission.

Fishburn, D. (ed), (1997) *The World in 1998.* London: The Economist Newspaper Ltd.

Hewstone, M. (1986) *Understanding attitudes to the European Community: A social psychological study in four member states.* Cambridge: Cambridge University Press.

Hilton, D.J., H. P. Erb, M. Dermot and D.J. Mullan (1996) 'Social Representations of History and Attitudes to European Unification in Britain, France and Germany'. Chapter 17 in G.M.Breakwell and E.Lyons (eds) *Changing European Identities.* Oxford: Butterworth-Heinemann.

Hofstede, G. (1980) *Culture's consequences: International differences in work-related values.* Beverly Hill, CA: Sage.

Hofstede, G. (1983) 'Dimensions of national cultures in fifty countries and three regions' in J. Deregowski, S. Dzuirawiec, and J.W. Berry (eds) *Expiscations in cross-cultural psychology* (pp. 335-355). Lisse, The Netherlands: Swets & Zeitlinger.

Hopkins, N., M. Regan and J. Abell (1997) 'On the context dependence of national stereotypes: Some Scottish data'. *British Journal of Social Psychology* 36, 553-563.

Hopkins, N., and S. Reicher (1996) 'The construction of social categories and processes of social change: Arguing about national identities'. Chapter 5 in G.M. Breakwell and E. Lyons (eds) *Changing European Identities*. Oxford: Butterworth-Heinemann.

Hussein, G. (1985) *An examination of the psychological aspects of money.* Unpublished MPhil thesis, University of Exeter.

Hutchinson, J. and A.D. Smith (eds) (1994) *Nationalism.* Oxford: Oxford University Press.

Jenkins, B. and S.A. Sofos (eds) (1996) *Nation and Identity in Contemporary Europe.* London: Routledge.

Lewis, A., P. Webley and A. Furnham (1995) *The New Economic Mind.* Hemel Hempstead: Harvester Wheatsheaf.

Lloyd, J. (1998) Interview: David Owen. *New Statesman,* 13th February, 18-20.

Moore, N.E.A. (1973) *The Decimalisation of Britain's Currency.* London: HMSO.

Muller-Peters, A., R. Pepermans and G. Kiell (eds) (1998) *The psychology of the European Monetary Union: A cross-national study of attitudes towards the euro.* Report submitted to the European Commission, DG X: Brussels.

Owen, D. (1998) 'Britain and Europe: Yes to Europe, no to federalism'. *The Economist,* January 24th, 35-36.

Reuters Ltd. (1997) 'Which countries want to join?' Chapter 3 in R. Pitchford, and A. Cox (eds) *EMU Explained: Markets and Monetary Union.* London: Kogan Page Ltd.

Routh, D.A. and C.B. Burgoyne (1998) 'Being in two minds about a single currency: a UK perspective on the Euro'. *Journal of Economic Psychology* 19 (in press).

Schlesinger, P. (1992) 'Europeanness: A new cultural battlefield?' *Innovation* 5(1), 12-18. Reprinted in J. Hutchinson and A.D. Smith (eds) (1994) *Nationalism.* Oxford: Oxford University Press.

Smith, A.D. (1991). *National Identity.* London: Penguin.

Smith, P.B., S. Dugan and F. Trompenaars (1996) 'National culture and values of organizational employees: A dimensional analysis across 43 nations'. *Journal of Cross-Cultural Psychology* 27, 231-264.

Tajfel, H. (1974) 'Social identity and intergroup behaviour'. *Social Science Information* 13, 65-93.

Tajfel, H. and J.C. Turner (1986) 'The social identity theory of intergroup behaviour' in S. Worchel and W.G. Austin (eds) *Psychology of Intergroup Relations.* Chicago: Nelson-Hall.

The Economist (1997a) 'A survey of the European Union: Europe's mid-life crisis'. May 31st-June 6th, Supplement.

The Economist (1997b) 'Towards EMU: Kicking and Screaming into 1999'. June 7th, 23-25.

The Economist (1998) 'Britain and Europe: Hopping on the juggernaut'. January 3rd, 27-30.

The European (1997) 'A comic pitch for the single currency'. Cover Story, 27th November, 8-13.

Tilly, C. (1975) 'Western state-making and theories of political transformation' in C. Tilly (ed) *The formation of national states in Western Europe*. Princeton, N.J. USA: Princeton University Press. Reprinted in J. Hutchinson and A.D. Smith (eds) (1994) *Nationalism*. Oxford: Oxford University Press.

Verkuyten, M. (1996) '"Twelve angry men". Accounting for Britain's minority position during the EU summit in Maastricht'. *Journal of Language and Social Psychology*, 15, 444-467.

Webley, P., S.E.G. Lea and G. Hussein (1983) 'A characteristics approach to money and the changeover from £1 note to £1 coin'. Paper presented at 8th International Symposium on Economic Psychology, Bologna.

Weller, S.C. and A.K. Romney (1990) *Metric Scaling: Correspondence Analysis*. London: Sage Publications Ltd.

Zelizer, V. (1994) *The Social Meaning of Money*. New York: Basic Books

Notes

1   This project was part-funded in Britain by NCR Corporation and part-funded in all fifteen states by the EC. The coordinators were Roland Pepermans in Brussels and Anke Muller-Peters in Cologne

2   Figures 1-5 are based upon Simple Correspondence Analysis using the Biomedical Data Package (BMDP) procedure, CA. Simple Correspondence Analysis is a useful method of identifying associations (both positive and negative) between the rows and columns of cross-classified frequency data, say between Countries and response categories. It is a specialised form of metric multidimensional scaling and permits the creation of a geometrical representation (map) in which each Country (say) is represented by one set of points and each response category (say) is represented by another set. The origin represents the 'average' Country and the 'average' response (for further details, see Weller & Romney, 1990). The points for countries, for example, represent complete country profiles, and their separation on the scale reflects differences between their profiles.

3   As noted earlier, the Italian authorities are planning to launch a 'Mickey-Mouse' story about the Euro (*The European, 1997)*; this would almost certainly be counterproductive in the UK.

4   In a two-dimensional solution, one needs to imagine directed arrows (vectors) emanating from the origin, and ending at the various points. A positive association between a row and column category is indicated when their corresponding arrows tend towards coincidence.

Monarchy and Nation in Britain Since the Eighteenth Century

Bruce Coleman

The British have become used to the Crown as the symbol and formal representative of nationhood. Though by historical criteria its forms of government can be called republican, the United Kingdom has retained a form of state that is monarchical. Though it is now very much a show monarchy – a matter of processions and good works – it retains enough constitutional significance to influence people's understanding of the state and to shape the national identity that supports it. This chapter examines the relationship between monarchy and nationhood since the early 18th century and assesses both what the monarchy has contributed to national identity and how a changing nation has shaped and reshaped the monarchy itself.

The subject is not a simple one. One reason lies with the multiple, overlapping and sometimes clashing identities embodied in the unions which created Great Britain and the United Kingdom. Only recently perhaps have historians started to explore freely the problematical status of the territorial conglomerate that came under the symbolic leadership of the dynastic monarchy. Another reason is that the constitutional theory of the monarchy has itself often been uncertain and has tended to lag behind the political realities of the countries of the United Kingdom. Though individual sovereigns and the Crown as an institution have often attracted strong loyalties as symbols of nationhood, they have rarely been able to control or shape the development of the nation. The Crown has, not always to its comfort, become more the servant than the master of the nation over which it has presided.

In 1603 the crowns of England and Scotland, each an ancient and self-governing nation, were joined in the person of James I and VI. Through the fortunes and misfortunes of the Stuart dynasty the two countries remained associated until they were united under one Parliament, that in Westminster, as well as one Crown by the Act of Union in 1707. By that settlement Scotland retained its own systems of religion, law and education. England brought other territories with it – Wales and, more problematically, Ireland had been conquered by the English Crown and then later consolidated as provinces under its authority and administration. Royal authority would, however, learn its own limitations. Parliamentary and sometimes popular resistance to Stuart essays in royal absolutism culminated in the 'Glorious Revolution' of 1688-89 which established, in effect, a constitutional monarchy dependent on parliamentary consent. Behind this constitutional drama lay the issue of the security of the Protestantism established by the 16th century Reformation. England and Scotland had different religious characters and their established churches represented different forms of Protestantism, but in both countries prevailing opinion rejected Roman Catholicism and the supranational authority of the Papacy. Rejected too were the Catholic main line of the Stuarts and the royal absolutism associated with the Papacy and the Catholic monarchies of Europe. The triumph of Protestantism was confirmed by the crushing of Catholic legitimist revolt in Ireland (William III's victory at the Boyne in 1690 would remain celebrated as the symbolic engagement) and by the 1701 Act of Settlement which established the succession of the Protestant Elector of Hanover to the throne. Worries that this succession would be less secure in Scotland than in England helped to produce the Union of 1707. The Hanoverian succession which occurred on Queen Anne's death in 1714 still had to be defended against Jacobite (and largely Catholic) rebellions in 1715 and 1745. Scotland was a more divided country in confessional terms than England, and the second rebellion had something of the character of a clash between the largely Catholic Highlands and the mainly Protestant Lowlands. The latter's triumph provided the final underpinning of the Protestant monarchy of the new Britain.

The early 18th century settlement had profound consequences for the future of both monarchy and nation. Though the political nation (or nations) had shown little enthusiasm for any republican alternative to monarchy, it had put in place a particular and unusual form of monarchy, not the type prevalent over most of the European continent. A parliamentary-based monarchy now had to rule within the law and seek a degree of consent. Though the Crown would still appoint and, in a sense, still head the executive, a parliament constituted by a system of representation had powers of veto over legislation and taxation, could limit government expenditure and could itself initiate and pass legislation. In this 'mixed constitution' sovereignty lay with the Crown-in-Parliament, not with the Crown itself. Thus the state which would shape and focus people's sense of nationhood was, though still a monarchy, not simply monarchical. A system which embodied the idea of 'the Englishman's liberties' had triumphed over the monarchical absolutism of the continent. In neither the United Kingdom nor any country within it could the Crown shape government and the state entirely in its own image. Patriotism would be identified with loyalty not simply to the Crown but to a broader-based form of state of which the Crown was one important component. The sense of British nationhood rested as much on Parliament and the rule of law as on the King. The Hanoverian dynasty reigned over the United Kingdom by the decision of the dominant political interests within the nation and pretty much on their terms.

The political nation which had settled its affairs thus was dominated by the landowning aristocracy and gentry. Despite some differences in forms and structures of landownership, England and Scotland were broadly similar in this respect. For these classes and for many others who deferred to them or aspired to rise into their ranks, landownership helped to define the nation. That view would colour the political culture and give the aristocracy much of its self-confidence far into the 19th century. The Protestant-inclined landed elite could view the nation as their creation more than the Crown's and the Hanoverians as a convenience dynasty to meet their needs. The attitudes which many of them displayed towards incumbents of the throne – attitudes that ranged from distant coolness through amused contempt to sharp irritation – reflected such assumptions. If the early-Victorian politician Henry Temple, Lord Palmerston, who worked to weaken the Crown's influence upon national policy, believed that he himself was a better focus for the nation's patriotic instincts than Victoria and Albert, he was probably right. Behind Palmerston and his abrasive Whiggery ('Lord Pumicestone' the royal couple called him) lay the realities of parliamentary politics. Over the two centuries after the Hanoverian succession the surviving powers of the Crown were subject to parliamentary scrutiny and their long-term atrophy transferred much of their exercise to the parliamentary leaders of landowning society. This aspect of landed oligarchy helped the integration of the several countries of the United Kingdom. The extent of intermarriage and inheritance, of shared education, culture and religion among the landed elites of England, Scotland and Ireland knitted them together as the ruling class of the United Kingdom and not just as local notables.

The Hanoverians were also an alien dynasty which initially had few roots, material or sentimental, in the kingdoms over which they now reigned. Arguably this foreign character and the limited sentimental appeal was part of the dynasty's acceptability. It would never be capable of building a Stuart-style absolutism upon such Tory Church-and-King loyalism as survived. Until 1837 British monarchs continued as Electors (from 1815 Kings) of Hanover. The practice of seeking royal marriage partners from other ruling houses and the requirement of the Act of Settlement that they be Protestant ensured that most were drawn from the Protestant dynasties of German and Scandinavian Europe. One consequence was a continuing German character to the monarchy which survived until the Great War forced its hurried abandonment. Another consequence was that such a monarchy provided an imperfect focus for the patriotisms of the United Kingdom and its component territories. Though there were attempts after George III's accession in 1760 to assert the Britishness of the Crown, the dynasty's marriage alliances and the nature of its extended family ensured that it remained semi-German. The loss in 1837 of Hanover, where female succession was barred, was countered soon by Victoria's marriage to the German princeling Albert of Saxe-Coburg and later by the marriage of their eldest child to the heir to the Prussian throne. (Had the succession not been by male primo-geniture, the future Kaiser Wilhelm II would have inherited the British throne.) Until the Great War this patriotic ambiguity of the Crown was not unduly damaging to its acceptability. For most of the two centuries after 1714 Britain saw France as its main rival and enemy and tended to construct anti-French alliances with German states. The struggle against Napoleon which culminated at Waterloo was a prime example. The credibility of a semi-German monarchy as a symbol of British national identity was powerfully assisted by the shaping of the latter by anti-French sentiment.

Another crucial element in the Hanoverian monarchy's relationship to British national identity was, of course, Protestantism. Indeed without the overriding importance of the struggle against Roman Catholicism there would have been no Hanoverians crowned at Westminster. (In 1714 there had been numerous Roman Catholics with a better hereditary claim to the Crown.) Religion brought its own complexities. In England the sovereign headed the established church and exercised considerable powers of patronage within it; in Scotland, the relationship with the Presbyterian kirk was more distant and ambiguous. The Hanoverians in Germany had been Lutherans, a variant of Protestantism little represented in either England or Scotland. But such distinctions could be blurred in a generalised anti-Popish identity that served to give the Crown considerable support among both the political elites and the populace at large. Its religious status was, however, more secure in England than elsewhere. Scotland was more divided by religion and the dissidence of the largely Catholic Highlands contributed to the troubles of 1715 and 1745. In Ireland, where a Catholic majority survived under a Protestant ascendancy based on the landowning classes and centred in Dublin, the Crown's Protestantism would be as much a weakness as an asset. Eventually, in the 20th century, majority opinion in Ireland would reject both the Crown and the particular nationhood it represented and create for itself a state both republican and Catholic. For the moment, though, Protestantism served as a buttress of the monarchy, as a cement of the relationship between Crown and Parliament, and as a central component of the national identity that developed around both. For two centuries after 1714 the sense of British nationhood would interact with a specifically Protestant interpretation of the Providential dispensation.

As we have seen, the Crown's position was different in each of the countries of the United Kingdom. It was securest in England, the most populous and powerful of the component countries; its greatest city, London, served as the seat of Court, Parliament and government, and the monarchy had a mutually supportive relationship with the church establishment. Traditional Church-and-king loyalism, once it had transferred itself from Stuarts to Hanoverians, was strongest in England. Scotland was more problematical, both because of its religious divisions and because of actual or potential resentment of English domination. Scotland also experienced a more troubled internal history in the 18th century than England. Though George III (who installed the first Scottish prime minister) and his successors worked to improve their Scottish credentials, various republican movements would tend to win more following in Scotland than in England. The greatest problem was, inevitably, Ireland where a Protestant monarchy represented not just the victory of a minority faith over the majority one and of a land-owning elite over the land-occupying classes, but also of a conquering race over a suppressed people. In the north of the island the earlier 'plantation of Ulster' by Scottish Presbyterians had given a different flavour to things, but an Irish patriotism already apparent in the late 18th century could still see the relationship between the kingdoms in terms of the triumph of Britannia over Hibernia. Here Crown and Parliament were always likely to be more divisive than in Britain. The grant of a Parliament with legislative powers to Dublin in 1782 reflected the weakness of the Crown, of Westminster government and of a British-centred definition of nationhood at a moment when the American colonists had defeated George III's forces and established independence and a republic for themselves. The Dublin experiment was shortlived. Revolt in Ireland in 1798, stimulated by the French Revolution and by renewed war between Britain and France, underlined the precariousness of the political order in the island. The 1800 Act of Union, which terminated the Dublin Parliament and brought Ireland under a form of direct rule from Westminster, albeit with some continuing administrative and legislative identity, was inspired by fears of the capacity of elements in Irish society for dissidence and turbulence. Always controversial, it amounted to an incorporation of Ireland into a British-dominated United Kingdom where Crown, Parliament and Protestantism defined a nationhood with which much of Ireland's population could only partially identify. Whatever its legal status, the United Kingdom as established in 1800 would remain an uncertain focus for national identity both in Ireland and, to some extent, in the other countries where it had little meaning except for Irish purposes. Perhaps significantly, the term never developed a corresponding adjective, as Britain and the separate countries had done, and has been little used outside legal and diplomatic contexts. Always an artificial construction of constitutional meaning rather than colloquial resonance, the United Kingdom of 1800 arguably did little to shape a sense of nationhood of its own.

The post-1800 United Kingdom did, however, possess some integrating influences. One, certainly, was the Crown itself, now strengthened as a symbol of conservative reaction and national resistance in the aftermath of the French Revolution. Another, as we have seen, was the land-owning elite, though more the great aristocracy, much of it owning land in more than one kingdom, rather than the petty gentry of merely local significance. Another was the armed forces; they recruited heavily from Scotland and Ireland, they developed loyalty to the Crown as symbol of nation and of authority, they fought the French and other foreign foes and Westminster was their paymaster. Perhaps the army and navy have been the most successful embodiments of the United Kingdom identity. Another force for integration was the scale and commercial importance of the colonial empire. The empire represented not just wider dominion and a sense of national success but also commercial and professional opportunity. It also offered settlement to land-hungry emigrants from the home kingdoms, Scotland and Ireland as well as England and Wales, and operated as a safety valve for pressures within the United Kingdom. Scotland was perhaps the most conspicuous beneficiary. The Union of 1707 had brought free trade with it and made Britain the largest free market in Europe. Access to the colonies' trade, land and jobs helped to cement Scotland into the Union. The nature of the Irish economy made that factor less important for Ireland, though much of the post-Famine emigration went to the empire and the late 19th century industrialization of the island's north-eastern corner helped to integrate its local economy with Britain and the empire. How far these integrating factors turned themselves into personal loyalties and conscious identities is another matter. Despite the mix of countries represented in his fleet at Trafalgar in 1805, Nelson still flew a signal that ran 'England expects ...' Despite its Irish regiments and recruitment the army remained a controversial force in many parts of Ireland during the 19th century while its standing elsewhere in the United Kingdom improved. What was not in doubt was the symbolic importance of the Crown itself for the purposes of any United Kingdom consciousness. One of the few institutions shared by all the countries of the United Kingdom conglomerate, it remained such even when some of the responsibilities of the Westminster Parliament and government were devolved, to the Irish Parliament in 1782-1800 or to the Northern Ireland Parliament from 1922 to 1972. As the colonial empire moved from administration by chartered companies to direct imperial rule, the Crown's symbolic importance increased. The centrality of the Crown to any definition of the United Kingdom was clear and the futures of the two institutions would inevitably be to some extent bound up together.

Some of these features have remained recognizably the same over the two centuries since the 1800 Act of Union; others have changed dramatically. The position has never been completely static. The challenge from an atheistic, republican, anti-aristocratic Jacobinism after 1789 had helped to lessen the exclusively Protestant and anti-Catholic resonance of the monarchy, just as it saw Britain form alliances with Catholic Austria and Catholic Spain. On the other hand the long wars with France between 1793 and 1815 confirmed the anti-French significance of both nationhood and the monarchy, which thereby achieved a peak of patriotic appeal. The war against republican France in the 1790s had triggered a loyalist surge across British society, so that George III had become a more conspicuous focus for patriotism than the Crown would ever manage to become again, at least in any European war. (This patriotic loyalism came to be labelled Tory, a revival in a new context of an ancient name with Church-and-King connotations.) The renewal of a threat from France and perhaps also a need to compensate for the American disaster had served to cement the Anglo-German monarchy in British affections and, indeed, to intensify the sense of British nationhood. The war threw up its patriotic heroes – the younger Pitt as the political 'pilot who weathered the storm', Nelson and Wellington as victors in battle. The final victory at Waterloo in 1815, won under an Anglo-Irish commander and with Prussian assistance, symbolized not just the endurance and success of Anglo-German relationships as represented in the monarchy but also the triumph of a patriotically aroused Britain over France and the victory, Europe-wide, of monarchies over both Jacobin republicanism and Napoleonic imperialism. 1815 thus represented a high point for British patriotism and identity, for the Crown and for the institutions of the state it headed.

That moment would, however, prove to be an artificial and ephemeral high. The political implications of loyalist patriotism had always been uncertain. Ironically, but significantly, the loyalist mood had coincided with the personal humiliations George had been forced to endure in the treatment of his supposed madness. George's reign, despite public approbation for his familial piety, had been condemned to end under the regency of his eldest son, a figure conspicuously lacking in the family virtues and in the aura of sanctity that his father had gained. But if the standing of the Crown would suffer from the personal unpopularity of the Prince Regent, the future George IV, there were also political realities re-asserting themselves. Even centre-right government in London had to distance itself from continental monarchism. Foreign secretaries Castlereagh and Canning concluded that association with the imperial monarchies of the Holy Alliance would be more than Parliament and British constitutionalism would tolerate. A Whig interpretation of national identity was emerging to counter-balance the Tory one of the anti-Jacobin years. By the 1820s Britain was shielding republican revolts in South America from the intervention of European monarchies. In 1830 France's restored Bourbon monarchy was overthrown to considerable approbation from British opinion. In Ireland the Ascendancy's control suffered as Daniel O'Connell organized the Catholic tenantry and made himself the hero of a new-style Irish (and pro-Catholic) patriotism. Britain itself, its economy disturbed by a series of shocks, witnessed revivals of both popular radicalism and aristocratic Whiggism. George IV was humiliated over his attempt to divorce his Queen Caroline in 1820; in 1829 his Tory prime minister Wellington forced him, over threats of abdication, to concede Catholic Emancipation for the sake of stability in Ireland. His brother and successor William IV would suffer defeats at the hand of the Whigs in 1832 (over parliamentary reform) and in 1835. In 1841 a telling defeat would be inflicted upon the young Queen Victoria, Whiggish herself, when she publicly backed her Whig ministry against the Conservative opposition in a general election. The Crown was being forced into retreat from overt political activity by the political parties and the organized public opinion they represented. Though monarchs retained partisan preferences and long continued to exert influence behind the scenes, they had to accept the dominance of the parties that controlled the House of Commons and contested general elections. A monarchical form of state survived but a republican mode of government was arriving.

This decline in the Crown's political strength, above all its inability to choose its own governments, dictated a modification of the style of a monarchy. The danger was that otherwise the monarchy and the popular sense of national identity would diverge dangerously, as has happened with various continental monarchies in the 19th and 20th centuries. A rethinking of royal strategy was provided by Albert, the Prince Consort, aided by German confidants who had, perhaps, a Central European sense of the precarious relationships between princely dynasties and national identities. The essence of Albertine monarchy was the Crown's withdrawal from overtly partisan political involvement, with all its evident dangers, to concentrate on a more disguised influence behind the scenes. The fragmentation of the political parties between 1846 and 1859, a development to which the Court contributed, offered considerable scope for this practice and the Crown would never again suffer a public humiliation like that of 1841. That did not, however, save the Court from continuing criticism and distrust or restore it as an unquestioned focus of patriotism. Albert, despite the respect some politicians felt for him, was dogged by a degree of unpopularity and never threw off the image of a German princeling on-the-make. Despite the royal couple's Russophobic enthusiasm for the Crimean War in 1854, it was Palmerston, their least favourite politician, who emerged as popular hero with victory in 1856 and who remained the embodiment of patriotic sentiment until his death in 1865. Albert's death in 1861 removed one hindrance to the Crown's development of popular and patriotic appeal, but for the moment its pro-German image remained a problem, particularly during the 1864 war over Schleswig-Holstein between Denmark and the German powers, and again in 1870-71 when Prussia defeated France and declared the German empire. The marriage of the Princess Victoria, the Queen's eldest child, to the heir to the Prussian crown had, despite their own liberal views by Prussian standards, helped to identify the Crown further with a Germany seen in Britain as militaristic, politically authoritarian and diplomatically overbearing. That was one factor, alongside the widowed Victoria's continued absence from public duties, in the spasm of republican enthusiasm in 1871. A few significant politicians were unwise enough to give it some countenance. Though this 'republican moment' was shortlived, it was a reminder that the Crown's standing as symbol of nationhood and focus for patriotism was not independent of its political acceptability to British society.

The next 40 years would see a strengthening of the monarchy's position and a closer identification between Crown and nationhood. The royal Jubilees of 1887 and 1897, the latter being a particularly spectacular celebration of Britain's world empire, were highpoints of this phase. Several features of this development related to Victoria herself. The Crown's earlier withdrawal from overt political partisanship had allowed her to establish a standing above public politics and, despite her private preferences, without the narrowly Tory image of her early 19th century predecessors. The culture of respectability and familial morality which the Queen and the Prince Consort had imposed upon their court had a strong appeal, not least to religious and middle class opinion. If this style of 'bourgeois monarchy' involved a resumption of the tone of George III's reign, it also anticipated developments under Georges V and VI in the following century. In all these cases the more moralistic elements in public opinion were largely supportive of the monarchy as representative of the best in British society.   The Queen and Albert had, furthermore, worked successfully to cultivate the Scottish dimension of the royal image. The development of Balmoral as a royal residence (journeys there would be the bane of ministers for the rest of the reign) and her publication in 1867 of *Leaves from a Journal of our Life in the Highlands* had a wider significance; the Crown, while still part-German, had at least given itself a British rather than a restricted English identity. Victoria even made clear her preference for the Scottish Kirk over the Church of England as representative of the rational Protestantism with which she identified.

There were, however, other influences that did not arise merely from Victoria's personal preferences or style. The most important was the development of a more self-conscious imperialism than the older British colonial system had produced previously. The causes of the late-Victorian expansion of the empire remain debatable, though challenges from the rival imperialist powers, France, Germany and the United States, were amongst them. Friction and rivalry with other powers stimulated the assertion of national identity and interests. As Britain's territories around the world multiplied and made up an empire on which, as a popular phrase had it, 'the sun never set', so national identity outgrew the British Isles. In this process the Crown had an important symbolic role and one no longer confined by systems of constitutional government or religious conformity.   In the 1870s the Tory politician Disraeli had seen the opportunity, following the death of Palmerston and with the Liberals now led by the internationalist Gladstone, to link Crown, empire and patriotism in one political identity and to commandeer them for Conservative party purposes. His enactment in 1876 of Victoria's own wish to assume the title of Empress of India reflected his personal enthusiasm for Britain's destiny as a great Middle Eastern power; it was also an attempt to neutralise the tendencies of both Liberalism and democracy. Despite the answering echo of popular 'jingoism' in support of Britain's backing of Turkey against Russia in 1877-78, Disraeli's translation of patriotic loyalism into a flamboyant foreign policy had both dangers and limitations, as his electoral defeat in 1880, after humiliations in colonial wars, would show. But he had established a new emphasis in the rhetoric and imagery of the political right. After his death the Primrose League, the Conservative party's populist rally, would combine patriotism, imperialism and loyalty to the Crown with established-church Christianity in a political confection of widespread appeal. That appeal would retain much of its power until the mid 20th century decolonization that ended the British Empire. But its apogee had arrived with Victoria's jubilees of 1887 and 1897, especially the Diamond Jubilee of the latter year, which, orchestrated by Conservative-dominated governments, focused patriotic pride on an imperial identity with which the Crown was crucially associated. Now, to the confused and sometimes competing national identities within the United Kingdom itself, had been added the British imperial identity.

The appeal of the latter did not, however, override all the problems of the former. By the 1880s Ireland had become the greatest problem. There the emergence of a new style of often nationalistic radicalism had been nourished first by Irish-American Fenianism (which looked to revolutionary and republican traditions) and then by acute agricultural depression which radicalised the tenant farmers class and worsened their relations with the landlord class of the Anglo-Irish Ascendancy. By 1885, aided by a more democratic franchise, the new Irish party had won most of the Irish seats at Westminster and were pressing for Home Rule (a subordinate Parliament in Dublin), though some of its figures had the grander vision of an independent and republican Ireland. Gladstone's proposal of Home Rule in 1886 split the Liberal party and introduced a new division in political life which followed, to some degree, the lines of controversy over empire. On the one side stood a liberal, internationalist standpoint which disliked militarism and realpolitik and which, distrustful of the emotional appeal of British patriotism and imperialism, was prepared to make concessions to subordinate national identities within the United Kingdom and to other national identities abroad. Against it

"NEW CROWNS FOR OLD ONES!"

(ALADDIN *adapted.*)

Punch's celebrated Cartoon of 1876 expressed a firm preference for the crown's traditional style and identity over its new Indian imperial pretensions stood a patriotic, sometimes militaristic and imperialistic, definition of British nationhood which saw the assertion and defence of British interests abroad and of the unity of the United Kingdom at home as the main task of government. It was inevitable that the latter standpoint more than the former emphasised the Crown as the symbol and particular focus of patriotic loyalty and of nationhood. This support was reciprocal; through the last decades of her reign Victoria identified herself firmly, if largely privately, with patriotism, Unionism and the empire.

What one might call the Gladstonian standpoint could, for all its distaste for the idea of a fully independent and republican Ireland, see Irish self-government as part of a larger and natural development by which a centralised United Kingdom transformed itself through the devolution of powers to the several component countries. The implication of this view was that the national identities of the separate countries were or would become more popular and compelling than an over-arching United Kingdom identity, though it was assumed that the latter would retain the force to operate for purposes of foreign policy, defence and empire. Though designed mainly to meet the case of Ireland, this view of nationhood found some late Victorian resonance within Wales, where the language issue and religious Nonconformity generated some antagonism towards the culture dominant in Westminster and Whitehall. For the moment they had rather less appeal in Scotland where the economic benefits provided by the empire limited the challenge that Scottishness could amount to Britishness. Scotland contained areas of strong anti-Irish and anti-Catholic sentiment, partly as a result of Irish immigration into its cities, and the Liberal split over Home Rule in 1886 showed Liberal Unionism to be a powerful force north of the Border. Even so, governments of both parties had agreed in the previous year to establish a Secretaryship of State for Scotland as a sop to any Scottish sense of separate identity. (Appropriately, the first holder of the new office was the Tory Duke of Richmond and Gordon, holder of both English and Scottish dukedoms and owner of major estates in both countries.) But the main influence of the prospect of a self-governing Ireland was to provoke a Unionist backlash in both England and Scotland which looked to defend the unity of the British Isles and of the empire. It also asserted the role of the Crown as the symbol of both. Ireland itself remained bitterly divided. Not all Home Rulers by any means were republicans, overt or covert; Unionists in Ireland came, however, to assert an emphatic loyalty to the Crown as the symbol of the unity of the United Kingdom and of a larger nationhood than the merely Irish.   As the local politics of Dublin, the vice-regal capital, came to be dominated increasingly by the Home Rulers, Irish Unionism found its safest stronghold in the north-eastern counties centred on Belfast, a fast-growing, industrialised city of national, indeed imperial, significance. Here Scots-Irish ethnicity based on earlier Scottish settlement and Presbyterian religion provided the underpinning for a militant Unionism and a fervent loyalty to the Crown as the symbol of Union. The working out of these divisions within Ireland, a country which by 1914 seemed to be on the brink of civil war, is a familiar story. The Easter Rising of 1916 and its aftermath would help to establish in power in most of the island a nationalism that would, in time, reject all further association with Britain and with the Crown. One consequence of the triumph of a fully independent and republican Ireland would be the continuing partition of Ireland itself and the continuing clash within it of the incompatible traditions of loyalism and republicanism, aligning themselves for and against the Crown, Unionists and separatists, for the most part Protestants and Catholics, celebrants of rival and highly tenacious national identities. What also stands out from the 50 year existence of a devolved government and parliament in the United Kingdom province of Northern Ireland is the continuing loyalty of the Loyalist majority there to the United Kingdom identity rather than a separate Northern Irish or Ulster one. This is one part of the United Kingdom where Unionism has remained a public cause and political identity. It is also the one part where the Crown has, with the majority community, retained its appeal as a political symbol as well as a focus of popular emotion, while in the minority community it has been rejected in favour of a professed republicanism.

No other issue within the United Kingdom has seen the Crown involved so centrally as a focus of national loyalties. Ireland remains still a special case. In the 20th century the rest of the once United Kingdom has, though, seen a general weakening of that patriotic loyalism which had reached a second peak in the late-Victorian period. It has also witnessed the monarchy reshaping itself in order to survive the coming of full political democracy, the changing relativities of the various classes and interest groups within British society and the changing status in the world of the United Kingdom and its empire. The Great War, by shaping the outcome of the crisis of national identities within Ireland, helped to emphasise the relationship of the Crown with a British rather than United Kingdom identity. (That view might be questioned in Northern Ireland but in fact the self-governing status of the province between 1922 and 1972 served to move it out of the mainstream of British culture and political development.) The war, the first great anti-German war, also forced the monarchy (with dramatic haste) to de-emphasise its Germanic roots and associations. The patriotic mood during the war damaged the careers of various public figures with German associations (Prince Louis of Battenberg translated his family name to 'Mountbatten') and persuaded George V that his Saxe-Coburg-Gotha dynastic identity had to be disguised as 'the House of Windsor'. The King's two eldest sons never had German brides sought for them and when the Duke of York succeeded as George VI in 1936 his queen, born Lady Elizabeth Bowes-Lyon, was the first British native consort of a reigning sovereign since the last wife of Henry VIII. (The second war against Germany would have a similar influence; when Princess Elizabeth married Philip Mountbatten in 1947 his German antecedents were de-emphasised to the advantage of his British and Greek ones.)

The last years of the Great War also generated another kind of nervousness. Russian Czardom had never enjoyed popularity in Britain; its fall in 1917 led Nicholas II to seek asylum in Britain for himself and his family. George V's personal refusal to afford them refuge – persuaded by fears about his own crown's association with a defeated, discredited and unpopular monarchy – condemned them, in effect, to death at the hands of the Bolsheviks. The political instabilities of the war's ending also toppled the imperial crowns of Germany and Austria-Hungary. At this point if anyone embodied a British patriotism successfully it was David Lloyd George, the Welsh Liberal politician whose coalition government had overseen victory (with the aid of the French and American republics). The settlement in Ireland showed the limitations of monarchy as a focus for patriotism and national identity even at the end of a successful war. One can only speculate how a less successful war would have left the monarchy's standing.

The period between the two great wars saw the arrival of full adult (including female) suffrage, the rise of the trade union-based Labour Party to become the second party in the political system and to form two minority governments, and growing resistance to British rule in India. National identities were changing their ideological complexion. These developments required a reshaping of the monarchy's image if it was to survive as a focus of national sentiment. (Contemporary events in Italy, Germany and Spain would show, as France and the USA had done before, how successfully republican regimes could represent patriotic feeling.) In Britain the *Almanack de Gotha* style of monarchy, already diminished by the Great War, would be replaced by something more domesticated and familial – less aristocratic, less militaristic, less imperialistic. The public ceremonials of these years, even George V's Jubilee in 1935 or the coronation of George VI in 1937, would not rival the bombastic magnificence of the 1897 Jubilee or the Delhi Durbar of 1911. Parallel to the evolution in these years under Stanley Baldwin of a 'New Conservatism', more bourgeois, domesticated and democratic than its pre-1914 equivalent, there developed a style of monarchy with some similar characteristics. George V, at least in his domestic life, suited this development more than his father would have done or his eldest son would do. It was a reversion to the image of familial domesticity and moral respectability which had marked the courts of George III and Victoria and Albert. Now it had firmer foundations in an extended middle-class electorate and culture strongly identified with formal Christian morality. The new female electorate was an influence too. The fragility of this family-based style of monarchy would show only in the late twentieth-century. When in 1936 the new king, Edward VIII, bucked the trend by his dalliance with an American socialite and divorcee, the Prime Minister Baldwin forced him into abdication and replaced him with the better domesticated Duke of York (complete with devoted wife and two young children) as George VI. This smooth replacement of one king by another, under pressure from the government, showed the inherent stability of monarchy as a national institution but also how little a particular monarch could control the political forces of the day or determine the nature of the nationhood he was required to represent. (Winston Churchill's attempt to rally a King's Party around Edward had failed pathetically.) The Crown had to be what the nation – or at least its dominant political culture – required it to be. Though monarchy would survive – and Baldwin, for all his brusqueness towards the Palace, never intended otherwise – it would do so in a form that could not be entirely of its own choosing.

Two other features of the period pointed in the same direction. One was the position achieved by the Labour party, which, like much of the Liberal party it had replaced as the main party of the left, did not share the type of patriotic identity promoted by Tory-dominated Unionism from the 1870s. Labour was cool about imperialism and its aristocratic trappings, it was anti-militaristic, it included pacifist elements and it was committed, at least in theory, to a semi-socialist internationalism. The first Labour government of 1924 was a shock to the Court. The second disintegrated over economic policy in 1931 in circumstances which saw George V play a significant role in the establishment of a National Government that split the Labour party, particularly its leadership, and inflicted a crushing electoral defeat upon it. There followed a brief spasm of republican sentiment in the rump of the Labour party and, even if the criticism of George's 'palace revolution' served as a cover for Labour's own failings, the dangers of such resentments on the political left were obvious. The background was of industrial depression and mass unemployment in some regions of the country. Fears for the Crown's potential unpopularity contributed to the decision to have the King make a Christmas radio broadcast in 1932 (the first of what became an institution) and to the expressions of sympathy with the unemployed by the Prince of Wales on visits to the depressed areas. It explained aspects of the Abdication crisis in 1936, including Baldwin's preference for a non-provocative, domesticated and moralistic style of monarchy over the more overtly plutocratic self-indulgence of Edward, and explained also the enthusiastic and highly public support of the new King and Queen for Neville Chamberlain's deal with Hitler at Munich in 1938. What came to be labelled 'appeasement' abroad and domestic piety, respectability and stability at home amounted to the style of monarchy required by the political circumstances of 1930s Britain. It was an appropriate (if far from heroic) symbol of nationhood at a time when prevailing opinion did not want the heroics of militarism or political confrontation.

Another feature of the period was the redefinition of the Empire as an Empire/Commonwealth through the 1931 Statute of Westminster which recognized the self-governing status of the Dominions and retained the Crown as the titular head of this looser form of association with the mother country. The rise of nationalism in India led to the concession of the 1935 Government of India Act which granted a limited self-government to the sub-continent and suggested, by implication, that it was moving towards Dominion status. (Churchill, now the personification of the romantic right, opposed this measure forcefully as he did Baldwin's policy over abdication and Chamberlain's over the Munich agreement.) The imminent ending of the Indian Empire and of the Empire at large was not intended or envisaged by most of those directly involved – George V remained wedded to the conception of his imperial status embodied in the 1911 Durbar and was bitterly hostile to Indian nationalism – but the way had been opened to a reformulation of the Empire in terms of popular self-government and consent, a liberal and more democratic understanding of post-imperial association. Though accelerated by the circumstances of the 1939-45 war, there was already under way a winding down of the British imperialism of the century's start and there would come with that process changes to Britain's own sense of nationhood and to the role of the Crown.

Though the wars of 1939-45 ended in a victory of a kind for Britain and its Empire and never gave the House of Windsor the problems of identity that had embarrassed it during the first war, the conflict and its outcome had implications for the Crown. Though George VI and his Queen, staying (though not normally sleeping) in London during the Blitz, worked their way back from the embarrassment of their fervent support for the 'appeasement' of 1938, the hero and personification of British resistance and survival was Winston Churchill. Ironically the royalist of 1936 now overshadowed the Crown as the embodiment of nationhood and patriotism. The national mood, one perhaps not wholly identified with Churchill's speeches of patriotic defiance in 1940, did not exclude the monarchy but it did subordinate and limit the representative and symbolic role of the Crown. There was also the fact that Churchill's wartime strategy – a preferred alliance with the republican USA and then a tactical, enforced alliance with the Soviet Union – had uncomfortable implications for the monarchy and for the type of nation it would have to represent in future. The Labour electoral victory of 1945 and the years of economic and social austerity that followed reduced the trappings allowed to the monarchy. At the same time the retreat from empire in the Indian sub-continent in 1947-49, the formal departure of the Irish Republic from the Commonwealth and from association with the United Kingdom, and the election of a Nationalist and less pro-British government in South Africa in 1948, the year after a high-profile tour by the King and his family, all pointed in the same direction. British nationhood and the Crown's representative role within it now found themselves in reduced circumstances. The 1956 Suez disaster and the burst of decolonisation in Africa and beyond in the late 1950s and early 1960s marked a sharp end of imperial pretensions for both Britain and its monarchy. A Commonwealth based on the voluntary membership of self-governing states would continue and the Crown's role as Head of the Commonwealth (even though many of its constituent states were republics) would be performed enthusiastically by Elizabeth II, but the status and glamour of both nationhood and the Crown were reduced by the process. Both were increasingly confined to the British Isles. Another consequence of the end of empire would, however, be that the bonds of shared national identity within the United Kingdom would themselves come under greater strain.

The Cold War being played out from the late 1940s had seen Soviet Russia, the wartime ally, re-identified as an enemy, to the immense benefit of British Conservatism. That confrontation and the NATO alliance which embodied it continued Britain's association with – indeed dependence upon – the United States. The rightward shift of American opinion early in the Cold War disguised some of the problems of this position, though the critical hostility of Washington to the Suez operation in 1956 underlined them cruelly. The domestic politics of the American republic made it less than wholly sympathetic to Britain's late-imperial pretensions, as later to its position in Northern Ireland. The influence and money of Irish

Americans helped to destabilize Ulster from the late 1960s and to encourage republicanism in the Catholic population there. Similarly the steady move of Canada into the United States ambit helped to weaken its links with Britain and to revive the ambitions of an anti-British and anti-royalist Francophone separatism in Quebec. Though the impact of these factors was softened for British opinion by the continuing anti-Soviet solidarity of the two countries and by the periodic closeness of their administrations, particularly during the Thatcher-Reagan era - perhaps also by the enthusiasm of American tourists for the monarchy and its trappings - the long-term affect of the United States was, on balance, unhelpful for traditional notions of British nationhood.

Another aspect of this period (again one largely encouraged by the United States for its own geo-political reasons) has been Britain's association with the European Community that was established by the Treaty of Rome in 1957. British governments applied for membership in 1961-62 (as part of Macmillan's post-Suez reconsideration of Britain's world position), 1968 and 1971-72, the last time successfully. Though the United Kingdom had no problem with those European associations involved in NATO or in the country's normal trading activities, the European Community, always controversial in British politics, has been quite another matter. Edward Heath's insistence on entry at all costs in the early 1970s raised questions about Britain's own constitution, democratic legitimacy, the relationship of the constituent countries of the UK itself and about Britain's relations with the Commonwealth, particularly the old Dominions. Whatever the benefits which pro-Community enthusiasts have claimed, particularly in terms of economic relationships, the political implications have been largely negative for British nationhood and for the monarchy's role within it. The tendency of the European Union – particularly of those forces within it that seek to create a European state – has been to weaken the traditional nation states in membership. The main issue involved here is that of national sovereignty and for the United Kingdom, which has one of the longest records of independence and self-government under its own law, that means the sovereignty of the Crown-in-Parliament. Unease over this aspect of the European involvement forced the only all-UK referendum on continuation in the EC in 1975 and has shown itself in opposition to the idea of a common European currency. Another effect of EC membership has been to encourage independence or devolutionist movements in Scotland ('independence within Europe') and Wales and, perhaps too, republican nationalism within Northern Ireland. The Palace has at various points signalled its unease with the policies of successive governments towards fuller European integration, but, though Europeanization is bringing into question the Crown's symbolic role at the head of a sovereign state, most of the opponents of that process have made relatively little of the Crown's position. The late Enoch Powell, the most resolute and articulate defender of national identity among recent politicians, stressed parliamentary sovereignty as the essence of the nation rather than the role of the monarchy itself. In this respect the development of the Crown into the symbol rather than the seat of power has left it with a modest significance. Perhaps only in recent debate about a common European currency has the issue of the Queen's head on the coinage served to make the monarchy's position a more central question. One should note in this respect that in recent wars, as in the great wars earlier this century, the figures to emerge (if any at all) as the embodiments of national resolve and eventual victory have been politicians, notably Margaret Thatcher in the Falklands War on 1982, not the monarch. Patriotic instincts identify themselves with the political power rather than the more formal institution that heads the state.

The late 20th century monarchy has thus survived in an attenuated form as the head and formal symbol of an attenuated nationhood. The steady incorporation into the European Community (now Union) from 1973 and the growth of nationalist (and perhaps largely republican) opinion in Northern Ireland, Scotland and Wales have blurred and brought into question the old identities and loyalties which had already been weakened by the decline of the monarchy's Protestant appeal since the Great War and by the loss of the empire in mid-century. The features which made the late-Victorian monarchy so successful as the focus of loyalty for an imperialistically-minded patriotism are, for the most part, not recoverable. The conspicuous strengthening of republican sentiment (though still a minority mood) in Britain in the 1990s should be seen as at least as much the result of these changes as of the marital problems of the House of Windsor. Ironically, though, a monarchy which had so successfully identified itself earlier with domestic piety and familial morality has suffered from the disintegration of those moral standards recently. Similarly the royal family's self-translation from a semi-German to a resolutely British identity has now begun to suffer from what may be a disintegration of the United Kingdom or at least its decline in appeal as against other loyalties, whether national or supra-national.

The late 19th century zenith of the monarchy as the focus of the emotions generated by a largely (despite Ireland) self-confident national identity can be seen as a temporary phenomenon produced by Britain's then economic strength, world status and imperial outreach. Though the monarchy survives with majority support in a head-of-state role, that state itself is now a cut-down version of what it once was and with its extent and identity in question. It may be more than semantic accident that it is now 'sovereignty' that seems to be at issue. Both national identity and the monarchy that symbolizes it have been diminished in their former glamour of economic success and imperial greatness. The old sense of a Providential dispensation has declined, if not disappeared. Romantic patriots like Powell have found that phrases like 'the sovereignty of the Crown-in-Parliament' have a diminishing resonance, perhaps because British traditions of parliamentary self-government are now neither special (as once they were) nor so particularly valued. The idea of 'the Englishman's liberties' has lost much of its popular appeal, if not always its rationale. The Crown can no longer present itself in terms of a Protestant Succession keeping a malignant Popery at bay (Prince Charles's evident wish to dissolve the Crown's religious identity into an idea of a generalised 'faith' shows how far the institution's former religious meaning has been dissipated) or as a contrast to autocratic monarchies on the European continent. Indeed the Windsor style of monarchy is often contrasted unfavourably, in all its aristocratic stiffness, with supposedly more liberal and 'democratic' styles of royalty in various European countries. One notes too how often recent holders of the premiership have been viewed (admittedly not always favourably) as 'presidential' in style or aspiration, an implicit analogy with republican regimes and above all with the United States. Perhaps in the long term the tension between an effectively republican form of government, with a liberal-democratic base, and a monarchical form of state has diminished the Crown's capacity to represent the loyalties of the nation. Patriotism in recent crises faced by the nation has looked more readily to political leaders, a Churchill or a Thatcher, to embody and represent national identity than to the monarch.

The nationhood which the Crown symbolises and seeks to represent is itself uncertain. National identity and assurance have been brought into question by the loss of empire, by the impact both political and constitutional of 'Europe', by the American acculturisation of British society, and, not least, by the rise of anti-British or anti-English dissidence within three of the four components of the United Kingdom itself. If the future of a sovereign United Kingdom is uncertain, so must be that of its crowned headship of state. Nations, nationhood, national identities are always to some extent political constructs, created partly by conscious political will, partly by less deliberated and more circumstantial developments. The effective character of the Crown has been created and recreated over the centuries and has had its phases of Protestant survival, of anti-Jacobin revival, of aristocratic imperialism, of Baldwinian pietism and of social democracy. In all this the monarchy has been more passive than active, more the outcome of forces outside itself than fully in control of its own fate. That weakness and malleability has been part of the secret of its survival. It has adapted because it has had to adapt to survive. That survival has often been celebrated as a marvel in itself and as a model of the continuity of national institutions. The historian has, however, to distinguish just what has continued from what has not. A continuity that is perhaps not much more than mere institutional survival through adaptation gives few clues to future developments. The British monarchy has, save in Ireland, faced very few serious challenges over the last two centuries. The extent of popular loyalty to it has rarely been put to serious test. It may soon find itself torn between the diminishing loyalties of the United Kingdom and pressure to transfer to a narrower and more secure (say English) identity. It may also find itself increasingly caught up in final struggles between a once-sovereign nation and the claims of a new and controversial 'European' identity.

Diana – 'England's Rose'

The view of a Group Analytic Psychotherapist

Joy Thompson

Introduction

In 1997, in the aftermath of the death of Diana, Princess of Wales, my colleague Nick Sarra and I, who are both Group Analytic Psychotherapists, arranged a large group meeting in which to reflect together on what had happened. Seventy people came, from a variety of backgrounds – mental health professionals, therapists, teachers, academics, doctors, clergy, a few young parents, etc. It was a fascinating exchange of experiences and reflections. What follows is a personal attempt to understand the national response.

Group Analysis is a form of psychotherapy in the group and by the group, so that the context of therapy is able to mirror the context of a person's life. It is rooted in a belief that we are what we are because of our relationships, and that the culture and context in which we grow up and live permeates us to the core. Group Analysts also believe that the ability to communicate is essential to the happiness and health both of individuals and of larger groups and institutions. It is also the basis for creating community and making democracy work.

At times, when public events evoke strong reactions, such as the Gulf War in 1991, or the Princess of Wales' death in the autumn of 1997, it is useful for a large number of people to meet and talk together so that they can share reactions and reflect on the meaning of what is going on in the public sphere. The larger group meeting both mirrors the scale of public feeling and provides a temporary container in which creative thinking can take place.

From the moment the death of Diana, Princess of Wales, was announced, there was a feeling of unreality and disbelief. I heard the news from a journalist who rang up at 7.50 a.m., before I had turned on the radio. The brutal fact of her death in a road crash suddenly disrupted the Sunday morning routine. Worshippers at the morning services in Exeter cathedral were told that candles and a lovely Orthodox prayer awaited them in the Lady Chapel. Some were in tears during the service. Everyone was stunned. As the day went on it was difficult to resist the constant output of radio and TV, describing what facts could be gleaned about the accident, recounting episodes of her life, repeating her own words from many occasions and especially from the Panorama programme she gave. And so it went on all week. All other news paled before this national obsession — an air accident in Iraq, even the death of Mother Teresa. It seemed we were all caught up, willingly or unwillingly, in an epic national story. Was it a tragic fairy tale, was it a true-life soap opera? Probably, it was a combination of both.

The fairy tale had begun with the announcement of Diana's engagement to the Prince of Wales. The unknown and innocent virgin with the shy smile and see-through dirndl skirt, with those round eyes which glanced seductively upwards; the glamorous and beautiful wedding in St Paul's, attended by the royal families of Europe; here was the stuff of fairy tales. Instantly her photographic potential was realised and her picture was never absent for long from the papers, both broadsheet and tabloid. 'The camera loved her', they said. The simple girl quickly became a fashion idol, yet in all the growing sophistication of her image, she never lost her human appeal; in fact, she steadily developed her capacity to communicate and to touch others, both in real encounters and through the media. Very quickly the public was hooked. Later, when she made known her suffering, the unhappiness of her marriage, the stress of living amongst the protocol of the royal family and her bulimia, the tragic tale unfolded. The marriage ended in divorce and she was seen as the victim of the establishment. She then became the true fairy-story suffering heroine, a Cinderella or a Snow White.

And the soap opera? Our royal family may be the most successful of soap operas, and Diana brought to it her charm and her beauty, her young motherhood, her good works, and later her sufferings and her love affairs: compulsive viewing. It seems, that by her identification with the marginalised, she brought to the image of royalty a new dimension, one which reflects the changes in our national culture, where increasingly the voices of minority groups, of the disadvantaged and of women, are coming to the fore, and where the status accorded to patriarchy, birth and family is diminishing.

On that fateful Sunday and throughout the ensuing week, the nation appeared to be swept along in the story. Millions of people were touched and, to some extent, involved. Was it a majority? We will never know how many went on living their lives as usual. Certainly the events of the week have no parallel in living memory. Crowds, which had begun to gather outside Kensington Palace on the Sunday morning, grew as the week passed. The queues stood silently through chilly September evenings, the old and the young together in the shared silence of grief. The hundreds of thousands of bunches of flowers, the candles, the books of condolence, all were repeated in every city and town of the land. There seemed to be no stopping the tide of grief.

Is it possible to make sense of this reaction? We can compare the public reaction to that evoked by other premature royal deaths; we can look at the use of the media and how much difference it may have made. We can try to understand the psychology of the week, from several different perspectives – whether historically it represents a cultural shift, whether it has made any difference, and what it tells us about our national life, and about our hopes and our needs today.

National Responses to Royal Deaths

In the 19th century the royal family suffered three shocking and untimely deaths among its closest members which had a repercussion on the public. They were the death in childbirth of Princess Charlotte in 1817, the death of Prince Albert in 1861, and the death of the Duke of Clarence, elder son of the Prince of Wales, in 1892.

In the 20th century the deaths of ruling monarchs have been significant events, evoking a strong public response. Dr John Wolffe, in a recent paper writes, that 'The deaths of prominent people, those so prominent as to be familiar figures to the great majority of the population, were important moments of definition of national identities in the British multi-national state and also served to promote states of mind that could legitimately be termed nationalistic'.[1] Whereas Wolffe presents the ways in which the response to royal deaths enhanced the popular appeal of the monarchy, Dayan & Katz[2] emphasise the primordial elements underlying each of three main types of ritual events, contest, conquest and coronations – a Royal death conforms to 'coronation', a rite of passage through which a nation is reminded of its cultural heritage.

In 1817, Thomas Chalmers said in a sermon in Glasgow: 'There never was an occasion [the death of Princess Charlotte] of such magnitude, and at the same time of such peculiarity. It does not wear the aspect of an affair of politics at all, but of an affair of the heart; and the novel exhibition is now offered of all party-irritations merging into one common and overwhelming sensibility. Oh! how it tends to quiet the agitations of every earthly interest and earthly passion, when death steps forward and demonstrates the littleness of them all.'

In 1861, Prince Albert died at the age of 42, leaving Victoria a widow in her early forties, with numerous young children and all the burdens of her royal position, from which Albert had done so much to shield her, and the public duties he had so ably shared. His death in Windsor Castle made it possible for the Queen to observe the rites of passage as privately as possible. There was no lying in state and no public procession, so that the crowds, which gathered at the foot of Castle Hill, Windsor, saw nothing but empty carriages. Yet the public response of sympathy and sorrow seems to have been nationwide. One contemporary pamphleteer, suggesting a close correlation between the monarch and the identity of the nation, wrote:

> Our beloved Queen is a widow and the Royal Family are fatherless. And never in the history of mankind has royalty been enshrined in the affections of a great and powerful people, as the sceptre of Victoria is, and has been in the heart of Britannia. Britannia weeps because Victoria weeps.[3]

The Times recorded, on 18 December 1861, that the public:

> felt real pain.... at hearing that a man of activity and genius, with high purposes and with the opportunities and energies for realising them had been suddenly cut off in the full vigour of life and in the full career of usefulness [thereby reaffirming what it had said on 13 December 1861 that] Prince Albert of the Queen's youth and our own.... is gone.

With no royal encouragement the nation mourned. Processions and church services throughout the land marked the day of Albert's funeral attracting larger numbers than normal church services. As Dr Wolffe observes, 'These events were therefore expressions of national solidarity centred on the royal family as well as occasions for more orthodox Christian reflection on the impermanence of life and the universality of death.'[4] A Leeds newspaper asserted that 'Never before was the unity of feeling in subjects and their rulers so strongly evident, so feelingly displayed.'[5] Statues and memorials to Albert rapidly appeared in the squares and parks of Britain. 'Stone Alberts, indeed, rapidly became more numerous in the streets, squares and parks of Britain than figures of any monarch or national hero. The Prince had chanced to die at a time when municipalities across the country were becoming wealthier and more conscious of their dignity, and emulation and local pride were no doubt a substantial spur to such efforts. The erection of a memorial to Albert was the ideal way in which a town or city could simultaneously both demonstrate its loyalty and sympathy for the Queen and thus its solidarity with the centre of national life, and at the same time assert its own status and distinctiveness.'[6]

Public identification with the Queen's bereavements grew as the years went on. Wolffe quotes a miner's verses on the death of Victoria's son, Prince Leopold, Duke of Albany, in 1884:

I don't know much about dukes
And such high folks like, I confess;
But the Queen's a mother, you'll grant,
And a duke's a son none the less.

She's nothing to you, you say;
Well, I'll not ask how that may be;
But I'd like to tell you, my mates,
Why she'll always be something to me.

When Prince Albert Victor, Duke of Clarence and Avondale, grandson of the Queen and elder son of the Prince and Princess of Wales died aged 28 in 1892, the 'somewhat feckless and allegedly dissolute' youth instantly became 'an ideal of British manhood. [...] It was a bereavement with which all age groups of the population could identify, whether as aged grandparent, despairing parent, or distraught fiancee. Moreover many others were succumbing to the epidemic which killed the Duke and so his death and funeral provided a royal and national focus for the personal griefs of others.'[7]

Clarence's funeral, unlike Prince Albert's, included a public procession and the sense of national identification was stronger than ever. When Victoria died large crowds gathered in the streets of London as the Queen's body was carried from Osborne to London. The bodies of Edward VII, George V and George VI all lay in state in Westminster Hall and there were funeral processions through the streets of London and Windsor.

In 1952, at the funeral of George VI, the whole ceremony could be watched on television for the first time, reducing the size of the crowds on the streets, but extending the possibility for the whole nation to be involved. As an undergraduate myself at the time I remember this as my first encounter with the (black and white) television screen.

Dr Wolffe's argument is that whereas in the 18th century Protestantism was central to the definition and articulation of national identity, during Victoria's reign the monarchy came to assume greater importance as a focus for the unity of the four diverse countries of the United Kingdom, and increasingly of the even more diverse components of the growing world-wide empire. And solidarity in grief played an important part in this process (as indeed did other pubic rites of passage such as jubilees and coronations).

Diana's death was very different in that she was both a Princess and not a Princess, in that her relationship to the Royal family was publicly ambiguous; an ambiguity mirrored in public responses. The involvement of television and mass communication is highly significant.

Yet, in reading these accounts of earlier royal funerals one can only be struck by many strong similarities which, because nearly all occurred before our lifetime, are so easy to overlook.

The part played by the media

At the large group meeting we convened subsequent to Diana's death, the reflections and expressions of feeling ranged over many aspects of the meaning of the public response, approached the task of understanding from many different perspectives and evoked strong differences of viewpoint and emotion. One point of discussion was the part played by the media which some believed had orchestrated the whole thing. From the moment Diana's death was announced most other programmes on radio and television were abandoned. Even for the remainder of the ensuing week it dominated, and endless accounts were given of the crowds and the flowers and the candles, endless on-the-spot interviews with members of the crowd, as well as flashbacks to Diana's life and words, and comments on this unique happening. How much was the public response inspired by the media coverage? In the cathedral, in Exeter, quite a modest queue formed on the Monday to sign condolence books, yet by the end of the week the queues had grown longer and longer, supplies of candles kept giving out, more books had to be bought. Would all these people have come had they not seen on their TV screens what the rest of the world was doing?

Many people have said that Diana herself was a creation of the media. The camera loved her, her picture sold newspapers and magazines, she herself spoke of 'my public' and clearly learnt to play to the photographers, to seek public attention through her image, to court the editors. Some say that without television she would never have become the best-known woman in the world. It was her picture, not her words, which was so insatiably bought and sold. After her death, Durrants, the press cutting agency which has monitored press output since 1880, reported that no other event had produced so many column inches, outstripping Kennedy's assassination, the Queen's coronation, and even the outbreak of the Second World War.[8]

Another point of view is that the media follows and only gives people what they want. Certainly radio and television were unprepared for the events of that Sunday, and responded hour by hour. It seems to me that these things are so reciprocal that linear cause and effect thinking is inadequate. The public took to their hearts the Prince's shy fiancée, the media recognised a photogenic young woman, the insecure Princess found solace in the public attention and admiration, and so the reciprocal cycle continued. Quite soon the photographers became an intrusion and there were reports of the Princess's rudeness to them quite early on in the marriage. Increasingly, in the unhappiness of her marriage and its eventual breakdown, she turned to 'her public' for reassurance, for confirmation of her identity. She came to live to quite an extent through the image she saw in the photographs; as many a public idol so easily can do. The girl, who had not been able to capture and hold the heart of her own mother nor of her husband nor of her lovers, sought to be 'Queen of Hearts' to her public.

The irony of the story, we were told in that week, was that the fatal crash was brought about by the pursuing paparazzi. A classic tragedy unfolded before our eyes as we saw the Princess brought to her death through the agents of those who had initially created her image, her fame, her identity, and her mind.

In our meeting in November as we reflected on the power of the media, memories of Nazi Germany surfaced and the way Hitler used the media of his time to create his myth and unify the nation behind him. Control of the media is essential to the control of all totalitarian states. Observing the crescendo of feeling following Diana's death, surmising that the media had a very large part in fuelling that crescendo, we are bound to be fearful of the immense power wielded by newspapers, radio and television, and by the visual images they create. Their reporting is by its nature always partial, (only the unusual or the controversial or the glamorous will sell papers). Photographs catch one perspective, one moment, not the next, and even the photograph may be doctored by modern technology. What we see we believe, even more than what we read. It is impossible for even the most highly educated people to maintain a critical approach all the time, let alone the mass of the people. 'So while the media reported a nation in mourning, this certainly was a media story [...] the coverage [...] reveals the media's ability to reconstruct history and so determine how an event is remembered.'[9]

There were two somewhat sinister aspects to the media coverage. One was the silencing of dissenting voices — future historians will be hard put to find them — and yet for the thousands who queued to sign books of condolence there must have been at least as many who carried on their lives much as if nothing had happened. Their voices were never heard. Instead grief for Diana claimed the moral high ground. I heard of people who were afraid to go for a walk on the Saturday of the funeral, for fear of the disapproval of neighbours. Failure to provide condolence books or special services was heavily criticised. All had to conform to the rituals and protocols of mourning for one who was herself perceived as the victim of protocol.

The second sinister aspect was the way in which the media redirected the palpable public anger, which initially focused on the paparazzi, towards the royal family. The unspoken message was that they were responsible for Diana's fate, and whatever they did it was wrong. It was wrong for the Princes to appear publicly at church on the Sunday. It was wrong for the family not to appear in London amongst the queuing crowds whose sorrow, it appeared, had a higher claim than the needs of the young Princes. In this there was an echo of popular anger with the widowed Queen Victoria for her withdrawal into private mourning.

An icon of the feminine

One of the comments we heard repeated over and over again at that time was that Diana had seemed like 'one of the family'. She was more real than the neighbours; her picture was, for many days, in the paper, or on the screen, as if its absence would have left too painful a gap.

The word 'icon' resonated continuously through the media coverage of that time. At first I reacted negatively, believing it to be a misuse of the word, but I have come to see that its meaning has indeed changed, a reflection no doubt of our current obsession with the visual image. An icon is, literally, simply an image. Traditionally, it has meant an image which in some way shows forth the sacred, a window, as it were, to the transcendent and invisible. However, in recent usage, it has come to mean a hero figure (or heroine), especially one that represents a particular movement or belief (like a 'pop icon').

There can be no doubt that images of women dominate the mass media and so therefore must command greater public interest. A male can hardly compete. Indeed images of Mary, the Mother of God, dominated western art for centuries, whereas today the camera has become the main purveyor of the feminine image.

In what way was Diana an 'icon'? I think what was meant was she was an image with which people could identify, which somehow represented widely-held aspirations and commanded adulation. She had the figure of a model, the kind of figure all fashionable women aspire to. The magic was in the combination of her beauty and glamour with her sufferings and her vulnerability, which she wore so publicly. On to her, could be projected the feminine images of virgin, wife, mother, princess. In her, women could find solidarity with their own experiences of failed love and broken marriages, their struggles as single parents or their childhood in broken homes. In her too, they could find encouragement in their struggle to overcome the problems, to grow up, to become independent.

Through her tragic death she became also an 'icon' of suffering and of marginalisation. Amongst the crowds who took to the streets was a very high proportion of marginalised groups; aids sufferers, the handicapped, ethnic minorities, etc. Her very public struggle with bulimia, her exclusion from the royal family, made her seem one with them, and they one with her. Her great wealth and privilege, her love of the high life and the expensive shopping sprees, were eclipsed and forgotten. Again and again, what was remembered was her ability to identify with those who suffered and her readiness to touch, literally, the untouchable.

During our evening meeting, someone who had once taught her spoke up, remembering how as quite a young girl Diana had not been especially pretty, not especially bright, a rather sad child, but she had organised a little group of girls to visit the Downs Syndrome children in the local hospital. Very early on, the motherless child had learnt to alleviate her own pain by caring for others; the suffering child in her could be projected on to them, and then, could be comforted.

The avalanche of grief which occurred suggests to me that behind the icon lay an archetype. In her Panorama interview, she wore a black suit and heavy black make-up. [It has been said that she became the Black Virgin. An archetype, as described by Carl Jung, is a universal image, occurring at many different times and places, and is normally accompanied by strong feelings and fantasies. It has a magical, transcendental quality, and can contain within it the opposites.] The black virgin contains both the destructive and the nurturing aspects of women. Elton John's song to 'England's Rose' also, probably unconsciously, links to the Virgin, the 'mystic rose' of medieval piety. The same thing happened with Eva Perron, helping to unify Argentinians in a national solidarity. In Diana's case, it seems that her archetypal appeal crossed national frontiers. As her brother said, 'A very British girl, who transcended nationalities'.

Grief is a complex process — shock and disbelief are usually followed by anger, guilt or remorse, by searching for the missing loved one, and sadness. Over a period of time, separation is achieved, making it possible then to internalise the lost one, as part of oneself. It could be that behind the unprecedented public reaction was guilt. We bought the papers with her pictures in them; it was through us that she was able to see reflected back in the photographs an identity she could claim. Without a market, the paparazzi who apparently chased her to her death, would not have pursued her.

The grieving, however, was not just for Diana. It seemed that this public death and its aftermath became the means whereby so many unresolved losses could be mourned. As a therapist, I heard, again and again, of men who had wept for the first time for years, and as in the Victorian verse quoted earlier, the public event gave permission for the private tears. The multitude of projections on to her acted as a condenser to release private feelings and allow them expression. In our cathedral this process seemed symbolised when the weight of wax in the box of sand where the candles were placed caused the whole thing to go up in flames. The massive collective movement of grief destroyed and dissolved years-old personal defences and the grief was released.

It could be said also that we were mourning for ourselves. The shock of this death, coming to one so young, so beautiful, so privileged, brought us up sharply to realise our own mortality, our own vulnerability. For many of the young it was their first personal encounter with death (and personal it seemed). In a world of technology and machines, a world where the touch of a switch brings us pictures from across the world, a world where we assume daily control of our environment and can so easily avoid the evidence of death and decline in the natural world, suddenly we were faced with the hard reality of our own mortality. 'Never send to know for whom the bell tolls. It tolls for thee.'

Has the world changed?

It has been suggested that we were mourning also for the 18 wasted years of Thatcherism – the ruthless, hard-edged, me-first days. Diana became a national symbol of opposite values – vulnerability and compassion. In her death we celebrate these new values, the values to be found in New Labour, the values which were endorsed in the May election in 1997. The real hope is that our country is in the midst of a cultural shift, of a fresh start, and both the general election and the corporate response to Diana's death can be seen as portents of this shift.

The same heady sense of democratic power was present in September. The people made themselves heard and changes followed. The flag was lowered. The royal family came to London to mingle with the people and join the public ritual. The funeral reflected the people's wishes and the people's tastes.

Unlike the elections, however, 'the people' were a minority given huge publicity by the media and it is unclear, as yet, whether that brief exercise of people power has any long-term significance.

The symbolic meaning attached to Diana is probably more important. The values attributed to her — compassion and care for the marginalised and the wounded — were essentially the feminine values, in contrast to Thatcherism's hard masculine values of the market place. The way the mourning was expressed, with candles and flowers, was in a very feminine way — spontaneous, intuitive, irrational even. It brings to mind the woman who anointed Jesus with expensive ointment and was criticised for doing so by the male disciples. The informal and the symbolic reigned. In Exeter, the Lord Lieutenant was criticised for wearing his uniform at the Thanksgiving service. ('Diana loved men in uniform', he replied.) Rarely, if ever, before have the traditionally Protestant British made such a display of the symbols of religion.

A case can be made for seeing the gradual re-establishment of feminine symbols and feminine values as being one of the most significant features of our time. Arnold Toynbee talked about the sub-plot in history, and the way that as it gathers momentum, the established plot becomes more and more strident. The Thatcher years had that quality. Whether New Labour really represents the sub-plot or not; in May 1997, the hope was certainly there. In terms of what is important to people in these islands there is a groundswell of activity in peace movements, women's movements, environmental groups, animal rights groups and so on, which is challenging the values of the establishment and the institutions. That groundswell found an outlet in the first week of September 1997.

A quotation from William Anderson's book, *The Face of Glory*, expresses a growing recognition of the importance of paying attention to the feminine principle, and to the importance of the feminine as a source of inspiration: 'The strongest images of the creative power of love [...] returning to us over the past decades have been those of the Eternal Feminine, whether as the Great Goddess of prehistory or as ideals, cults and symbols from later civilisations and societies or as a state of calm and unified experience. These images have appeared or been discovered synchronously with the surges in society that have brought about great changes in the political and social position of women. What is remarkable is that the images of the Feminine have arisen in many unconnected fields [...] Thus archaeologists have revealed the matriarchal character of the earliest known religions from the time of the earliest European art onwards. Scholars have found the long-repressed evidence of the great role played by women and the feminine principle in early Christianity. All this has been quite independent on the one hand of the movement for the ordination of women and on the other of the promulgation of the Doctrine of the Assumption by the Roman Catholic Church, itself a return to and a reinterpretation of an event implicit in the past. Others have traced the transformations of the images of Isis and Horus and other female deities into the appearance of the Black Virgins of the early Middle Ages and even followed the fortunes of the Virgin taken by the Nestorian Christians to China [...] In science, not only has the name of the goddess Gaia been revived to name the unified processes of the biosphere but what is often regarded as the most important discovery of the life sciences of the past fifty years, the way in which DNA transmits genetic information, is based on the helix, or spiral, one of the fundamental images of the Great Mother. In art similar images, including the recurrence of the biomorphic form, have given influential themes to western artists. More recently we have seen many attempts to reinterprets history as a sequence of oppressive patriarchal systems. Memory is personified as female: the scientific imagination has pursued and wooed, often brutally, the memory of the past. It is now time for a marriage in which that imagination with its knowledge will be transfigured by the love of the Eternal Feminine.'[10]

It seems that in her death the image and idea of Diana assumed not only a symbol of national identity but also the archetypal power of the eternal feminine at a time in our history when a weariness with the old patriarchal institutions and structures is opening the way for creative new ways of thinking.

Old wine in new wineskins

One remarkable aspect of the new way of being was the pervasive presence of a surprising number of expressions of belief in the spiritual, in life after death, in heaven, in the power of prayer. Suddenly, in a nation dedicated to raising the GNP, to consumerism, to the acquisition of material goods, there was an eruption of spirituality. The descriptions of the public response to royal deaths in Victorian England have the same flavour, although no candles were lit in the streets. Sudden and tragic death seems to trigger what could be called either a regression to primitive religious beliefs or perhaps a return to ultimate truths; certainly to a search for meaning. An accident such as this is a fearful affront to our assumed control of our destiny, an assumption encouraged by our daily technological control of our environment, by the flick of a switch or the start of an engine. When this control is called into question we naturally look to a higher power. But whereas Victorian England was still a country where Christian belief was the norm and pervaded most aspects of public life, England of the 1990s is a secular society where Christians are a minority; where there are many different religions and religious beliefs, and large numbers of people apparently reject all religious belief and practice. For two or more centuries, since the tide of the Industrial Revolution brought people from country communities into the towns and cities, since improved mobility allowed people to travel to find work, to travel to work, since the motor car and the television, and much more, the network of community life in which people traditionally lived has been methodically dismantled. Not entirely by chance, this breakdown in local community has gone hand-in-hand with the diminishment of institutional religion and the religious rituals which knit people together in a shared sense of meaning. What we see today, with a few exceptions, are conglomerations of people living cheek by jowl, yet isolated and alone, not part of a community, not known to their neighbours, unsupported in times of need and sickness.

All societies need rituals and rites of passage. Through our participation in them, our individual experiences, in themselves, often seeming meaningless, can become part of a larger story, even a universal story, and so can be given a meaning and be made bearable.

'Religion' means of course to bind together, and it is our common beliefs and our common ways of expressing them that bind us together. In secular Britain our common belief is in the importance of material goods, and our communal ritual which expresses this is the ritual of shopping. Diana loved shopping. Yet although we shop as part of a crowd it is an individualistic activity, and to some extent a selfish and competitive activity. It has taken the place of other family weekend activities such as going for walks or playing games and of course going to church. It does not bind us together. In 1970 Sogyal Rinpoche wrote: 'What disturbed me deeply, and has continued to disturb me, is the almost complete lack of spiritual help for the dying that exists in modern culture [...] I have been told many stories of people dying alone and in great distress and disillusion in the West without any spiritual help. Wherever I go in the West, I am struck by the great mental suffering that arises from the fear of dying, whether or not this fear is acknowledged'.[11]

In that September week, when Diana's death gave us all a shared experience, new rituals emerged spontaneously and naturally to express the shared feelings of loss, shock and fear, and the search for meaning. Where once a majority could find satisfying rituals in the church and chapel ceremonies and services, now, for an unchurched nation, new rituals had to be found and created. The lighting of candles, the placing of flowers, the signing of books, the waiting in silence, all these became a great corporate ritual, simple but expressive and meaningful. Ways to come together, to express a shared grief, became necessary and in the process individuals and families were knitted into a larger whole, sharing a sense of belonging and a sense of meaning. People who felt excluded and marginalised were able to join in; as one single parent expressed it: 'For the first time I felt part of society'.

We must remember of course that what we saw and heard was not the whole nation, but a very visible minority. Although the beliefs expressed were often vague and rather unorthodox, thousands of people took almost for granted spiritual realities and meanings which seemed quite natural to them in the wake of tragedy, and thousands converged on the cathedrals and parish churches of the land to express their grief and solidarity, and demanded services of Thanksgiving the following weekend. It seemed abundantly evident that, despite all the years of rational positivism and materialism, not far below the surface many, many people have an innate spiritual faith and belief in a spiritual power and turn naturally to prayer.

Final thoughts

All conclusions must as yet be provisional and to an extent subjective. The response to Diana's death was unique, and yet had features in common with other similar events. The media played a large part, and yet they also tapped into real and deep feelings, so strongly indeed that dissent was silenced. Diana became a fairy tale princess, a soap opera heroine, an archetype of the feminine, a symbol of national identity. Crowd mentality was powerful and potentially dangerous, but it may have been expressing the 'sub plot' of our time, the growing sense of the need for a shift in values; a shift from pure reason to make room for the spiritual, a shift from the institutional and formal to the personal and the connected. Above all the need for corporate rituals became very clear; the need for ways to help fragmented communities and a fragmented nation to connect, and to find a shared sense of meaning.

For some decades royal popularity had been declining and with it pride in being British. In quite large sections of society, the inner cities for instance and the world of social work, both practical and academic, value has increasingly been attributed to the un-British, to members of ethnic groups and to those seen to be excluded from the historic establishment. In an increasingly plural and multi-ethnic society, what does it mean to be British and what can people find in the royal family, that bastion of traditional values, that speaks to their condition? Diana appears to have provided an answer, a bridge between different worlds. She retained the glamour of royalty, wealth and beauty, and importantly her rootedness in the traditional landscape of our capital city and its life, but combined all this with her powerful identification with the disadvantaged, the victimised and the feminine. Even her romance with Dodi Al Fayed, Muslim and un-British, could be welcomed as a sign of new patterns emerging.

In death, she was very much a Princess, very much part of the royal family. For a brief time she provided a focus of national identity on the very streets where royal pageantry traditionally belongs, but where now anyone could take part and have that sense of being 'part of society'. The paradox lies in the fact that it was her exclusion from the royal family which gave her that place in the hearts of the marginalised, so that in death she represented the inclusion of the excluded. The rejected wife and single mother was accorded a royal funeral in Westminster Abbey. A ritual of mourning and a rite of passage were found which could include everybody.

These both connected us to our historical roots and made new connections. They brought together the under-privileged, the rich, the handicapped, the immigrant. By participating in the streets or watching on the television anyone could feel included and could resonate not only to the old traditional hymns but to the pop culture represented by Elton John.

Diana, 'England's Rose', was full of contradictions, but those very contradictions became a focus for a nation in the process of great changes, so that very private experiences and feelings could be expressed publicly and become part of a larger and meaningful corporate, national whole.

Notes

1   J. Wolffe (1997) *Dying before Diana: Religion & Nationalism in Responses to the Deaths of the British Royalty 1817 -1997.* Manchester University Press
2   D. Dayan & E. Katz (1992)*Media Events; the Live Broadcasting of History.* Harvard University Press.
3   Blenkinsop (1862) *Britain's Loss & Britain's Gain,* quoted in J. Wolffe, op. cit.
4   J. Wolffe, op.cit.
5   *The Leeds Intelligence,* 28 December 1861, quoted in J. Wolffe op. cit.
6   J. Wolffe, op. cit.
7   J. Wolffe, op. cit.
8   Carol Sellars, *The Psychologist,* November 1997.
9   Danielle Aaron & Sonia Livingstone, *The Psychologist,* November 1997.
10 William Anderson (1996) *The Face of Glory: Creativity, Consciousness and Civilisation.* Bloomsbury.
11 S. Rinpoche (1995) *The Tibetan Book of Living & Dying.* Random House Audio Books.

Elm Bank Publications

Multimedia CALL: Theory and Practice *Keith Cameron (ed)*
Published 1998.VII + 307pp. 0-9502595-9-4. £24.99/$44.95

A Tragic Farce: The Fronde (1648–1653) *Wendy Gibson*
Published 1998.VII + 148pp. 0-9502595-8-6. £14.99/$24.95

Dialogues 1: Ricochets *Susan Bainbrigge (ed)*
Published 1998. 96 pp. 1-902454-00-6. £9.99/$17.95

Dialogues 2: Endings *Ann Amherst and Kate Astbury (eds)*
January 1999. 100 pp. 1-902454-01-4. £9.99/$ 17.95

Contemporary French Pronunciation *Aidan Coveney*
January 1999. 100 pp. 1-902454-02-2. £9.99/$17.95

***The Coach** and **The Triumph of the Lamb**: **Marguerite de Navarre** *Hilda Dale*
February 1999. 150 pp. 1-902454-04-9. £15.99/$29.95

Francophone Voices *Kamal Salhi (ed)*
February 1999. 150 pp. 1-902454-03-0. £24.99/$ 44.95

Francophone Studies: Discourse and Multiplicity *Kamal Salhi (ed)*
March 1999. 250 pp. 1-902454-05-7. £29.99/$49.95

André Breton – The Power of Language *Ramona Fotiade (ed)*
July 1999. 250 pp. 1-902454-06-5. £29.99/$49.95

Matthew Arnold's 'Church of Brou' and other poems: a new look *G.A. Featherston*
September 1999. 200 pp. 1-902454-07-3. £24.99/$44.95

Robert Garnier: Les Juifves *Keith Cameron (ed)*
Published 1996. X + 85pp. 0-9502595-7-8. £5.00/$9.95

As Mighty As The Sword: A Study of the Writings of Charles de Gaulle *Alan Pedley*
Published 1996. VII + 226pp. 0-9502595-3-5. £24.99/$44.95

Jonquils: A Florilegium of Literary Translations *Keith Cameron and Martin Sorrell (eds)*
Published 1996. V + 96pp. 0-9502595-5 1. £9.99/$17.95

Variability in Spoken French: A Sociolinguistic Study of Interrogation and Negation *Aidan Coveney*
Published 1996.V + 271pp. 0-9502595-4-3. £24.99/$44.95

The Short Story: Structure and Statement *William J. Hunter (ed)*
Published 1996. IX + 198pp. 0-9502595-2-7. £19.99/$34.95

Translation: Here and There, Now and Then *Jane Taylor, Edith McMorran & Guy Leclercq (eds)*
Published 1996.VII + 185pp. 0-9502595-6-X. £24.99/$44.95

Elm Bank Publications are distributed by
Intellect, FAE, Earl Richards Road North, Exeter EX2 6AS, UK.
Tel/Fax 44 (0)1392 475110 elmbank@intellect-net.com

- All US orders should be made to the US distributor, ISBS. Call Toll free 1 800 944 6190.
- Further information on these books and how to order them is available on Intellect's website, **www.intellect–net.com**, or can be supplied on request.